13

Things

Mentally

Strong

PARENTS

Don't Do

Also by Amy Morin

13 Things Mentally
    Strong People Don't Do

13

Things

Mentally

Strong

PARENTS

Don't Do

RAISING

SELF-ASSURED

CHILDREN

AND TRAINING

THEIR BRAINS

FOR A LIFE

OF HAPPINESS,

MEANING,

AND

SUCCESS

AMY MORIN

WILLIAM MORROW
An Imprint of HarperCollins *Publishers*

This book contains advice and information relating to health care. It is not intended to replace medical advice and should be used to supplement rather than replace regular care by your doctor. It is recommended that you seek your physician's advice before embarking on any medical program or treatment. All efforts have been made to assure the accuracy of the information contained in this book as of the date of publication. The publisher and the author disclaim liability for any medical outcomes that may occur as a result of applying the methods suggested in this book.

The names and identifying details of many of the individuals discussed herein have been changed to protect their privacy.

HarperCollins books may be purchased for educational, business, or sales promotional use. For information, please e-mail the Special Markets Department at SPsales@harpercollins.com.

A hardcover edition of this book was published in 2017 by William Morrow, an imprint of HarperCollins Publishers.

FIRST WILLIAM MORROW PAPERBACK EDITION PUBLISHED 2018.

Images throughout © by Shutterstock

Designed by Bonni Leon-Berman

Library of Congress Cataloging-in-Publication Data has been applied for.

ISBN 978-0-06-256575-4

22 23 24 25 26 LBC 13 12 11 10 9

To all those who seek to make
a difference in the life of a child

CONTENTS

INTRODUCTION   1

CHAPTER 1:   They Don't Condone a Victim Mentality   9

CHAPTER 2:   They Don't Parent out of Guilt   33

CHAPTER 3:   They Don't Make Their Child the Center of the Universe   57

CHAPTER 4:   They Don't Allow Fear to Dictate Their Choices   81

CHAPTER 5:   They Don't Give Their Child Power over Them   105

CHAPTER 6:   They Don't Expect Perfection   129

CHAPTER 7:   They Don't Let Their Child Avoid Responsibility   155

CHAPTER 8:   They Don't Shield Their Child from Pain   179

CHAPTER 9:   They Don't Feel Responsible for Their Child's Emotions   205

CHAPTER 10: They Don't Prevent Their Child from Making Mistakes   231

CHAPTER 11: They Don't Confuse Discipline with Punishment   257

CHAPTER 12: They Don't Take Shortcuts to Avoid Discomfort   285

CHAPTER 13: They Don't Lose Sight of Their Values   305

CONCLUSION   329

REFERENCES   333

ACKNOWLEDGMENTS   343

INTRODUCTION

Early on in life, I decided that when I grew up I was going to help kids in need. Throughout my childhood, my parents always helped anyone they could. Both of them were postmasters who seemed to have a special knack for recognizing an underdog. Whether they made anonymous donations to someone in need or they lent a helping hand to someone down on their luck, they were generous with whatever we had.

It's no wonder both my sister and I became social workers. Both of our parents were unofficial social workers for years. But long before I ever got my social-work license, my goal was to become a foster parent.

I had grown up knowing that there were kids who didn't have families. Some of them didn't have homes. And many of them had never felt loved. So I decided that someday, when I had my own house, I'd take in kids who needed a place to live.

When I was in college, I met Lincoln—my future husband. He was an adventurous person who loved to travel, meet new people, and try new things. Early on in our relationship, I told him my goal was to become a foster parent. Fortunately, he loved the idea. Right after we got married—while I was still finishing graduate school—we bought a four-bedroom house and started the foster-care licensing process. We chose to become therapeutic foster parents, which meant we would raise children with serious behavior problems or emotional issues. There were classes to take, a home-study process to complete, and modifications that had to be made to our home to meet the foster-care licensing requirements.

But about a year later, just as we were finishing up the licensing process, my mother passed away suddenly from a brain aneurysm. At her funeral, I heard countless stories—many of them from people I'd never met—about how she helped them in some way or other. Hearing those stories of all the lives she touched reminded me about what was really important in life—the legacy you leave behind. My mother's generosity fueled my desire to help children more than ever.

Within a few months, our therapeutic foster-care license came through and our journey as foster parents began. By then, I was working as a psychotherapist at a community mental health center. I worked exclusively with children, many of whom had behavior problems, and their parents. Becoming a foster parent gave me an opportunity to apply the principles I was teaching parents in my therapy office to the children who came into our home.

Lincoln and I loved being foster parents and we began to talk about adoption. None of the children who stayed with us were available for adoption, however. They all had plans to return to their birth families or to be adopted by other relatives. So we started looking at the adoption waiting lists to see if we could find a child who might fit into our family well.

But on the three-year anniversary of my mother's death all of our hopes for adopting a child changed in an instant. Late that Saturday evening, Lincoln said he didn't feel well. A few minutes later, he collapsed. I called for an ambulance and the first responders rushed him to the hospital. I called Lincoln's family and they met me in the emergency room. I wasn't sure how to explain to them what happened. It had all happened so fast.

We just sat there in the waiting room until a doctor came out and invited us into the emergency room. But rather than take us to see Lincoln, he took us to a small, private room and sat us down. The words that came out of his mouth changed my life forever. "I'm sorry to tell you, but Lincoln has passed away."

And with that one sentence, I went from planning to adopt a child to planning my husband's funeral. The next few months were a blur.

We later learned he'd died of a heart attack. He was only twenty-six and didn't have any history of heart problems. But ultimately, it didn't matter how he died. All that mattered and all I knew was that he was gone.

Fortunately, we didn't have any children living with us at that particular time. I could only imagine how traumatic it could have been for a foster child to have been there. We'd actually had plans for a little boy to move in later that week. When his guardian heard the news, he found him a different foster home.

For a while I wasn't sure I wanted to be a single foster parent. I worked a full-time job, and with foster children, there are always lots of appointments, visits with birth families, and meetings with guardians and lawyers. It would be a tough job from a practical standpoint, but also an emotional one. I took about a year off from foster parenting. With help from my faith in God, the love of my friends and my family, and the knowledge I had about grief from my work as a therapist, I put one foot in front of the other.

It took about a year for the fog from grief to start to lift. But once I felt like I was in a place where I could be an effective parent, I notified the foster-care administrators that I was ready to be a foster parent again.

I began my new adventure as a single parent by doing mostly weekend respite work. That meant I cared for foster children whose full-time foster parents either needed a break for a few days or they needed to attend to family affairs without their foster child present.

The transition back into foster parenting went smoothly and gave me something to look forward to on the weekends. As a young widow, I found that staying active was sometimes a challenge. But caring for children gave me a sense of meaning and purpose.

It took a couple of years to establish a new sense of "normal" in my life without Lincoln. Many of the things I enjoyed doing with Lincoln weren't as much fun without him. And although some people encouraged me to start dating, I wasn't interested.

But that all changed when I met Steve. He was different from anyone I'd ever known. And it didn't take long to fall in love. Fortunately, he wasn't scared away by the fact that I was a widow or that my goal was to continue being a foster parent.

After dating for about a year, we eloped to Las Vegas and began a new chapter in our lives. Steve had to go through the foster-care licensing process too—background check, classes, and a home study. But it was faster this time around since my home already met the foster-care licensing standards. Within a few months, Steve was a fully licensed foster parent.

Our lives melded together quite nicely and life was smooth sailing for a while. But then, Steve's father, Rob, was diagnosed with cancer. At first, he was given a good prognosis. But despite multiple treatments, his health deteriorated. A few months later, doctors said his condition was terminal.

The news hit me like a ton of bricks. I'd already lost my mother and Lincoln. Rob and I had grown close and I couldn't imagine losing him too. I started thinking about how unfair it was that I had to lose another person so close to me in such a short amount of time.

But before I let myself host a lengthy pity party, I reminded myself that mentally strong people don't feel sorry for themselves. Through my work as a therapist and my personal experiences with grief, I knew bad habits like self-pity could rob me of mental strength, if I let them. And with that, I sat down and I wrote a list of all the things mentally strong people don't do.

I published my list of the thirteen things mentally strong people don't do to my blog, hoping someone else might find it useful. Within days my list went viral and it was read by tens of millions of people. But very few people knew that I'd written that article as a letter to myself during one of my lowest points.

Just two weeks after that article went viral, Rob passed away. And throughout my grief I reminded myself not to do the things mentally strong people don't do.

That viral article led to the opportunity to write a book about the thirteen things mentally strong people don't do. It was an honor to be able to share those lessons I've learned about resilience. And while I have received many questions from readers, there was one question I kept receiving over and over again: *How do we teach these skills to kids?*

I've also heard many readers say, "I wish I could have learned this stuff a long time ago." So I'm excited to be able to provide a guide for teaching kids how to build mental strength. Developing mental muscle early will prepare them for a brighter, better future.

Through my work as a therapist, and my experience as a foster parent, I know it's possible for kids of all ages and backgrounds to become mentally strong. But it's essential for the adults in their lives to be invested in helping them practice the exercises that will help them become stronger.

The Benefits of Raising Mentally Strong Kids

Frederick Douglass once said, "It's easier to build strong children than to repair broken men." As a therapist, I know this is true. It's much easier to gain mental muscle during childhood. And childhood is full of opportunities for growth.

You can't prevent your child from facing adversity. He's going to fail and get rejected. He's going to experience loss and heartache. And he's going to face hard times.

But if you give him the tools he needs to build mental strength, he'll be able to turn those hardships into opportunities to grow stronger and become better. No matter what circumstances he faces in life, and no matter what sort of hand he was dealt, he'll know he's strong enough to overcome it.

That's not to say your child won't still struggle with his emotions or have difficulty handling stress. But mental strength will help him cope with hardship in a productive manner. It will also give him the courage to tackle problems head-on, gain confidence in his skills, and learn from failure.

The Components of Mental Strength

As kids grow and learn, they develop core beliefs about themselves, other people, and the world in general. If you're not proactively helping your child establish a healthy outlook, however, he may develop beliefs that limit his potential.

Core beliefs influence how children interpret events and how they respond to their circumstances. More importantly, those beliefs may turn into self-fulfilling prophecies. A child who labels himself as a failure, for example, won't put effort into improving his life. Or, a child who believes he can't succeed in life because other people will hold him back, isn't likely to fulfill his potential.

Your child's core beliefs influence how he thinks, feels, and behaves. Here's an example of how core beliefs influence two different children who don't make the basketball team:

Child #1

Core belief: I'm not good enough.

Thoughts: I'll never be good at basketball. I'm just not athletic.

Feelings: Sad and rejected.

Behavior: He quits playing basketball.

Child #2

Core belief: I'm a capable person.

Thoughts: If I practice, I can get better. Maybe I'll make the team next year.

Feelings: Determined and hopeful.

Behavior: He practices basketball every day after school.

While core beliefs can be modified later in life, it's more challenging to alter them as an adult. After holding on to a certain belief for decades, it's difficult to "unlearn" what you've always held to be true. And the unhealthy thoughts, behaviors, and feelings that reinforce that belief will be harder to change.

In addition to helping your child build healthy core beliefs, you also need to teach her how to regulate her thoughts, manage her emotions, and behave in a productive manner. Here are the three components of mental strength:

1. **Thoughts**—Exaggeratedly negative thoughts, harsh self-criticism, and catastrophic predictions will prevent your child from reaching her greatest potential. But the solution isn't to just teach your child to be optimistic. Being overly confident and ignoring realistic dangers can leave her ill-equipped and unprepared for the realities of life. Teach her how to have a realistic outlook so she can perform at her peak.

2. **Behavior**—Unproductive behavior, like complaining and staying inside her comfort zone, will interfere with your child's education, relationships, and future career. Teach your child how to challenge herself and make healthy choices, even on the days when she doesn't feel motivated.

3. **Emotions**—Getting stuck in a bad mood, losing her temper, and avoiding fear are just a few ways your child's inability to regulate her emotions could limit her ability to live a rich and full life. Teach your child how to manage her emotions and she'll enjoy many lifelong rewards, such as improved self-control and better communication skills.

Why the Focus Is on What Mentally Strong Parents Don't Do

In a world where one in thirteen U.S. children take psychiatric medication for emotional and behavioral problems, and 31 percent of teens report feeling overwhelmed by stress, it's clear that today's young people aren't learning how to develop mental strength. Yet most parents have no idea how to help their children build mental muscle.

Whether it's an anger management problem or a body-image issue, every week parents bring their children into my office asking, "Can you help my child?" While I'm always happy to try, teaching a child to change the way he thinks, feels, and behaves is a slow process when I only see him once a week for an hour-long therapy appointment. But if I can teach the parents how to coach their child, they'll see results much faster.

As a parent, you have an opportunity to help your child gain mental muscle every day by giving him exercises to practice. And, you'll be right there with him during some of life's most teachable moments. Whether he's having a bad day or he's struggling with a particular problem, you can coach him right on the spot.

As I explain in my first book, building mental strength is a lot like building physical strength. If you want to become physically strong, you need good habits, like going to the gym. But if you really want to see results, you also need to give up bad habits, like eating too much junk food.

Building mental strength requires good habits too. But it also requires that you give up the unhealthy thoughts, behaviors, and feelings that hold you back. Quite often, parents inadvertently inhibit their child's growth. It takes only a few bad parenting habits to interfere with a child's ability to gain mental muscle.

Mental strength exercises train the brain the same way physical exercises strengthen the body. Helping your child practice the exercises in each chapter will help him build mental muscle.

Refusing to do the thirteen things mentally strong parents don't do will give your child opportunities to use his mental muscles, which can, in turn, help him grow even stronger. Giving up those bad parenting habits will also help you work smarter, not harder. You'll be teaching your child the skills he needs with less effort.

You can't teach a child how to be mentally strong by handing him a list of bad habits to give up. Saying, "Don't feel sorry for yourself," isn't likely to put an end to the pity parties he hosts when he's had a bad day. And telling him not to give up after his first failure won't miraculously boost his confidence.

But there are steps you can take to show your child how to avoid those thirteen unhealthy habits that will rob him of mental strength. The parenting strategies described in this book will help you teach your child to avoid the things mentally strong people don't do, in a kid-friendly manner.

Each chapter provides strategies to help your child develop healthy core beliefs that will make his attempts to grow stronger more effective. You'll also find specific exercises—both for you and your child—that will help your child reach his greatest potential.

They Don't Condone a Victim Mentality

*"Cody has ADHD and the school doesn't care!" fourteen-year-old Cody's
mother exclaimed. "Rather than help him get caught up on his work, his
guidance counselor suggested he get therapy!"*

*In this first therapy session both Cody and his parents expressed concern
that the teachers gave him too much work. Cody had fallen behind and he
didn't think he was ever going to get caught up. His parents didn't think he
needed counseling, but they had brought him to the appointment in hopes I
could advocate for him at school.*

*Cody had been diagnosed with ADHD the previous year. Since then, his
pediatrician had been prescribing medication to improve his attention span
and decrease his hyperactivity. "He's much calmer now that he's taking medication. We definitely notice a difference when he forgets to take his pill," his
father explained.*

*Interestingly, however, Cody's grades hadn't improved. He was still failing
several classes. And his parents expressed frustration that the school wasn't
helping him. They signed the necessary paperwork that granted me permission
to talk to his teachers and his pediatrician. So after his appointment, I called
the school to gain more information.*

Cody's teachers had put several accommodations in place, such as seating him near the front of the classroom to reduce distractions and giving him extra time to complete tests and classroom assignments. Additionally, they were asked to sign off on his assignment book each day to ensure that he understood the homework assignment. Cody was also invited to stay after school every day to attend the homework club where he could receive additional help from teachers.

All of his teachers said the same thing—he was failing because he wasn't applying himself. He never finished his homework. He never stayed after school. And he never took advantage of the extra time he was allowed to have on his tests.

I contacted Cody's pediatrician, who confirmed, that by all accounts, Cody's medication was helpful. His teachers and his parents had completed reports about his behavior after he started taking it and they all agreed that he was calmer and more attentive.

When Cody's parents attended his appointment with him the following week, I presented the information I'd gathered. They agreed with the basic facts—the medication works, the school makes accommodations, and Cody has an opportunity to stay after school to get extra help. "But extra time and extra help aren't enough," his mother said. "He has ADHD. He shouldn't be expected to do the same amount of work as the other kids."

That statement clarified everything. Cody's parents believed ADHD should excuse him from doing his work. And they'd sent that message to Cody. He'd bought into the notion that ADHD meant he couldn't keep up with the other students. So he'd stopped trying.

Cody's parents wanted him to perform better in school. But before he could do that, the family had to make some serious changes.

It appeared the real problem was:

1. **Cody's family believed ADHD made it impossible for him to succeed.** Cody's parents thought his ADHD meant he couldn't possibly do the same work as the other kids.
2. **Cody had given up trying to do his work.** Cody stopped applying himself because he believed he wouldn't be able to keep up.

The three biggest issues I wanted to address in treatment:

1. **Cody's parents had to support his education.** Cody's parents thought they were fostering his education by advocating that the school implement more changes. The real change needed to start in the home.
2. **The family needed an education on ADHD.** With more information, Cody's parents could learn how to help Cody manage his symptoms.
3. **Cody had to view himself as capable of success.** Cody needed to know that ADHD didn't need to be a roadblock to success. He could find ways to overcome the challenges.

I spent the next few weeks educating the family on Cody's diagnosis and the steps they could take to help him succeed. Cody was surprised to learn that most students with ADHD are able to keep up with their peers.

He was excited to discover several musicians, athletes, and famous entrepreneurs who had been diagnosed with ADHD as well. It gave him—and his parents—hope he could still do whatever he wanted in life, regardless of his diagnosis.

His parents became invested in supporting his education by helping him catch up on all of his overdue work, one step at a time.

They didn't want to make Cody attend the homework club after school—because they thought he should have time to get some energy out after a long school day. So they decided that after school, he could come home and shoot hoops or ride his bike before starting his homework. Then they'd assist him with getting his work done. He'd only be allowed to use his electronics once his nightly homework—and at least one overdue assignment—was complete. And his parents would check his assignment book each day and monitor his grades.

Once Cody's parents held him accountable, Cody got his homework done every night. Within a few weeks, his grades improved and his teachers noticed a difference in his attitude at school. He felt less overwhelmed by his overdue work and more empowered to tackle his assignments.

All the family had to do was shift their thinking. Rather than view Cody as a victim of ADHD and an unsupportive school staff, they just had to see that ADHD was a challenge Cody could handle.

Do You Condone a Victim Mentality?

Some parents see themselves as victims of unfortunate circumstances. Their belief about their inability to succeed or find happiness may stem from their own childhood. They may even view themselves as a victim of their child's bad behavior. Other parents don't feel like victims, but they inadvertently endorse their child's victim mentality. And that can have serious consequences. Do any of these statements resonate with you?

In your personal life:

○ You think someone else—or some unfortunate circumstances—prevent you from being your best.

○ You think other people are generally luckier and more fortunate than you are.

○ While certain solutions may work for other people, your problems are exceptional.

○ You spend a lot of time complaining about other people's behavior and how it affects you.

○ You believe nothing ever goes right in your life.

In your parenting life:

○ You think your child's misbehavior is proof you're being punished by the universe (or a higher spiritual power).

○ You make excuses for your child's failures or shortcomings.

○ You feel sorry for your child.

○ You spend more time talking to your child about problems than solutions.

○ You think your child is helpless sometimes.

Why Parents Raise Kids with a Victim Mentality

Cody's parents had no idea that ADHD wasn't the problem—it was their belief about ADHD that was the issue. Rather than empower their son to rise to the challenge, they insisted everyone else needed to coddle him.

They thought they were doing the right thing by advocating for him to be given less homework. But in doing so, they'd sent him the message that he wasn't capable of being a good student.

Even if your child doesn't have a diagnosis like ADHD, consider the life lessons you're teaching when he faces hardship or unfair circumstances.

THE VICTIMHOOD CULTURE MAKES EVERYONE A VICTIM

In the past, you might be considered a victim if you endured a violent crime. But today, people consider themselves victims when the housing market crashes.

Mainstream sociologists say our "victimhood culture" is evidenced by the increased complaints from individuals who claim to be victims whenever they encounter minor offenses. And modern-day victims don't just want to be heard. They're demanding other people stop offending them.

Take, for example, the Starbucks red cup controversy during the holiday season of 2015. When the retailer sold coffee in solid red cups—as opposed to winter-themed cups—customers were outraged. Suddenly people blamed Starbucks for "waging war on Christmas." Angry customers turned to social media to express their offense at the company's decision to "take Christ out of Christmas." Strangely, however, past holiday cups had featured images like snowflakes and a dog sledding down a hill—nothing specifically related to a Christian celebration.

Rather than boycott Starbucks, angry customers wanted to publicly express their anger. Ironically, they were happy to exercise their right to free speech while simultaneously trying to stifle a private business's ability to express itself through its products.

The news is filled with examples of people claiming to be victims, and sometimes there's a fine line between helping people who are marginalized and encouraging a culture of victimhood. An article published in *Comparative Sociology* titled "Microaggression and Moral Cultures" outlines that shift in victim mentality.

The authors of the piece, sociologists Bradley Campbell and Jason Manning, describe how culture dictates the appropriate way to respond to an offense. In an honor culture, like in the Wild West or in modern-day gangs, physical aggression is often used. In a dignity culture, like the twentieth-century West, most people respond to minor offenses quietly. A minor offense may lead the aggrieved person to cut off the relationship and a major offense could lead to a call to the police so the matter can be resolved by authorities.

In today's culture, however, people complain to third parties over minor offenses. They advertise their oppression and demand assistance each time they feel offended. Then they try to gain support for their cause by claiming the minor offense they experienced is part of a much bigger cultural problem.

Social media is a common tool people use to convince others to see themselves as victims. Messages like "They're discriminating against us," might be an attempt to get others to join forces. While banding together to solve a problem or fight injustice can be healthy, sometimes those messages lead to a mob mentality.

Research by the University of Leeds demonstrates how easy it is for a crowd to be influenced by just a few people. Throughout a series of experiments, people were asked to walk randomly in a large hall. A few people were secretly given details about where to walk. They were not allowed to communicate and they had to stay within arm's length of each other. In all cases, the informed individuals were able to get everyone to follow them. The 5 percent of people who were told where to walk were able to influence the entire crowd's movements. The other 95 percent had no idea they were being influenced.

Raising a mentally strong child who accepts personal responsibility for his life can be extra challenging when everyone else is trying to convince him he's a victim. Failing a class, being overlooked for a job, and being benched by a coach doesn't necessarily mean he's a victim. But if he has a victim mentality, he'll view criticism and failure as proof that other people are trying to prevent him from succeeding.

A VICTIM MENTALITY CAN BE INHERITED

Parents who grew up believing they were victims raise children with a victim mentality. Even if the word "victim" is never used, children receive a message that says, "You won't succeed, so don't bother trying." Parents with these beliefs often view their children as further evidence that they're victims. They say things like, "He acts bad just to punish me," or "My child abuses me just like everyone else in the world." That way of thinking—and relating to their child—is incredibly destructive. And sadly, it sets a child up for failure.

Healthy parents don't intend to raise victims. But many of them inadvertently teach their kids that "other people will hold you back," or "you can't do anything about the bad things that happen to you in life." Sometimes, their subtle actions lead kids to believe they're helpless.

Here are a few ways you might be instilling a victim mentality in your child without even knowing it:

- **Role-modeling a victim mentality.** Saying things like, "Why do these things always have to happen to me?" when you encounter a setback sends the message that you're a powerless victim. A defeatist attitude is contagious and your child will come to believe she has little power to control her destiny.
- **Feeling sorry for your child.** Sometimes parents secretly feel sorry for a child who has a disability or who has endured traumatic circumstances. But pitying your child—even when it's never openly discussed—teaches your child he's a victim.
- **Underestimating a child's capabilities.** Whether your child has a physical disability or a cognitive impairment, or you just doubt his

abilities in general, focusing on what your child *can't* do, rather than what he can, leads to a victim mentality.

- **Refusing to watch a child struggle.** Watching a child grow frustrated by her inability to do something is tough. But rescuing your child at the first sign of a struggle teaches her that she must depend on others to do things for her.

Raising a Child with a Victim Mentality Will Turn Him into a Victim

Cody's parents assumed his ADHD diagnosis meant he couldn't succeed. They viewed their child as a victim of a callous school system rather than a child full of potential. The longer they held on to the belief that Cody couldn't do the work, the further behind he fell.

While it's important to teach your child to stand up for himself and to help others who are oppressed, it's also important to ensure your child doesn't grow up believing he's an unfortunate victim. The belief that he can't succeed will hold him back more than any obstacle, disability, or lack of talent.

A VICTIM MENTALITY LEADS TO VICTIMIZATION

Leanne had been bullied ruthlessly as a child. She hated every minute of school. The torment she endured affected her grades and her self-esteem. Even as an adult, her past continued to haunt her.

Now that Leanne was a parent, she resented the fact that she had to send her kids to school. She feared they'd get picked on and she worried bullies would ruin their lives, just like they'd ruined hers.

From a young age, she taught them that "other kids are mean." She cautioned them that other kids would bully them and the adults might not do anything about it.

She shared stories of her own experiences being bullied: how the other kids picked on her for being overweight or stole her lunch money. She said the teachers even joined in sometimes by laughing at the names kids called her or by punishing her for tattling when she tried to get help.

What Leanne didn't realize was that her stories and warnings weren't protecting her kids. Instead, her childhood horror stories caused her children to accept the same fate.

When her daughter was teased, she didn't speak up. And when her son got pushed down at recess, he didn't bother to tell a teacher. Both kids assumed no one was going to help them and there was no sense in trying. Their mother had convinced them that bullying was something to be endured—not a problem to be addressed.

In fact, Leanne's message to her kids about bullies led her kids to be standoffish with their peers. Rather than make friends, they became loners. And some of the bullying stemmed from their withdrawn behavior.

When her kids came home from school crying because they were getting picked on, it was too much for Leanne to bear. It conjured up painful images from her own childhood and she couldn't stand the thought of her children going through the same things.

That's when she sought therapy. She thought her only option was to homeschool her children. But she was a single mother with a full-time job.

Leanne hadn't intended to raise her children with a victim mentality. But ultimately, that's what she did. And she saw the fact that her children were being picked on as further proof that *she* was a victim.

In many cases—just like in the case of Leanne's children—a victim mentality becomes a self-fulfilling prophecy. Kids who view themselves as victims aren't proactive. They don't take steps to keep themselves safe or to improve their situations. Ultimately, their attitude increases their risk of victimization.

No one is ever dealt a perfect hand in life and it's likely your child may have to deal with some type of hardship. Whether he's the shortest kid in the class or you have less money than everyone else in the neighborhood, no one's life is perfect. But allowing your child to believe he can't handle disadvantages does him a disservice.

Tough circumstances won't make your child a victim. It's your attitude about those circumstances that matters.

A VICTIM MENTALITY IS A HARD CYCLE TO BREAK

When kids believe they're victims, it affects the way they think and the way they behave. A child who feels hopeless might think, "There's nothing I can do to make this better." As a result, he is likely to stay inactive.

I see this all the time with children and teens I work with. Whether they fall behind in their schoolwork or they have trouble getting along with their peers, they allow their problems to pile up.

Researchers refer to this as "learned helplessness." One of the most famous studies on the subject was performed in 1967 by Martin Seligman at the University of Pennsylvania. In the first part of his experiment, Seligman subjected dogs to electric shocks. One group of dogs could stop the shocks by hitting a lever. The other group had no way to stop the shocks.

During the second part of the experiment, all of the dogs were placed in a crate that had a low partition separating one side from the other and they were subjected to shocks. They could escape the shock by jumping over the partition. The dogs who had been able to stop the shocks in the previous experiment jumped over the partition to stop the shocks. But the dogs who had no control over the shocks in the previous experiment didn't try to save themselves from the shocks. Instead, they lay down and took no action.

Even when offered rewards, the dogs didn't move. So researchers used other dogs to demonstrate how to escape the shocks. But the dogs still didn't try. It was as if they'd concluded they were doomed to suffer.

Albeit disturbing, this study shows how learned helplessness becomes pervasive. A child who learns "I can't do anything to make my life better" will give up trying to improve her situation. Consequently, her suffering will continue. And it's hard to change those beliefs once they're ingrained.

What to Do Instead

Cody's parents stopped viewing him as a victim once they learned that ADHD was a common obstacle that many people overcome. When their attitude changed, their behavior changed. They began problem-solving how to best manage the symptoms of ADHD and they found strategies that helped Cody be successful in school.

If they hadn't learned more about ADHD, Cody may have always believed he was incapable of learning. He may have insisted he couldn't do as much work as his peers. And he may have spent much of his life thinking he was a victim when the world couldn't accommodate his demands. Because that's what happens when people see themselves as victims—no matter what others do for them, it's never enough.

Examine the ways you may be reinforcing your child's victim mentality so you can take steps to teach him he's a capable kid who can deal with life's inevitable challenges.

LOOK FOR WARNING SIGNS OF A VICTIM MENTALITY

Kids who have a victim mentality carry around a pervasive belief that says, "The world is a bad place and everyone is out to get me." That core belief affects how they perceive events, how they think about the future, how they behave toward other people, and how they feel about themselves.

Here are some clues that your child might think he's a victim:

1. **Hosting pity parties.** A child with a victim mentality may insist that no one likes him or he might say he'll never be able to pass math class. Rather than look for solutions, he'll stay focused on the problem. He'll likely complain, sulk, and mope as he sits around feeling sorry for himself.

2. **Focusing on the negative.** It's hard to see the good in the world when you have a victim mentality. A child might talk about the one

mean kid in school and ignore the fact that the rest of the kids are really nice, or he may be quick to exaggerate the hardships he endures.

3. **Misinterpreting events.** When someone is kind or when something good happens, kids with a victim mentality are suspicious. Your child might say, "He wasn't actually being nice when he said I did a good job. He was really making fun of me."

4. **Acting helpless.** Your child might not make any attempts to improve his situation. And if you offer suggestions for how he might take positive action, he'll insist your ideas won't work.

5. **Seeking sympathy.** Your child may work hard to make sure others view her as a victim. She might try to convince them they are victims too or insist on telling everyone that what happened to her was unjust and unfair.

BE A GOOD ROLE MODEL

A victim mentality is mostly a learned behavior. If you tend to be a glass-half-empty kind of person, you might be unintentionally teaching your child he's a victim of life's unfortunate circumstances.

Complaining about your life—without actually taking any action—convinces your child that you're a helpless victim. Or, blaming other people or certain groups of people for holding you back in life teaches your child that other people have the power to prevent him from reaching his goals.

Here are a few ways to be a good role model:

- **Be positive.** Be aware of how much you complain about other people and tough circumstances. Whether you insist the heavy traffic isn't fair or you complain you can't afford a better house, your gripes will affect the way your child views the world. Offer more positive statements than negative ones.
- **Resist the urge to vent.** Although you might think rehashing your day with your friends and family is helpful because it lets you "get

out your frustration," venting does more harm than good—for both the listener and the speaker. So while it can be helpful to process your emotions, make sure you aren't unleashing your negativity on a daily basis

- **Create positive change.** Show your child that you can make a difference in the world—or at least in someone's world. Perform acts of kindness and help other people. Teach your child that everyone has the ability to make the world better.
- **Be assertive.** If someone cuts in front of you in line, speak up politely. Or, if you receive poor service, talk to a manager about it. Your child will learn he doesn't have to be a passive victim when he sees you're willing to speak up for yourself.

GO AFTER THE GOOD

Lilly didn't like school. And every day she couldn't wait to burst through the door and tell her mother about all the problems she encountered. One day she'd say, "Mom, you're not going to believe what happened at lunch today. The teachers made us eat in silence because some of the kids were being too loud!" The next day she'd say, "Mom, the kids on the bus were so mean today. I don't want to ride the bus ever again!"

Every day her mother, Holly, listened intently to all the injustices her daughter suffered. She responded by saying things like, "That's horrible. I'm sorry you had to go through that." Holly thought lending her daughter a sympathetic ear was the best thing she could do.

What she didn't realize was that she was giving her daughter positive attention for being a victim. She encouraged her to keep talking about everything that went wrong. The longer this went on, the more Lilly focused on all the reasons she hated school.

Changing Lilly's "poor me" attitude required Holly to change their daily afterschool interactions. Rather than continue to invite Lilly to complain about all the bad things that happened, Holly needed to go after the good.

That meant asking questions like, "What was your favorite part about school today?" or "Start by telling me the best thing that happened to you today." Instead of allowing her daughter to dwell on all the unfairness and maltreatment she'd suffered, Holly could help her recognize a few positive aspects.

If your child focuses on the negative, avoid questions like "How was your day?" Instead, go after the good by asking, "What was the happiest part of your day?" Be willing to hear about the difficult parts as well—but don't make hardship the focus of your conversation.

How to Teach Kids to See Themselves as Strong

In the case of Cody and his ADHD diagnosis, the solution to his educational problems was to shift the family's beliefs. Once his parents began viewing him as capable, Cody believed he could improve his grades. Teach your child to believe in himself and he'll strive to reach his greatest potential.

HELP YOUR CHILD FOCUS ON WHAT HE CAN CONTROL

Whether you're going through a divorce or your child hates school, it can be easy to convince yourself that your child is a helpless victim. But the truth is, no matter what your child is faced with, he always has the ability to control something.

An organization called Kids Kicking Cancer proves that even kids who find themselves in the most difficult of circumstances can find control over something. This group has made it their mission to help kids with cancer recognize that although they can't control their health or their treatments, they can gain some control over their pain and discomfort.

Kids are taught mind-body techniques, such as martial arts, breathing techniques, and meditation. The goal is to help them regain a sense of control over the chaos and to feel empowered in their own healing. Some kids who have been through the program report they're able to sit still during blood draws (where in the past it had taken several nurses to hold them down) and others say they're able to stay still during their scans thanks to the breathing techniques they learned.

If kids with life-threatening illnesses can discover things they have control over, there are definitely things you can help your child feel like he has control over. Even when he can't control the environment, he can control his thoughts, his effort, and his attitude.

When your child complains, ask questions like:

- What can you control in this situation?
- What are your choices?
- What kind of attitude are you going to choose?

DIFFERENTIATE BETWEEN BLUE AND TRUE THOUGHTS

Your child needs to recognize that just because he thinks something doesn't mean it's true. When he's had a rough day or he's in a bad mood, his thoughts are likely to be overly negative. And believing those negative thoughts will not only make his mood worse, but it could reinforce the idea that he's a victim.

While there are several kinds of thinking errors, the acronym BLUE is a good way to help kids remember when their thoughts might be too upsetting to be true. Developed by PracticeWise, it's a common tool used in therapy to help kids combat negative thinking. Here's what you can be on the lookout for:

- **Blaming everyone else.** Thinking things like "My teacher never tells us what to study for tests, so I always get bad grades" prevents your child from seeing how he can do better next time. While you don't want your child to take on extra responsibility (like assuming a team's loss is *all* his fault), don't let him blame other people and external circumstances.

- **Talk about responsibility.** Talk about how to accept personal responsibility for his share of the outcome. Ask questions like "Is it really *all* your teacher's fault?"
- **Looking for the bad news.** Kids with a victim mentality screen out all the good things that happen to them and only focus on the bad. So rather than celebrate that he went swimming, a child who sees himself as a victim might say, "It was horrible! It started raining so we had to come home early!"
  - **Point out the good.** When your child insists nothing good happened, take a moment to point out the positive. Ask a question like "Did you have fun before it rained?" Help him see that good things happen, even during his toughest days.
- **Unhappy guessing.** A victim mentality leads kids to make catastrophic predictions. Thinking something like "I'm going to fail my test tomorrow" may cause your child to believe there's no use in studying.
  - **Encourage your child to take action.** When your child predicts bad things will happen, don't let her be a passive victim. Ask questions like "What can you do to prevent that from happening?" If it's something she has no control over (like she predicts it's going to rain), help her think about how she'll cope when faced with difficulties.
- **Exaggeratedly negative.** It's easy for kids to let their imaginations get the best of them, especially when they're upset. A child who thinks she's a victim might say things like "Everyone in the whole school is mad at me!" after having an argument with two friends.
  - **Look for exceptions.** When your child insists things *never* go right or she's *always* in trouble, help her find exceptions to the rule. Say something like "Well, what's one time when things did go right?"

When your child starts feeling sorry for himself, ask, "Is that a BLUE thought or a true thought?" Teach him to identify the BLUE thoughts that contribute to his victim mentality and remind him that although some things might feel true, his thoughts won't always be accurate. Help him see that stretching the truth—even in his mind—isn't helpful. Then help him replace his internal monologue with more realistic thoughts.

SPEAK UP OR SHUT UP

Kids with a victim mentality either become overzealous in proclaiming that their rights have been violated or they become overly submissive and allow bad things to happen to them. While it's important for your child to learn to speak up for himself when he encounters certain injustices in life, it's equally important that he not declare he's been victimized every time he disagrees with someone else.

There are times when it's appropriate to push back against authority and times when it makes sense to stay respectfully silent. But deciding on the best course of action is a sophisticated skill.

Talk about the following scenarios with your child and come up with situations of your own. Discuss the pros and cons of speaking up and the risks and potential benefits of staying silent. Listen to your child's insights as well as the reasons behind them. Offer your own words of wisdom about when to speak up and when to stay silent:

- An umpire makes a call you disagree with.
- A teacher gives you a grade you don't think you deserve.
- A child is calling another kid names on the playground.
- Someone shares an inappropriate joke on social media.
- A teacher is scolding a child for not getting his work done.
- A friend borrows something from you and doesn't give it back.
- A coach yells at you because you're not paying attention in the game.
- A friend says only certain types of kids can sit at the lunch table.

GIVE YOUR CHILD FREE TIME TO PLAY

Today's kids spend the majority of their free time engaging in structured activities that are monitored by adults. Basketball practice, guitar lessons, scouts, and summer camps involve adult-led activities and adult-created rules.

And according to sociologist Steven Horwitz, too much adult intervention fuels a victim mentality. Rather than learn how to negotiate, create rules, and follow social norms as a group, kids automatically turn to an adult to referee at the first sign of a disagreement.

Then, the adult decides who is "right" and who is "wrong." The kid who sought adult help gains validation that he needs someone else to fight his battles. The other kids get the message that you can't offend anyone or a third party will be notified to solve the conflict.

Give your child unstructured time to play. Don't hover when he's playing with friends and don't rush in to intervene every time there's a hint of trouble. Give him an opportunity to practice resolving conflict on his own.

Of course, it's important to get involved if there's a child who is clearly being taken advantage of repeatedly. But there are times when your child will figure things out on her own when there aren't adults there to make sure everything is "fair."

Teach Preschoolers to Recognize Their Choices

There are many things preschoolers can't do. After all, their fine motor skills aren't yet developed and their decision-making skills are still evolving.

There will be plenty of times when you need to say no or tell your child to stop doing something. Set firm limits and give your child opportunities to practice dealing with the rules and limits placed on him.

But constantly saying, "No, you can't do that!" will teach your child that he doesn't have say over anything. Whenever possible, give your child two options—just make sure you can live with either choice. Here are some examples:

- Do you want peas or carrots?
- What do you want to put on first, your shoes or your coat?
- Do you want to wear your red shirt or blue shirt?
- You can't go outside right now but you can play indoors. Do you want to play with blocks or color a picture? It's your choice.

Giving your child options will help him stay focused on what he *can* do rather than what he can't. It will help shape his thinking as he learns to recognize he's a competent person who possesses a certain degree of control over his circumstances.

Teach School-Age Kids to Look for the Silver Lining

School-age kids can learn to recognize that difficult situations aren't all bad. Good things can come out of really bad circumstances. So, it's a great time to practice looking for the silver lining.

When your child has little control over an event or the outcome—she gets cut from the soccer team or she doesn't get invited to a birthday party—acknowledge that she can't do anything about it. She can't control other people's choices and she can't go back in time and change things. But what she does have control over is her attitude.

Help her learn to change her attitude by looking on the bright side. While it may be hard to have younger siblings, being the oldest may mean she gets to enjoy certain privileges first. Or while not making the soccer team is disappointing, it could mean she'll have more time to ride her bike.

Just don't ask her to look for the silver lining when her feelings are still so raw. It may take a few hours, or perhaps even a few weeks, for her to gain some new perspective.

When she's had sufficient time to process her emotions, ask questions like:

- What's one good thing that could come out of this?
- What's a positive way to look at this situation?
- How could you look on the bright side, even when something like this happens?

Offer ideas when your child struggles to find them. With practice, she'll learn to start looking for the silver lining on her own.

A child who is able to recognize the silver lining in a tough circumstance is less likely to view herself as a victim. Instead, she will see that there are opportunities to learn and grow, even when she's faced with hard times.

Teach Teenagers Healthy Ways to Get Their Needs Met

Teenagers can be dramatic by nature, so it's easy for them to assume their lives are harder than anyone else's and that no one could possibly understand their hardships. And the Internet now gives teens a global platform to share their perceived injustices.

Posting vague messages on social media like "I can only be hurt so many times before I give up" might be a way to gain support for a victim mind-set. And saying, "We can't let the teachers get away with treating us this way!" can be a way to get other teens to see themselves as victims to gain support for a cause.

So it's important to educate your teen about the ways social media can fuel a victim mentality:

1. **Discuss what your teen shares.** Talk about her intent in announcing an injustice or sharing how she was offended by someone else's behavior.
2. **Talk about the herd mentality.** Joining forces with friends, sharing memes, or using specific hashtags that indicate she's a victim without thinking about what that really means could be damaging to her reputation and her future.

Encourage your teen to avoid complaining, gossiping, and judging in general, but especially online. Make sure your teen knows her words are powerful and they can influence how others perceive themselves and their circumstances.

Teach your teen healthy ways to get her needs met. If she's sad, encourage her to use direct communication. Calling a friend and saying, "I'm having a bad day. Can you talk?" will likely help her gain more support than a cryptic social media message. Just make sure to remind your teen that maintaining friendships requires her to be a good friend to others. Encourage her to be there for her friends and to treat them with kindness when they're struggling with problems as well.

Empowered Kids Become Resilient Adults

Jim Abbott was born without a right hand. But his parents weren't going to let that stop him from realizing his dreams.

When young Abbott announced he wanted to play baseball, his parents asked, "Why not?" and they signed him up for Little League.

With only one hand, he learned how to pitch. That meant he had to balance the glove on his left arm, throw the ball, then quickly put the glove back on his right hand so he could field. And when the ball was hit to him, he had to field it, take the glove off, and throw it to first all with his left hand. But somehow, he made it work.

And it kept on working. He was a standout pitcher in high school and he went on to play in college, where he won a multitude of awards. By age twenty-one, he'd even won a gold medal in the 1988 Olympics.

His skills captured the attention of Major League Baseball. He was drafted by the California Angels without ever playing a single game in the minor leagues. He spent ten years in the major leagues, where he won eighty-seven games, including a dramatic no-hitter.

Abbott's parents acknowledged the extra challenges he faced without a right hand, but they taught him he could overcome those challenges. Abbott says his father—who was only eighteen when Abbott was born—did everything with him that other fathers did with their sons. They fished, rode bikes, and played ball. "When I went out into the world and felt like I'd been spit out the other side, my father would turn me around, open the front door, and send me back out," he explains in his book, *Imperfect: An Improbable Life.*

When a child refuses to play the role of the victim, he won't waste time throwing a pity party. Instead he'll take action. He'll believe he has the power to make his life—and other people's lives—better. He'll be invested in making the world a better place because empowered kids turn into unstoppable adults.

Mentally strong people don't feel sorry for themselves. And if you want to raise a child who will turn into an adult who refuses to engage in self-pity, don't condone a victim mentality. Empower your child to deal with life's challenges head-on, rather than insist he's a powerless victim.

Life isn't always easy. And it's healthy to acknowledge that to your child. But make it clear that even though life is tough, you're tougher. Give your child the skills he needs to create the type of life he wants to live—and the confidence to overcome the obstacles that stand in his way.

Troubleshooting and Common Traps

Be careful that you don't inadvertently reward your child for being a "victim." If your child says he got picked on at recess, resist the urge to say, "Let's go out to eat at your favorite restaurant tonight," to make him feel better. Otherwise he'll learn that being a victim leads to rewards.

Similarly, if your child is going through a difficult time, don't cut him too much extra slack. Letting your child avoid chores because you're going through a divorce or giving your child permission to stay home from school because he's overwhelmed by his work will only reinforce the idea that he's a victim who deserves special treatment.

On the opposite end of the spectrum, parents sometimes minimize a child's feelings. In an effort to "toughen him up," a parent might be tempted to say things like "Stop acting like you're the victim here." But being too cold could reinforce your child's victim mentality, as he'll start to think you don't care.

Show empathy by saying things like "This must be really hard" or "I know this is tough right now." But make it clear to your child that no matter what circumstances he faces, he has options in how he responds. When you show that you have faith in his ability to deal with hard times, he'll feel confident he can handle adversity.

Don't let your child's victim mentality distract you from the real problem. If your child insists he's failing because his teacher doesn't like him, don't waste time arguing about whether the teacher actually likes him. Instead focus on what he's going to do to improve his grades.

WHAT'S HELPFUL

- Looking for warning signs of a victim mentality
- Going after the good
- Replacing BLUE thoughts with true thoughts
- Giving your child two options
- Focusing on what your child can control
- Looking for the silver lining
- Giving your child unstructured playtime
- Teaching your child healthy ways to get attention

WHAT'S NOT HELPFUL

- Feeling sorry for your child
- Attending your child's pity parties
- Rewarding your child for being a victim
- Minimizing your child's feelings
- Pointing out the negative more than the positive
- Underestimating your child's capabilities

They Don't Parent
out of Guilt

Joe's eight-year-old son, Micah, was almost a hundred pounds overweight. Despite warnings from the pediatrician that Micah was at risk for serious health problems, Joe kept feeding him whatever he wanted.

When the pediatrician threatened to call Child Protective Services, the gravity of the situation set in. Joe entered therapy because he knew he needed help changing his parenting habits.

During the first appointment, Joe acknowledged he gave Micah second—or even third—helpings at dinner and he let him eat snacks whenever he wanted. He said, "I know I feed him too much, but I can't stand to see him hungry. He's a big boy. He needs to eat, and no eight-year-old boy wants to eat carrot sticks."

I asked whether he was concerned about Micah's health and he said, "Yes, I've seen what can happen to people when they're overweight. My father has diabetes. I have high cholesterol and I know I could stand to lose a few pounds."

He felt guilty that Micah was overweight, but he felt even guiltier when Micah cried and begged. To alleviate his guilt, he always let him eat one more snack or one more serving.

But he didn't want to do that anymore. He was terrified that if he didn't *take action right away, the pediatrician would call Child Protective Services.*

Joe's goal was to help Micah lose weight. So together, we decided the problems that needed to be addressed were:

1. **Joe lacked basic nutrition information.** He didn't know how much food his son should eat and he didn't know what types of food were high in fat and calories.
2. **Joe couldn't stand feeling guilty.** He needed confidence that he could say no and tolerate feeling bad.

My recommendations to Joe included:

1. **Take Micah to see a dietitian.** Joe needed reassurance his son wasn't being deprived if he limited his food intake and he also needed to learn how to feed his son the right types of foods.
2. **Write a list of all the reasons why it was healthy to set limits with food.** As Joe's guilt rose, his rational thinking declined. Creating a list of reasons why he needed to help Micah maintain a healthy diet could help him keep things in perspective. Reading that list when he was tempted to give in could help him stick to his limits.
3. **Create a discipline plan for dealing with the backlash from Micah.** Since Micah wasn't used to being told no, it was quite likely he was going to scream louder and beg longer the first few times Joe said no. Joe needed a strategy to deal with that behavior.

Joe agreed with the plan, and with help from the dietitian, he began to understand the importance of setting limits on how much food his son consumed each day. The more knowledge he gained, the more motivated he became to help his son lose weight.

He struggled to tolerate his guilt when he said no to his son's requests for more food. So we had to change his thinking. He needed to stop believing that he was depriving his son. Instead he had to start thinking about the benefits his son would experience when he ate healthy portions and fewer snacks.

Over time, it became easier to say no. Joe still felt bad when Micah claimed he was starving or when he said things like "If you loved me, you'd let me have a snack!" But his confidence in his ability to handle guilt and his desire to do what was best for his son helped him resist the temptation to give in.

Micah lost a little weight over the next few months. More importantly, he stopped gaining weight. His progress satisfied his dietitian and Joe promised to continue helping him eat a healthier diet and he also agreed to help him become more active.

During his final therapy session, Joe said, "I used to feel guilty almost all the time because I knew Micah wasn't healthy. Eating junk food made him happy. And when he felt happy, I didn't feel guilty—at least for a minute or two. But over time, letting him eat too much wasn't good for either of us."

Is Parenting Guilt Getting the Best of You?

Feeling guilty after you've done something hurtful is a good sign. But many parents carry around excessive guilt. Take stock of the way you handle guilt and consider whether any of the following statements sound familiar:

- ○ I have trouble saying no to my child because I feel guilty.
- ○ I regularly beat myself up for not being as good of a parent as I think I should be.
- ○ Watching other parents causes me to think I should be doing more for my child.
- ○ I frequently spend a lot of time thinking about mistakes I've made as a parent.
- ○ Even though I can't specifically identify why, I'm convinced I'm somehow going to mess up my child for life.
- ○ I feel guilty over things I have no control over.
- ○ I sometimes give my child extra things because I feel guilty.

○ I give in when my child says things like "But all the other kids get to have one!"

○ No matter how much time I spend with my child, I feel like it's never enough.

○ I think if I feel guilty, it must be because I'm doing something wrong.

Why Parents Feel Guilty

Joe convinced himself that denying his son food was wrong. He thought if he said no when Micah was hungry, he would cause him to suffer.

Like Joe, many parents exchange short-term discomfort for long-term pain, even when it's at their child's expense. Micah was the one who was going to suffer long-term health problems, but allowing him to overeat relieved Joe of his immediate guilt. Joe felt guilty that Micah was at risk of serious health issues but he felt even worse when he denied Micah a second helping.

While you might not see such dire consequences stemming from parenting out of guilt, it's likely that your feelings of guilt sometimes shape your parenting practices. Consider how these feelings can lead to unhealthy behavior.

TYPES OF PARENTAL GUILT

There are three main types of guilt parents experience:

1. Appropriate guilt

A guilty conscience can be a good thing. Feelings of remorse may signal that your actions aren't in line with your values, which could motivate you to create positive change.

Feeling guilty after yelling at your children could be a wake-up call that you need to find a new way to discipline them. Or feeling bad after you lose your temper might be a sign you need to reduce your stress level. Either way, that uncomfortable guilty feeling may prompt you to repair the relationship and change your behavior.

2. Unnecessary guilt

One day you might say, "It was such a nice day today. I should have played outside with the kids." But then, the next day, you find yourself saying, "I shouldn't have stayed outside so long with the kids. They were hot and now they're itchy from all those bug bites."

Even though your behavior isn't actually harmful, you might convince yourself that you let your child down. But in reality, your actions aren't damaging your child's health or your relationship in any way.

3. Chronic guilt

Perhaps you feel guilty all the time, without a clear reason why. Maybe you assume you're doing something that will scar your child for life or maybe you worry that you're just not doing enough to prepare your child for the future.

Whenever your child struggles, you might draw sweeping conclusions that link his "inadequacies" to your parental failures. You might also make negative predictions about how your present choices will cause your child problems later in life.

EXCESSIVE GUILT STEMS FROM INCORRECT BELIEFS

While many parents experience guilt, working mothers seem to be the most susceptible to it. In a survey by BabyCenter, a whopping 94 percent of moms reported feeling mommy guilt.

In the decades since it became commonplace for mothers to enter the workforce, many working moms feel torn as they strive to find the "perfect" work-life balance. While some working parents claim you really can "have it all," most mothers have discovered limits to their superhuman abilities. Any mothers who strive to climb the corporate ladder while keeping their hat in the ring for "mother of the year" will likely feel as though they fall short somehow.

Mommy guilt seems to stem from the romanticized notion that before mothers entered the workforce, stay-at-home moms were all like June Cleaver. They made home-cooked meals, kept a neat house, and spent copious amounts of time with their children every day.

But in reality, studies show that since 1985, the number of hours parents spend with their children each week has been on the rise. A 2016 study published in the *Journal of Marriage and Family* reports American parents spend more time with their children than any other parents in the developed world. Yet there's still this idea that parents should devote even more time to their kids.

Another study published in the *Journal of Marriage and Family*, this one in 2015, found that the quantity of time you spend with your child doesn't really matter all that much. Researchers discovered that the time mothers spent with their child had no effect on behavior, emotions, academics, or overall well-being.

There was one exception—adolescence. When mothers spent more time with a teen, fewer delinquent behaviors were reported. But that's it. It didn't matter whether the mother had been a stay-at-home mom for fifteen years or whether she'd been a working parent all her child's life.

And oddly, the time when kids reach adolescence is precisely the time that many mothers enter the workforce. After all, the kids are finally old enough to start fending for themselves. But research shows the teenage years are the critical time period when kids actually do need to spend more time with their parents.

That's not to say that time with children isn't important—clearly, it's an integral part of healthy development. But the quality rather than the quantity of time is what matters most.

Being a stay-at-home mom doesn't absolve parents from guilt, however. I've seen plenty of mothers in my therapy office who feel guilty that they don't love every minute of being a stay-at-home parent. And I've seen work-at-home moms who get a double dose of guilt—they feel bad they aren't at the office and feel guilty that they aren't able to play with their kids all day.

SOCIAL COMPARISONS CAUSE YOU TO FEEL INADEQUATE

It's easy to judge how you're doing as a parent by drawing social comparisons. When you scroll through Facebook you're likely to see plenty of people who look as though they should be nominated for parent of the year. Fun family vacations, extravagant birthday parties, beautifully decorated nurseries, and parents who make it all look easy.

And it's not just social media. Maybe you overheard your neighbor say she signed her son up for a soccer clinic and you start to think, "Should I have done that?" Or you drop your child off at a birthday party that makes your child's last celebration look incredibly lame and you think, "My child deserves better than what I give her."

Of course, marketers know how to prey on your guilt as well. Whether it's a product that will teach your child to read at the age of three, or it's the latest toy that will give your child endless hours of fun, companies send the message that your child not only deserves it, but needs it to be truly happy.

To keep up with the Joneses, parents are buying more gifts than they can afford. A survey conducted by *Parenting* magazine found that 76 percent of parents spoil their children during the holidays because they want to ensure their child won't be disappointed, because if she's disappointed, they'd feel guilty.

But don't think having more money to buy your child more stuff will automatically alleviate your guilt. In a recent PBS special, singer and actress Jennifer Lopez talked about the mommy guilt she experiences. Despite her estimated net worth of over $300 million, and an entire staff to help her care for her children, she said she often feels like she's not doing enough for her kids. So rest assured, even if you did have everything at your disposal, you'd likely still feel some sense of guilt.

Parenting out of Guilt Sends an Unhealthy Message

Guilt is an uncomfortable emotion that can be hard to tolerate. Quite often, it's tempting to take drastic measures to rid yourself of it.

In Joe's case, he gave in to his son's demands to gain some temporary relief from his guilt. But ultimately, it caused more long-term problems.

Guilt can also cloud your judgment. And if you're parenting your child out of guilt, you'll struggle to make the best parenting choices.

GUILT CAN KEEP YOU STUCK IN A PATTERN OF BAD HABITS

Feelings of guilt can influence your behavior. You might be tempted to do things that will relieve your guilty conscience, even when it's not in your child's best interest.

Here's what parents do when they parent out of guilt:

- **Fend off guilt**—In an attempt to ward off that uncomfortable guilty feeling, you might take drastic steps to avoid anything that could cause you to feel like a "bad" parent. So perhaps you deny yourself time alone because you'd feel guilty taking a break. Or maybe you don't buy things for yourself because you'd feel bad not spending that money on the kids.

- **Alleviate guilt**—Sometimes parents alleviate their guilt by giving in to their kids' requests—such as Joe did with his son Micah. When your child cries or insists you're the meanest parent in the world, it can be tempting to give him what he wants. Even if it isn't in his best interest, giving in helps you feel better—at least temporarily.

- **Overcompensate for guilt**—A parent who feels guilty for yelling at her child earlier in the day may allow him to stay up late. Or a parent who feels guilty because he got divorced may allow his kids to do whatever they want during his weekend visitations. Even though those actions don't mitigate the problem, they might ease a parent's guilty conscience.

GIVING IN TO GUILT TRIPS SENDS THE WRONG MESSAGE

If you say, "Oh, fine, go ahead!" after your child gives you the puppy-dog face, or you agree to loan money to a relative who insists, "Good families help each other," you are teaching your child she should succumb to guilt trips as well.

Also, giving in after your child whines, begs, or sticks out his bottom lip makes him question your decision-making abilities. Kids need consistency and an authority figure who can keep them safe.

If you change your mind to relieve the guilt you felt for saying no, your child may become anxious as he sees that you're a bit wishy-washy when it comes to decisions. Although kids appear as though they want you to give in, doing so undermines their overall confidence in you. Your child wants to see that you're a strong leader who can withstand the pressure to give in when the going gets tough.

Kids learn how to pour on the guilt as well. While one parent may give in to a child who says, "But I haven't seen you all day!" the other one might be more likely to back down when she hears, "But all the other kids do that!" You certainly don't want your child to learn to manipulate people with guilt trips.

What to Do Instead

In Joe's case, he had to learn to tolerate feeling guilty when he said no. And he had to see that feeling guilty didn't necessarily mean he was doing anything wrong. In fact, in his situation, feeling guilty meant he was setting limits with his son.

I've worked with many parents who say things like "I let my kids play way too many video games," or "I don't spend nearly enough time with my kids." But they aren't sure whether the solution is to change their behavior or change their emotions. Acknowledge the reasons for your guilt and notice how it affects your behavior. Then, you can decide what action to take.

CHANGE YOUR BEHAVIOR WHEN GUILT IS WARRANTED

To determine whether your guilt is justified, ask yourself these four questions:

1. **Did I do something that negatively affected my child?** Perhaps you've become too relaxed with screen time and your child is spending most of his time watching TV. Or maybe you overreacted out of anger and said something you shouldn't have. If your actions are harmful, change your behavior.

2. **Is there something I can change?** If you feel guilty because you got divorced three years ago, you can't go back in time to change it. But if you're feeling guilty because you aren't encouraging your child to do his homework, you can rectify the problem.

3. **What can I do differently?** Identify one small step you can take to become a better parent. Create a specific plan that will help you change your habits. So instead of scrolling through your phone while you're spending time with your child, commit to giving her your undivided attention. Or rather than eat dinner in front of the TV, create a rule that says no electronics during meals.

4. **Is there something I should do to make amends with my child?** While you don't need to apologize to a three-year-old for being stressed out, make amends when it is appropriate to do so. Say, "I am sorry I yelled at you. I was angry and I should have found a better way to handle my anger." Show your child how to make reparations after you've made a mistake.

If you can't change your behavior (like quitting your job to become a stay-at-home parent), try changing the way you think about guilt. Beating yourself up or convincing yourself that you're doing damage (even when there isn't any evidence) isn't helpful.

STOP MAKING CATASTROPHIC PREDICTIONS

Just because you feel bad doesn't mean you've actually done anything wrong. Yet many parents predict one small thing they do today will somehow prevent their child from reaching her greatest potential down the road. But there's a good chance your assumptions about the impact your parenting has on your child aren't accurate.

Here's a scenario:

A mother forgets to sign her ten-year-old up for baseball camp. She starts thinking things like "I am such a disorganized parent. I don't get him involved in enough activities. All of his friends are going to camp together, where they'll create lifelong memories and my son is going to be left out. All the other kids are going to improve their skills, and my child probably won't make the baseball team next year."

This parent predicts her child is going to become a social outcast who will never be able to play baseball because he missed out on one week of baseball camp. She might spend the rest of her life believing her disorganization prevented her son from making the major leagues.

Rest assured, I've yet to have an adult enter my therapy office because he didn't get to go to summer camp. I'm much more likely to see people who say, "My parents were so stressed out all the time because they were afraid of being 'bad' parents that we never had any fun."

I once worked with a mother who strongly believed that all good mothers always had clean houses. So she spent the majority of her time cleaning carpets, scrubbing floors, and washing windows. She refused to let her kids use art supplies and she never allowed them to have friends over because she was afraid they'd mess up the house. Ironically, her desire to be a "good mother" with a clean house prevented her from having time to play with her kids.

So while a cluttered house or unswept floor weren't likely to scar her children, her stress about the cleanliness of the house left an unhealthy impression on them.

You have no way to predict how some of your child's experiences might shape her—or how she'll even look back on them when she's an adult. When she's thirty, she might not even remember that incident you thought would scar her for life.

I have a friend who describes her childhood as a wonderful experience. She speaks highly of both of her parents and talks about the great effort they put into cooperating with one another after they got divorced.

But if you talked to her brother, you'd swear they were raised by different people. He describes their parents as selfish and he recalls their divorce as a turning point in his childhood—saying that he had to grow up too fast as a result.

Two kids enduring the same situation may have very different experiences. Of course, they may perceive situations quite differently depending on their ages, but you just never know how it will affect them. So before you conclude you've damaged your child, remember, your predictions might not be accurate.

REFUSE TO DRAW INACCURATE CONCLUSIONS

Connecting the dots between cause and effect helps us make sense of certain situations. After all, that's the lesson we try to teach kids, right? *You threw the ball, so it's your fault the vase broke. Or, you hit your sister, so it's your fault she's crying.*

But sometimes we leap to conclusions even when there isn't any proof because we feel as though we need some sort of explanation. And quite often that conclusion isn't accurate.

I once met a mother who was convinced her child's learning problems stemmed from the fact that she drank a few cups of coffee during her pregnancy. "Sometimes, I just needed a little pick-me-up because I was so tired all the time. I knew it was wrong to have caffeine but I did it anyway," she said.

I've worked with many mothers who were convinced something they consumed (or didn't consume) or something they were exposed to during pregnancy explained the problems in their children's lives. I had to assure one mother that the one glass of wine she drank before she learned she was pregnant probably didn't cause ADHD and had to convince another mother that the nonorganic vegetables her child ate as a toddler didn't cause his anxiety.

While it is important to be healthy during pregnancy and throughout your child's life, there are studies that show it might not be as life-altering as some parents predict. A 2011 study published in the journal *Neurotoxicology and Teratology* found that babies born addicted to crack cocaine end up doing just as well in life as babies who weren't born addicted to drugs. So if crack doesn't harm your child's chances at lifelong success, it's unlikely your insatiable appetite for salmon during pregnancy is the sole reason he's not an honor student.

Consider the types of conclusions you've drawn to explain something in your parenting life and ask yourself if it's possible there might be some alternative answers. If you blame yourself excessively for something, be open to the possibility that it might not be your fault. It might be time to start changing the story you tell yourself.

FORGIVE YOURSELF FOR THE MISTAKES YOU MAKE

Gabrielle had only stepped out of the room for a minute when her curious three-year-old son, Tyson, peered over the kitchen counter. He couldn't quite see what was up there, so he grabbed the electrical cord to the crock pot in an attempt to pull himself up. The Crock-Pot slid off the counter and spilled boiling hot soup onto the little boy.

Tyson spent the next several weeks in the hospital getting treatment for the burns that covered much of his body. And although he recovered from his injuries, he would always have scars on his arms and face.

Gabrielle started therapy a few months after the accident. And when we met for her first session she said, "Every time I look at the scars on his face I feel so bad that I let that happen to him. I'll never be able to forgive myself."

In fact, Gabrielle was convinced she *shouldn't* forgive herself. She thought she didn't deserve to be happy and feeling guilty was her penance. The only reason she came to therapy was to help make sure she didn't make such a "stupid mistake" again.

It took a long time for Gabrielle to acknowledge that what happened to her son was an accident. And accidents can't always be prevented.

She had to see how beating herself up every day wasn't healthy for her son. He needed an emotionally present mother who loved herself.

Over the course of several months, Gabrielle was able to acknowledge that the accident didn't serve as evidence that she was a bad parent. She was a kind and loving mother.

Slowly but surely, she was able to let go of some of her guilt by changing the way she thought about the accident. Rather than punish herself for what happened, she focused on enjoying the time she had with her son and she tried to prevent the same thing from happening to other families.

A little guilt isn't a bad thing. But convincing yourself you're a bad person or a horrible parent does more damage than good. Don't allow self-condemnation to get in the way of becoming the best parent you can be.

STRIVE TO BE GOOD ENOUGH

Earlier today, I stumbled across an Internet meme that said, "Good enough is never good enough." And while it wasn't specifically referring to parenting, I think that's the attitude many modern-day parents have adopted.

But being a "good enough" parent actually could be the best thing for your child, at least according to research conducted by the late D. W. Winnicott, a pediatrician and psychoanalyst. He interacted with thousands of mothers and their children and he concluded, "To be a good mother is to be a good enough mother." Later, the conclusion was expanded to include fathers.

Winnicott recognized that good enough mothers felt conflicted about being selfless and self-interested. They were dedicated to their child, yet still experienced resentment. They made plenty of mistakes, yet through their imperfect and human ways, good enough mothers raised healthy and resilient children.

It definitely makes sense when you think about it. After all, let's imagine you were the "perfect" parent—whatever that means. You did everything "right" all the time.

What would happen to your child when he becomes an adult? He'd struggle to survive in an imperfect world filled with human beings who make mistakes. There will be times when his future partner, his boss, and his neighbors fail him. He needs to know how to deal with disappointment, hurt feelings, and imperfect people.

Each parenting mistake you make is an opportunity for your child to build mental strength. That doesn't mean you should go out of your way to speed up his strength-building process, but it does mean you can give him real-life learning experiences through your own failures.

So don't beat yourself up for not being a perfect parent. Because even if you were perfect, you wouldn't be doing your child any favors. Instead give yourself permission to be a good enough parent, flaws and all.

Just like you love your child even though she's imperfect, your child will love you for being a good enough parent. She'll appreciate your efforts, and someday she'll recognize the sacrifices you made to raise her to become a responsible adult.

How to Teach Kids About Guilt

Whenever Micah begged Joe for a snack and Joe gave in, he was teaching Micah that guilt was intolerable. It was an unhealthy message and he needed to teach him that guilty feelings didn't have to dictate his behavior.

If your child breaks someone's toy or says something mean, you want him to feel guilt. The lack of a conscience could be a sign he's a psychopath.

But on the opposite end of the spectrum, you also don't want a child who feels guilty all the time. A child who apologizes for everything or who blames himself unnecessarily may be more susceptible to mental health problems, like anxiety and depression.

TELL YOUR CHILD TO LISTEN TO HIS SHOULDER ANGEL

Do you remember watching cartoons that depicted a character with a devil on one shoulder and an angel on the other? The shoulder devil tries to convince the character to make bad choices while the shoulder angel tries to convince him to do what's right. If you ever took Psychology 101, you might recall this as Freud's psychoanalytic theory of personality.

Talk to your child about how everyone experiences times when one part of their brain says to break the rules and the other part says to do the right thing. If he's never seen a cartoon with the devil and the angel on each shoulder, a quick online search can help you find an example.

Explain the importance of listening to his shoulder angel (which is really his conscience). Here's a sample dialogue:

Parent: Have you ever seen a cartoon character who has a devil on one shoulder and an angel on the other and they're both telling the character to do something different?

Child: Yes.

Parent: Well, that's sort of what happens in real life. Although we don't see an actual devil and a real angel, part of our brains tells us it's okay to break the rules or hurt someone's feelings. But the other part of our brains says, "No, don't do that! It's wrong!" Does that ever happen to you?

Child: Yes. When you told me I couldn't eat a cookie, part of my brain said, "Just take one anyway!"

Parent: That sounds like something the shoulder devil would say. What did your shoulder angel say?

Child: He said, "No, don't do it! You have to listen to your mother."

Parent: So you listened to your shoulder angel?

Child: Yes.

Parent: Good work! It's important to listen to your shoulder angel as much as you can.

Talk about the potential consequences of not listening to the shoulder angel. Making bad choices can hurt other people's feelings or can damage relationships. It's also likely to cause your child to feel guilt.

Point out that guilty feelings can serve as a reminder that you made a bad choice. And sometimes that means you have to take steps to make reparations. But make sure your child knows that an apology or an attempt to make amends won't undo the fact that he made a mistake.

INSTILL GUILT *NOT* SHAME

I used to work at a junior high school and many of the kids referred to therapy were the ones who got sent to the principal's office on a regular basis. One particular day, the school called a meeting to discuss a twelve-year-old boy whose behavior was out of control.

His mother took the afternoon off from work to attend. Her embarrassment and frustration were evident as she listened to the teachers go around the table, one by one, explaining all of his bad behaviors. She apologized repeatedly for her son's outbursts and defiance.

The boy was invited to join the last few minutes of the meeting so the teachers could explain the newest disciplinary plan. As soon as he walked through the door, his mother started in.

"How could you do this to me? You've turned into such a bad kid! Look at what you've done. I've had to sit around for an hour listening to your poor teachers talk about how bad you are." She went on for at least five minutes and it was clear she felt guilty that her son wasn't exactly a model citizen. And she was trying to shame him for his misbehavior.

But shaming kids doesn't motivate them to change. It causes kids to believe they possess character flaws that render them incapable of behaving. A child who believes "I'm bad" will likely fulfill that label and he won't be motivated to make good choices.

It's easy to confuse shame and guilt. In fact, many researchers struggle to agree on a clear definition between the two. Here are three ways to distinguish the two emotions:

- **Guilt involves feeling bad about a behavior.** Feeling bad about what you did indicates guilt. Feeling bad about who you are constitutes shame. Thinking, "I shouldn't have made that mean comment," is guilt. Thinking, "I'm such a horrible person for saying that," is shame.
- **Guilt is usually private.** Guilt is usually a private emotion, but shame tends to involve public knowledge of what you did. So while you might feel guilty for cheating on a test, you might experience shame if all of your friends and family condemn you for it.
- **Guilt stems from not doing the right thing.** Guilt occurs when you fail to make a good choice. Shame usually stems from doing something wrong and it often involves breaking a moral code. So you might feel guilty if you don't help your friend move, but you are more likely to experience shame if you stole something from your friend.

While it's helpful to ensure your child develops a healthy amount of guilt, avoid shaming your child. Children who experience shame struggle to feel good about who they are, and they often give up trying to make healthy choices.

Teach Preschoolers Basic Concepts About Guilt

Researchers report children as young as two start to show signs of guilt when they do something wrong. For instance, toddlers avert eye contact when they feel bad. Of course, they don't yet fully understand what guilt means.

When your child hurts someone, place your attention on the victim and model how to respond. Say things like "Oh no, I'm so sorry Johnny kicked you. Are you hurt?" Offer to get a Band-Aid or give a hug.

Once you've tended to the victim, follow through with a consequence for your child. Place him in time-out or take away a privilege. You can also instill a consequence that will help make amends.

For example, make him loan his favorite toy to the victim for twenty-four hours. Or have him do an extra chore for his brother. Doing a kind deed for the victim can go a long way toward showing him the importance of making reparations.

Start using the word "guilt" in your language with your preschooler and role-model how to give an apology. Say things like "I'm very sorry we can't go to the playground today because it is raining. I feel guilty that I promised you that we would, but it just wouldn't be safe to go when the slides are all wet."

It's a good time to also start pointing out examples of times when you listened to your shoulder angel. Say something like "I'd really like to park right next to the door since it's raining outside but my shoulder angel reminds me that it wouldn't be right to park in that space meant for people who have trouble walking. I'd feel guilty if I didn't listen to my shoulder angel." Over time, your child will learn what it means to feel guilty and he'll recognize the importance of striving to make the right choice.

Teach School-Age Kids How to Deal with Guilt

Researchers have found that when children between the ages of five and eight do something hurtful, they just want to forget the event ever happened. They're more likely to look for an escape route—like running into the other room—rather than take responsibility for their behavior.

So don't be surprised if your child struggles to take responsibility at this age. You can help her face guilt head-on by showing her how to deal with it in a healthy manner.

When your child hurts someone physically or emotionally, brainstorm together how he can make amends. Ask questions like "You lied to your friend. What do you think you should do about that?" or "You broke your sister's doll. What can you do now?".

Somewhere around the age of nine or ten, kids show more interest in wanting to repair the relationship. They're more likely to apologize or want to make amends on their own. Start conversations about guilt so your child will learn to recognize when he's feeling it.

Ask questions like "Did you feel guilty when you threw that ball and it hit that girl?" or "Did you feel guilty when you lied?" Point out that feeling guilty is a good sign because it shows he's trying to be a good person and wants to do better next time.

Apologize to your child when you make a mistake. This will serve as a good role model about how to repair a relationship. Say things like "I'm sorry I yelled at you earlier. I was stressed out about work and I took it out on you." Make it clear that you plan to change your behavior and you'll teach your child how to apologize when he makes a mistake.

Teach Teens Guilt Trips Don't Work

A teen is likely to have a good understanding of guilt and he may try to guilt-trip you into doing what he wants. You're likely to hear things like "But everyone else's parents let them do it!" or "You *never* let me do anything fun!"

When your child says these things, respond with a simple answer like "I love you and it's my job to keep you safe." You don't need to offer a lengthy explanation. But whatever you do, don't give in to guilt trips.

Acknowledge when you feel guilty by saying, "I feel bad that you are the only one of your friends who isn't allowed to go to that party but I'm not going to change my mind." Teach your child that you're going to make wise decisions, even when it's uncomfortable to do so.

Additionally, don't use guilt trips on your teen. Saying things like "If you really cared about me, you wouldn't make me worry so much" isn't healthy. Parental guilt trips have a profoundly negative effect on teens. A study at the University of Virginia discovered that teens who are subjected to guilt trips are more likely to struggle to develop healthy friendships and relationships later in life.

Set limits and follow through with consequences, but leave the guilt trip out of your discipline. Teach healthy relationship skills and model how to get your needs met in a healthy way.

Your teen may experience excessive or unnecessary guilt at times and she may need help handling those emotions. Disagreements with friends may lead to guilty feelings, even when your teen does the right thing. Tell your child, "I think you made a good decision but not everyone will always be happy with the choices you make. And you might feel guilty about that, but it doesn't mean you did anything wrong."

Kids Who Understand Guilt Become Adults
Who Set Healthy Boundaries

Imagine your twelve-year-old's friend asks to copy his homework. When your child declines, his friend says, "If you were really a good friend you'd help me out." Would you want your child to give in to that type of guilt trip?

Or what if your teenage daughter goes on a date with a boy who says, "If you loved me, you'd have sex with me?" Would you want her to give in because he guilted her into it?

Your child learns how to deal with guilt by watching you. If you succumb to guilt trips, he'll do the same. Refusing to give in, working to make amends, and tolerating healthy guilt will help your child develop a moral compass. He'll learn to recognize that he can tolerate guilt trips from others and he can deal with difficult emotions, like guilt, in a healthy manner.

Mentally strong people don't try to please everyone. Instead they're able to make healthy decisions, even when others disagree with their choices. When you refuse to parent out of guilt, you'll show your child that guilty feelings don't have to lead to unproductive behavior or unhealthy shame.

He'll grow up knowing that he can set healthy limits with other people. Whether he says no to a peer who tries to pressure him into underage drinking or he refuses to be treated like a doormat at the office, he'll recognize that his job isn't to make other people happy.

Troubleshooting and Common Traps

Forcing your child to apologize usually isn't a good idea. If your child walks up to someone and says, "Sorry," but he doesn't mean it, he won't actually be doing anything to relieve his guilt or make amends. So rather than force an apology, focus on role-modeling apologies. Then, when your child is old enough to understand what it means to genuinely say "I'm sorry," he'll be more likely to offer a sincere apology.

Unfortunately, many kids run around saying, "I'm sorry," with no intention of changing their behavior. Teach your child that apologies are only meaningful when she is intent on trying to change her behavior.

Be careful not to fall into the trap of trying to alleviate your child's guilt too soon. Saying, "Oh, that's okay that you broke that lamp," might cause your child to think her behavior wasn't a big deal. Make sure she knows that her behavior hurts other people. It's healthy for her to experience some level of guilt because that guilt can lead to positive behavior change.

Be on the lookout for excessive guilt in young children, however. Quite often, they experience magical thinking, where they believe they have the power to control certain things that happen in the universe. Sometimes this way of thinking leads to excessive self-blame when something bad happens.

A child who says, "I hate my brother!" might feel it's his fault when his brother gets hurt. Or one who dislikes having to help care for his dog might believe he's at fault if the dog gets hit by a car. If you see signs of unnecessary guilt, reassure your child that he had nothing to do with those types of outcomes.

WHAT'S HELPFUL

- Evaluating whether your guilt is warranted
- Striving to be good enough
- Refusing to go on guilt trips
- Practicing self-forgiveness
- Teaching your child to make amends
- Sticking to your limits even when your child tries to guilt you into changing your mind
- Encouraging your child to listen to his shoulder angel
- Role-modeling how to apologize

WHAT'S NOT HELPFUL

- Aiming to be a perfect parent
- Comparing yourself to other parents
- Punishing yourself for your mistakes
- Assuming your feelings of guilt must mean you did something wrong
- Giving in to alleviate your guilt, even when it's not in your child's best interest
- Shaming your child for his misbehavior

They Don't Make
Their Child the Center
of the Universe

Carol and Tom brought their fourteen-year-old daughter, Brittany, to coun-seling because they weren't sure what to do with her anymore. "She refuses to listen to us," Carol explained. "She won't do what we say and she doesn't care what anyone thinks."

Tom said, "I just don't know what happened to our little girl. We gave her everything she could have ever wanted and this is how she treats us?"

Carol and Tom were older parents by most standards. Carol was forty and Tom was forty-three when Brittany was born. And Brittany was their "mir-acle" baby. After trying to conceive for nearly a decade, they were just about to give up hope when Carol became pregnant. From the minute she was born, Brittany was the light of their world.

They spent almost all their time together as a family. Whether they were headed to the beach or they were off to Disney World, the three of them were always together, doing whatever Brittany wanted.

Her parents showered her with all the possessions she ever wished for. She rarely did any chores because her parents wanted her to have fun. And she had few responsibilities because her parents thought she should "just be a kid."

They began having problems with Brittany when she was about twelve. She became defiant and argumentative, and over the years, their conflict increased.

The seriousness of the situation hit home when they overheard one of Brittany's classmates describe her as one of the "mean girls" in school. It was a horrifying revelation to both Carol and Tom to think that their daughter's disrespectful behavior had spread beyond the confines of their home. They wanted to put a stop to it but they weren't sure how.

Brittany wasn't invested in changing, so if her parents wanted her to behave differently, they needed to change their behavior. Carol and Tom attended the second appointment without Brittany so we could talk about strategies that would help their daughter.

The problems appeared to be:

1. **Brittany thought she was the center of the universe.** Her parents doted on her to her own detriment.
2. **Her social skills were suffering.** Brittany was having trouble getting along with other kids because she lacked basic social skills, like how to empathize and take turns.

If Carol and Tom wanted to help Brittany, they needed to make the following changes:

1. **Set limits with her.** That meant saying no and sticking to it, even when she got upset.
2. **Do things that didn't involve Brittany.** Setting aside time for themselves as individuals and time together as a married couple could help Brittany see that their lives didn't revolve around her.
3. **Make Brittany earn privileges.** Rather than giving her anything she wanted regardless of her behavior, Carol and Tom needed to show Brittany that privileges must be earned.

At first, Carol said, "But we don't mind doing all those things for Brittany. She's our only child and we want to give her everything we can." I pointed out whether they "minded" or even enjoyed doing nice things for their daughter wasn't the point. It wasn't good for Brittany to be given unlimited attention and material possessions without any responsibilities.

After a lengthy conversation about how things had gotten to this point, both parents acknowledged the role they played in the way Brittany viewed herself. They treated her like a little princess, and over time, she started believing she was extra special.

Over the next few weeks, Brittany's parents began setting more ground rules and giving her more responsibilities. They stopped showering her with praise and material goods, and for the first time, Brittany had to do chores to earn an allowance.

At first, her behavior got worse. She dug in her heels and refused to do anything. But her parents stood their ground. They stopped making everything about "Brittany." They made her earn privileges based on her good behavior. They began emphasizing kindness. And they stopped giving in to all of her demands.

They realized that they weren't going to change the way Brittany viewed herself overnight. It had taken her years to develop the belief that she was the center of the universe, and it was going to take time to show her that that belief wasn't accurate.

But they were invested in making it happen. They didn't want their spoiled teenager to turn into an irresponsible adult.

Does the World Revolve Around Your Child?

While you might think it's healthy to make your child the center of *your* world, doing so teaches children that they're the center of the entire universe. Do any of the following points sound familiar?

- ○ I love to shower my child with praise and accolades.
- ○ I think my child is more special than other kids.
- ○ I'm happy to drop whatever I'm doing to respond to my child's requests.

○ I'm pretty sure my child is better than average in most things.
○ I love to remind my child of all the areas where she excels.
○ I think it's impossible for kids to have too much confidence or too much self-esteem in today's world.
○ I devote a lot of time toward doing all the things my child wants to do.
○ I feel okay about overindulging my child.
○ I believe my child deserves special treatment.

Why Parents Make Kids the Center of the Universe

Spoiled. Entitled. Narcissistic. Self-absorbed. Call it whatever you want. But parents who make their child the center of the universe cause them to think they're exceptional.

Remember that guilt we talked about in the previous chapter? Those guilty feelings often drive parents to make kids the center of the universe. Parents who believe in the common misconception that "good parents do everything for their kids" dote on their children to a fault.

That's what Carol and Tom did. They were thrilled that they were able to have a child and they wanted to be the best parents they could be.

They thought being really nice to their child would teach her to be really nice to other people. What they didn't realize was that "being nice" didn't mean they had to do whatever their daughter wanted. Rather than teach her to be a kind and loving person, they had taught her to be a demanding and entitled child.

They thought saying no to something Brittany wanted somehow meant they weren't being good parents. They figured it was their duty—since they were so lucky to finally have a child—to make sure that they gave her anything and everything she ever wanted. And they made everything in their lives revolve around Brittany.

Their identities were wrapped up in being parents. They were no longer

"Tom the engineer" and "Carol the librarian." Instead, they saw themselves almost exclusively as "Brittany's parents." Clearly, that wasn't good for their marriage or their personal well-being.

Even if you don't dote on your child to the extent that Carol and Tom doted on Brittany, there may be some ways you still send a message to your child that he's "extra special." Perhaps you set up meetings with the teacher to inquire about why your child wasn't promoted into the higher-level reading group even though her grade is only mediocre. Or maybe you regularly point out your child is the *only* one in the class who knows her math facts and the *only* kid on the soccer team who can score on a penalty kick, which reinforces her belief that she's exceptional.

THE FUZZY LINE BETWEEN HEALTHY SELF-ESTEEM AND NARCISSISM

During the nineties, low self-esteem was discussed as if it were a health epidemic that was infiltrating neighborhoods and school yards like a contagious disease. To stop the "self-esteem crisis," kids were taught they were special. Everyone was given a trophy. And children were promised that they were "the best." Somewhere along the way, the difference between healthy self-esteem and detrimental narcissism was lost.

According to Jean Twenge, the author of *The Narcissism Epidemic,* kids have been given too much undeserved praise and it's led to the rise of narcissism over the past few decades among Western youth. Twenge argues that kids have overinflated egos and it's their parents' fault.

Quite often, parents believe that if a little compliment leads to a little self-esteem, an over-the-top compliment must lead to great self-esteem. Rather than telling a child, "Great job on the soccer field today," parents are more apt to say, "You're the best soccer player in the whole world."

Adding fuel to the fire is the emergence of social media and selfies. Young children pose for photos and ask parents, "Can you share that one on Facebook?" Then, once kids are old enough to get their own social media accounts, the competition to gain fans, likes, and followers begins. Many teens' attempts to become an online celebrity in this way only further their notion that the world revolves around them.

At the same time, parents are told kids are struggling with body shaming, eating disorders, cyberbullying, and mental health problems. So of course, parents wanting to combat those potential problems shower their children with messages that they are beautiful, perfect, and lovely in every way. While honest and accurate feedback validates kids for who they are, empty praise and unrealistic accolades actually lead to insecurity. Parents who don't understand where the line is between healthy self-esteem and narcissism may easily go overboard.

OVERCOMPENSATING FOR YOUR CHILDHOOD

For some parents, making their child the center of the universe is about healing their own childhood. A father who grew up without much money may be tempted to spoil his child so she never feels poor. Or a mother who never felt "good enough" as a child may shower her child with tons of accolades to ensure she feels good about herself.

Take Dave, for example. From the minute his son, Nathaniel, was born, Dave vowed to make his childhood better than his own. Growing up, Dave was never given much attention from his father, who worked long hours. But even when he was home, he rarely gave Dave any attention because he strongly believed that children should be seen and not heard.

Dave never wanted Nathaniel to experience the same sting of rejection or the pain of loneliness. So he invested all of his time into ensuring his son felt the love he himself never experienced as a boy. And Dave was proud of himself for being such a hands-on dad.

Which is why he was surprised when Nathaniel's preschool teacher approached him to say she was concerned about his behavior. Nathaniel was aggressive toward the other children, and quite often, he was defiant.

Dave's guilt was apparent from our first session together. He came into my office saying, "I feel like a failure. I did everything I could to make sure my son was a happy, well-adjusted child. But apparently, I didn't even do that right."

Dave knew his father hadn't been a very good parent. So he thought if he just did the opposite of what his dad had done, it would mean he was being a good parent. What he didn't realize was that there existed a happy medium between undernurturing and overparenting. It was just a matter of figuring out what exactly that happy medium was.

He had to see that his son's behavior didn't mean he was a "bad" parent. It meant his son needed more support. And he had to accept that more support meant more rules and more consistent consequences, not endless amounts of attention.

Making Your Child the Center of the Universe Will Make Him Self-Centered

When children are young, they believe that the world stops when they go to sleep and that the day begins for everyone the moment they wake up. And for a while, that egocentric view is part of normal child development. But if you continue to send the message that the sun rises and sets for your child, he'll never learn that the world is much bigger than he is.

In the case of Brittany, her parents made their world revolve around her. Getting whatever she wanted, whenever she wanted it, led to an unhealthy superiority complex. It interfered with her friendships, and other kids thought she was mean.

GRANDIOSE SELF-BELIEFS CAUSE KIDS TO LASH OUT

Telling your child "You're a genius in math," or "You're the prettiest girl in the whole world," may help in the short-term. When she's five, she might believe those things are true. But at some point, she'll start to realize that the rest of the world doesn't agree.

If she's grown up hearing she's the world's best basketball player, yet she doesn't make the all-star team, she has to somehow reconcile the two. Rather than conclude that your statements are inaccurate, she's more likely to decide other people don't recognize greatness when they see it. So she may say, "I didn't make the team because the coach is dumb," or "The other kids only made the team because the coach feels bad for them."

A 2012 study at the University of Florida found that kids who feel extra special are more likely to become aggressive in the face of criticism. They struggle at hearing words they don't like and they're more likely to lash out and blame other people.

THE NEED FOR ADMIRATION IS NEVER SATISFIED

The parents I work with often say things like "It's a tough world. I've got to build my child up because the world is going to tear him down." But their methods of "building their child up" usually involve offering undeserved and exaggerated praise.

Excessive accolades won't build him up in the way you might think. In fact, exaggerated praise causes kids to become preoccupied with feelings of superiority. This can turn into a vicious cycle where the child requires even more admiration and attention. They never feel satisfied and always strive for more external validation.

Here are a few more immediate problems that stem from kids thinking the world revolves around them:

- **Diminished empathy**—It's impossible to consider other people's feelings when kids think their feelings are the only ones that matter.
- **Chronic dissatisfaction**—Kids are unappreciative of everything when they're given anything they want.
- **Reduced persistence**—Entitled kids think they shouldn't have to try very hard to get what they want.
- **Unpleasant to be around**—Kids become irritable, bossy, and demanding when they believe everything is about them.

- **Expect immediate gratification**—They expect everything to happen according to their desired timeline.

SELF-CENTERED KIDS BECOME NARCISSISTIC ADULTS

There used to be a widely held belief that narcissism, which is characterized by grandiose views of oneself and a constant craving for admiration, stemmed from growing up with cold and unemotional parents. But research has debunked that theory and shows that in fact, the opposite is true. Parents who "overvalue" children give their kids a grandiose sense of self-importance that increases the likelihood they'll turn into narcissistic adults.

What's the problem with being a narcissist? Well, for starters, narcissistic adults aren't happy people. They report feeling empty and they're never able to fully satisfy their craving for admiration. Their selfishness interferes with their ability to maintain healthy relationships.

Unlike mentally strong people, who feel grateful for what they have, narcissistic people think the world owes them something. They walk around with a chip on their shoulder and they feel like they never get the attention, admiration, and power they deserve.

What to Do Instead

In the case of Tom and Carol, the solution to their spoiled daughter Brittany's sense of entitlement was a complete parenting overhaul. Tom and Carol had to stop treating her like she was more special than everyone else.

Teach your child to focus more on what he can give, rather than what he can take from others. Prevent your child from believing the world revolves around him by replacing:

- Selfishness with kindness
- Entitlement with gratitude
- Narcissism with healthy self-esteem
- Self-importance with humility

OFFER GENUINE PRAISE AND AFFECTION

Eight-year-old Billy was brought to therapy by his parents after he started misbehaving at school. His teacher said he was disrupting class and having trouble getting along with the other kids. In fact, he was downright disrespectful much of the time.

As I asked some questions during the first appointment, Billy's mother took some earbuds out of her purse and handed Billy her phone. She instructed him to play one of his favorite racing games. Once the earbuds were in his ears and he was preoccupied with his game, she whispered quietly, "I'm pretty sure he's acting out because he feels bad about his speech issues." Billy had been in speech therapy for the last few years, and although there was an improvement, some of his words were still hard to understand.

After she explained his speech issues and the problems they were experiencing, I asked about his strengths. Before she answered, she motioned to him to put the game away and told him to tune back in to the conversation. Once she was sure she had Billy's attention, she said, "Well, Billy is good at a lot of things, right, Billy?" He nodded and smiled and listened to his mother list his extraordinary talents.

"For starters, he's the fastest runner I've ever seen! And he can kick a soccer ball from one end of the field to the other. He's really smart too. He's been advanced in math since preschool."

His father chimed in and said, "He has a real mechanical mind. He loves to take things apart just to see how they work. Then he puts stuff back together even better than before. He took my watch apart just the other day and put it all back together again."

At that point, Billy's mother took another turn at listing his impressive accomplishments. Their accolades for Billy went on and on.

And while it was refreshing to see parents who could readily identify their child's strengths (sometimes parents of misbehaving kids have trouble naming one good thing about them), their reports about his extraordinary skills clued me in on why Billy was having problems.

Billy's misbehavior didn't stem from deep-rooted self-esteem issues caused by a speech impediment. Instead he was acting out because he thought he was superior to the other kids.

Billy's parents had worried so much that he was going to be made fun of for his speech issues that they tried to compensate by showering him with praise. And unfortunately, much of the praise they gave him wasn't accurate. Clearly, Billy's superiority complex wasn't doing him any favors in the friendship department.

Billy's parents had to start being more honest with Billy—and themselves. They had to stop telling him he was extraordinary in everything he did. They also had to see that it was okay to talk about his speech issues with him—it wasn't a secret. He'd been in speech therapy for years and talking about his speech problems openly could ensure that he didn't feel ashamed by them.

Many parents make the same mistakes as Billy's parents. They praise their kids for the sole purpose of boosting their self-esteem. Unfortunately, exaggerated and insincere feedback does more harm than good.

Praise is healthy when it builds character. It's not healthy when it over-inflates your child's ego. Here are a few examples of healthy vs. unhealthy ways to praise kids:

1. Praise compassionate behavior.

Point out kind behavior so your child sees that it's important to treat others with respect. Keep the emphasis on how his kindness affects other people rather than how great a person it makes him for doing a good deed. Then he'll be invested in helping others even when you're not there to praise him for his choices.

Situation: Your child shares his snack with a friend.

Unhealthy praise: "You're the most generous kid ever!"

Better praise: "That was nice of you to share your snack with your friend. He looked really happy that you shared with him."

2. Praise your child's efforts instead of the results.

Whether your child scores ten points in a basketball game or he makes the honor roll, praising his success teaches him he needs to excel to gain your approval. Praise his effort and attitude and he'll see that you value hard work more than excellence.

> **Situation:** Your child gets a hundred on his math test.
>
> **Unhealthy praise:** "Great job getting everything right!"
>
> **Better praise:** "You've been working hard this year. Your effort is really paying off!"

3. Praise things your child can control.

Praising your child's innate characteristics, like how pretty she is or how smart she is, isn't helpful because those things are out of her control. Praise her for what she does rather than who she is.

> **Situation:** Your child scores a goal in the soccer game.
>
> **Unhealthy praise:** "You're such a great athlete!"
>
> **Better praise:** "You really hustled out on the field today. I could tell you were trying hard."

PROVIDE THE KID TREATMENT, NOT THE ROYAL TREATMENT

I see a lot of blended families in my therapy office who are dealing with a variety of complicated family issues. And Alyson and Matt were no exception. Matt and his wife Alyson had weekend visitation with Matt's eight-year-old daughter, Kiera, from his previous marriage.

Matt and Alyson didn't feel close to Kiera. Matt said, "It's impossible for us to have a healthy father-daughter relationship when I only see her on the weekends. And even though Alyson has been with me for three years, she hardly has much of a relationship with Kiera either."

Matt said they enjoyed their weekend visits, but he said, "We're not there for the everyday things, like homework and softball practice." Alyson agreed, saying, "We have a pretty formal relationship with her."

They explained how they squeezed as much fun into each weekend as they possibly could. They went to the park, watched movies, ate out at restaurants, and played games almost every time she visited. Yet they just didn't feel like Kiera could open up to them.

We discussed how their weekend visits might look different if Kiera lived with them full-time. They said if Kiera were with them all week, they'd likely spend their weekends relaxing, running errands, and doing jobs around the home.

I asked them why they didn't do those things with her now and Matt said, "Because our time with her is so limited, we don't want to waste it doing ordinary things." Of course, that was understandable. But as long as they treated Kiera like a special guest rather than their daughter, they weren't going to have a normal relationship with her.

They rolled out the red carpet for her every weekend. Whatever she wanted to do, they did. No wonder she didn't feel at home with them.

They agreed to start treating her more like a family member. And slowly, over the course of a few weeks, they made their weekends comparatively mundane. They went to the grocery store, cooked meals at home, and went about their business in a more usual fashion. Kiera was still included in their activities, but the focus was no longer on providing constant entertainment.

To their surprise, Kiera didn't complain about their shift in activities. Instead she seemed content to help her father clean the garage and she was happy to go to the grocery store with her stepmother. She spent time in her room alone too—which was new—and Matt and Alyson recognized that she seemed to be more "at home." Although they thought they had been doing the right thing by showering her with tons of attention, they were happy to learn backing off a bit was best for her.

No matter what type of family you have—blended or otherwise—your relationship with your child benefits when you don't treat her like she's the center of the universe. Treat her like a loving, respected member of your family by expecting her to contribute her fair share. When she has realistic expectations of how she should be treated, and how she should treat others, she'll be better equipped to create healthy relationships with other people.

How to Teach Kids They Aren't the Center of the Universe

While some kids dedicate their teenage years to raising money for charities or serving the less fortunate, others devote their spare time to thinking about what they're going to wear on Saturday night. Your child doesn't have to set out to change the whole world—but it's important that she see the world doesn't revolve around her. Strive to raise a kind and caring child who recognizes the needs of others, in addition to her own.

In the case of Brittany, the spoiled only child, her parents had to show her she wasn't entitled to everything she wanted. They had to teach her that she needed to think about other people's feelings and she needed to learn how to deal with her emotions in more socially appropriate ways.

WALK A MILE IN SOMEONE ELSE'S SHOES

It's easy for kids to get caught up into thinking their point of view is the only way to look at a situation. Teach your child that his actions impact other people and it's important to think about other people's feelings.

When your child hurts someone else, physically or emotionally, it can be tempting to just give him a consequence and tell him to "be nicer" next time. But until kids understand how to think about other people's positions, it's hard for them to treat others with more respect.

So while it can be helpful to ask your child, "What can you do differently next time?" there are better questions that can help kids think about how their behavior affected someone else. If your child hurts someone, ask him to complete the "someone else's shoes" questions before he can earn his privileges back.

Here are four questions to ask your child:

1. What mistake did I make?
2. How did my behavior affect the other person?
3. What would I have done if I was the other person?
4. What can I do better next time?

If your child hits his friend, place him in time-out. Then, once he's done serving his time-out, tell him he can play with his toys again once he talks to you about "someone else's shoes." Here's an example:

Parent: What did you do wrong?

Child: I hit Avery.

Parent: How did that affect Avery?

Child: I made his arm hurt. And I hurt his feelings too.

Parent: Yes. That's right. What would you have done if you were Avery?

Child: I probably would have hit back.

Parent: What could you do next time so you don't hurt Avery?

Child: I could come tell you that he took my toy from me.

Parent: That'd be a good choice because then you wouldn't hurt Avery.

The point of the exercise should be to help your child think more about how he can be respectful of others in the future, not necessarily how he can avoid consequences. Holding regular conversations like this each time your child breaks the rules can remind him that other people have feelings too.

INSTILL A SENSE OF GRATITUDE

Your child won't insist he deserves more attention, more appreciation, and more material possessions when he's grateful for what he already has. Instilling gratitude in children provides many benefits, including increased life satisfaction and lower levels of envy, materialism, and depression.

Express gratitude for simple things in life, such as the rain that waters the plants and the sun that keeps you warm. Help your child see that there is always something to be thankful for.

Here are a few ways to teach your child gratitude:

- **Establish a daily gratitude ritual.** Whether you ask, "What are two things you feel thankful for today?" before going to bed, or you take turns going around the dinner table to say why you feel thankful, make it a daily habit.
- **Construct a gratitude jar or bulletin board.** Take turns writing down what you're thankful for and hang it up or place it in the jar. Seeing those slips of paper add up will help the whole family see how many good things you have in your life.
- **Encourage your child to write in a gratitude journal.** Writing in a gratitude journal every day can significantly boost a child's emotional and social success. Encourage your child to start a simple journal where she lists three reasons why she's grateful every day.

ACKNOWLEDGE POSSIBLE ALTERNATIVES

There will likely be times when your child insists other people's behaviors are about her. When you notice your child assuming the world revolves around her, offer possible alternatives. Here's an example:

Child: Eva must be mad at me. She never replied to my text message.

Parent: Is that the only reason she wouldn't have replied?

Child: Yes, she always replies.

Parent: Is it possible she's doing something where she can't have her phone on?

Child: I doubt it.

Parent: Or maybe her battery went dead? Or perhaps she got in trouble and her phone got taken away. Any other possible reasons she didn't reply?

Child: I guess. Maybe she fell asleep or something.

Parent: Right. Although her being angry at you is one possibility, I think there are possibly hundreds of other reasons why she hasn't replied yet.

Acknowledge that it's easy to assume other people's choices have something to do with us. Look for opportunities to gently remind your child that other people's days—and lives—don't revolve around her. When you help her develop realistic expectations of other people, and she is able to see things from another point of view, she'll be equipped to deal with the realities of the real world.

Teach Preschoolers Empathy

Although empathy is a complex concept, preschool is an opportune time to begin teaching your child how to consider someone else's feelings. One of the most effective ways to teach empathy is by showing empathy to your child.

If your child cries because she skinned her knee, say, "I'm so sorry to see you're hurt. Skinned knees don't feel very good." When you give her a hug, kiss her boo-boos, and bandage her scrapes, you show her that you care about her well-being.

Respond similarly to emotional pain. Say things like "I know you feel really scared right now" or "I feel sad when you're sad." Try to problem-solve together by saying things like "What can we do to make you feel better?"

Responding to your child's pain with empathy will help her learn to recognize when other people are struggling. She'll be more likely to pitch in and help out when she sees someone in need.

Teach your preschooler basic emotions, like happy, mad, sad, and scared. Label how you're feeling when you hold conversations by saying things like "I am happy that we are going to visit Grandma today" or "I'm sad that you aren't feeling well." Point out other people have emotions too. When you see a child crying, say, "That boy looks sad," or "That little girl looks really angry that she has to go home."

Research shows talking about the emotional content in stories increases children's emotional comprehension. In one study, conducted by researchers from the University of Milano-Bicocca, kids were divided up into two groups—one group drew pictures about what they read and the other group discussed the characters' emotions. After two months, the kids in the conversation group showed better emotion comprehension and greater empathy.

Reading books and watching TV with your kids are great opportunities to pause and talk about how characters might be feeling. Ask questions like "How could you tell he was mad?" and "Why do you think he felt sad?" Recognizing body language and verbal cues as feelings, and saying those types of things out loud, will help your child better understand that other people have feelings too.

If you really want to help your child empathize, ask her to show you how the other person feels. Researchers have found that imitating facial expressions leads to changes in the brain that correspond to a specific emotion. Making a sad or angry face can even change your heart rate, skin conductance, and body temperature.

When you tell your child to show you how someone else feels, he'll gain more insight into the other person's emotions. Say things like "Make a face that shows me how you think Avery felt when you hit him." When your child tries to make his face look sad, by frowning or looking down, he'll actually feel sad.

You can also use this to teach your child how his prosocial behavior affects people in a positive way. Say, "Make a face that shows me how you think Grandma felt when you drew a picture for her." When your child smiles, he'll feel happy and he'll recognize how his behavior influences others.

Teach School-Age Kids to Volunteer

When your child refuses to eat his broccoli and you say, "There are starving kids in the world who would love to eat that food," that type of logic isn't likely to foster a sense of global compassion. But volunteering as a family at a food pantry might open his eyes to other people's problems outside of his own.

Children who volunteer empathize more with others. Additionally, being involved in a community service project gives children a sense of meaning and purpose. Volunteering at a young age increases the chances they'll volunteer during the teen years and throughout adulthood.

When your child is actively involved in volunteer work, he'll learn that other people have problems too. He'll think more about how to help them and the community in general, instead of demanding that all his needs be met all the time.

Rather than fund-raise for an online charity or send money to a third-world country, get your child involved in hands-on activities whenever possible. Here are some volunteer activities that your school-age child could do with your help:

- Mow an elderly neighbor's lawn
- Serve food in a soup kitchen
- Make care packages for the homeless and donate them to a homeless shelter
- Volunteer at an animal shelter
- Make cards or small gifts for a nursing home or children's hospital
- Participate in a community cleanup project

Show your child there are many things he can do to make a difference in the world. When he views himself as someone who has worthwhile gifts to give others, he'll spend less time thinking that the world revolves around his needs and wants.

Teach Teens the World Is Bigger Than They Think

In an environment that encourages young people to broadcast every aspect of their lives on social media with selfies and personalized videos, teaching teens to be less self-absorbed poses some interesting challenges. One key to helping your teen see that there's more to the universe than just him is to inspire awe.

Researchers from the University of California, Berkeley, found that feelings of awe provide a new perspective on the world and our place within it. Awe can lead us to feel smaller, and help us see that we're in the presence of something greater than ourselves.

When your teen experiences awe he'll feel connected to the world around him. But at the same time, he'll see that he's not the center of the universe.

Feelings of awe are so powerful that they tend to trigger a

physiological response within your body. When you get goose bumps when you overlook the Grand Canyon or when you look up at the sky on a starry night, it's because feelings of awe activated your sympathetic nerve system. Your muscles under your skin contract and make your hair stand up. That's powerful.

So how can you evoke feelings of awe in your teenager? Natural wonders, whether it's a spectacular mountain range or an oceanic view, are instrumental in conjuring up feelings of awe. But not everyone feels awe-inspired by the same things.

So while one teen may be moved by a canoe ride in a lake, another teen may feel a sense of awe when staring at a T. rex skeleton in a museum. So look for things that produce awe in your teen. And the good news is, you don't have to be a world traveler to encourage awe.

Looking at pictures in a book or watching educational videos may inspire a sense of awe. If your teen isn't likely to be impressed by nature, don't worry. For some teens, hearing true-life stories about people who accomplish incredible acts of kindness or who overcome great adversity can also inspire a sense of awe.

Kids Who Know Their Place in the World Become Adults Who Contribute to Society

Every year the Prudential Spirit of Community Awards honor kids and teens who perform exemplary community service. Many of these kids have accomplished things that adults might deem impossible.

The 2016 list included kids like Kayla Abramowitz, a fourteen-year-old from North Palm Beach, Florida, who started a nonprofit organization called Kayla Cares 4 Kids. She's collected over ten thousand DVDs, books, and other items for hospitals and Ronald McDonald houses in all fifty states.

Eleven-year-old Grace Davis of Louisville, Kentucky, helped raise more than $140,000 for premature babies. Only in the fifth grade, Grace distributes piggy banks to students in her community and encourages them to fill them up.

Ten-year-old Jackson Silverman of Charleston, South Carolina, packs weekend lunch bags for kids who don't have much food at home. He persuaded a local food bank to let him start a youth volunteer program that has packed more than fourteen thousand lunches.

There are many kids working hard to help other people. But they wouldn't be able to do so if they viewed themselves as the center of the universe.

Mentally strong people don't think the world owes them anything. They focus more on giving, rather than taking, and they recognize they have the power to create positive change. Rather than saying, "Someone should do something about that," they recognize they are the ones who can take action. If you raise your child to see that he's only as special as everyone else, he'll be a kinder, more compassionate person who is committed to making the world a better place.

Troubleshooting and Common Traps

Don't fall into the trap of believing that the more you give your child, the better parent you'll be. And don't start thinking the more you give your child, the more he'll give to others. Those strategies will backfire.

Make an effort to talk to your child about what he has to give, not just what he wants to gain. So instead of talking about how much money he wants to earn in a future career, ask him what he hopes to contribute to society. Or rather than focus on what presents he wants to open on the holidays, help him make a list of gifts he wants to give other people.

Another common problem is when parents devote all of their time to kids' activities. While extracurricular activities can fill up your spare time fast, don't devote every second of your time to becoming your child's chauffeur, cheerleader, and entertainment coordinator.

It's healthy to set aside time for yourself and to do activities that don't involve your child. Whether you go on a weekend getaway once in a while or you make going to the gym a priority in your life, it's good for your child to see you take care of yourself.

Finally, don't insist that your child is the exception to the rule. Asking the band director to let your child be in the band even though he didn't make the cut, or requesting that a coach let your child play in the game even though he missed practice, only reinforces your child's belief that he's extra special.

Let your child follow the rules and protocols just like everyone else. Regardless of whether you think it's fair, remind yourself that making him follow the rules will teach him that he's not superior.

WHAT'S HELPFUL

- Offering genuine praise
- Evoking awe
- Volunteering as a family
- Creating gratitude rituals
- Teaching empathy
- Helping your child walk a mile in someone else's shoes

WHAT'S NOT HELPFUL

- Offering exaggerated praise
- Giving your child special treatment
- Emphasizing your child's success over his efforts
- Insisting your child is the exception to every rule
- Making your entire life revolve around your child's activities

They Don't Allow
Fear to Dictate
Their Choices

Anna brought her twelve-year-old daughter, Zoey, to counseling because she was afraid Zoey's behaviors were getting out of control. "Look at her hair! She dyed it last week without my permission," she said as she pointed to her daughter's obviously dyed-blond hair.

Anna's husband Paul worked long hours. So, as a stay-at-home mom, Anna took on the majority of the parenting duties for Zoey and their four younger children. Anna said she ran a tight ship to prevent their kids from going out and doing things "like this." "I let her go to a friend's house for a few hours and she comes home looking like this. It just goes to show we need to be stricter with her because we can't trust her at all," Anna said.

But as Anna described their household rules, her phrase "running a tight ship" took on more and more substance. Her household seemed more like boot camp than a kid-friendly home.

Zoey and her younger siblings had almost every minute of their day planned. Anna made sure Zoey got exactly nine hours of sleep each night. She monitored the kids' exercise and ensured they got their recommended sixty minutes each day. Anna described the other steps she took to promote good health, such as buying organic produce and making sure everyone applied hand sanitizer when they were out in public. "You never know what kind of germs you might pick up!" she exclaimed.

In addition to "exercise time," there was a mandatory two hours of studying and homework time each day. The kids had a lengthy list of chores to complete and they were allowed thirty minutes of educational screen time, as Anna believed other kids spend too much time in front of screens. "It's bad for their eyes, not to mention their brains."

It was rare for Anna to allow any of the kids to visit friends' homes. But now that Zoey had gone to a friend's house and dyed her hair, Anna made it clear she wouldn't be allowed to visit with her friends again.

Anna was worried that this "act of rebellion" might be signaling a deeper-rooted problem. Aside from her concerns about the "toxic chemicals" Zoey had put in her hair, she thought Zoey might have a body-image issue or a mental health problem. Anna assumed Zoey's decision to lighten her hair meant she didn't feel good about herself, which is why she brought her to therapy.

Although Anna had hoped the treatment would involve "fixing Zoey," there wasn't anything wrong with the girl. Instead my recommendations were that Anna change her parenting habits.

The real problems seemed to be:

1. **Anna's rules were rigid.** The strict rules were likely stifling Zoey's development.
2. **She viewed normal child behavior as proof her kids needed more structure.** She believed any deviation from her rules was proof that the kids were "out of control."

My recommendations included:

1. **Learn about child development.** Anna had to change her mind-set before any real change could take place. I recommended she read several child development books to learn about Zoey's needs.

2. **Schedule free time.** Zoey needed time to create, explore, and just be a kid, which meant she needed less structure. I recommended that Anna schedule at least one hour per day to let Zoey do whatever she wanted.

3. **Give Zoey opportunities to make choices.** Zoey needed to learn to make good choices and solve problems on her own, without her mother interfering and offering suggestions. Letting her make small decisions, like whether to do her homework or her chores first, would give her a chance to assert her independence in a safe manner.

4. **Relax some of her rules.** It was important for Anna to see that letting Zoey stay up a little later one night or allowing her to eat a few sweet treats once in a while wasn't going to lead to complete chaos.

Anna was hesitant to let go of some of her rules. She was fearful that if she let go of an ounce of control, the result would be complete anarchy. Micromanaging her children's lives helped her feel as though she had more control, and this helped keep her anxiety in check.

So part of the family's treatment involved helping Anna learn skills to manage her anxiety. Once she learned she could tolerate uncertainty, she was able to make parenting choices that were best for her kids, not for her anxiety.

To Anna's relief, relaxing her rules a little bit didn't lead to utter anarchy. When she gave Zoey a little bit of freedom, Zoey became motivated to demonstrate she could be responsible, because she wanted to earn more privileges.

How Many of Your Parenting Choices Stem from Fear?

Raising a child in today's world can feel scary. But if you allow fear to dictate your choices, there's a good chance your child might suffer the consequences. Do any of these statements sound like you?

○ I go to great lengths to make sure my child doesn't feel afraid.

○ I'm overprotective of my child much of the time.

○ I worry about my kids more than most parents do.

○ I rarely allow my child to go places or do things without me.

○ There are many things I don't allow my child to do because I worry that he'll get hurt physically or emotionally.

○ I think it's my job to prevent my child from being criticized.

○ I devote a lot of energy into thinking about the worst-case scenarios my child might experience.

○ When my child is scared, I am quick to jump in and rescue him.

○ I spend more energy calming my child than teaching him how to calm himself.

○ Much of my energy goes toward reducing all types of risks my child might face.

Why Parents Parent out of Fear

To keep her anxiety in check, Anna developed hard and fast rules. She became rigid about her children's schedules and restricted their activities. And while she had good intentions, parenting became more about controlling *her* anxiety.

It might feel safe and comfortable as a parent to err on the side of caution. After all, your child isn't likely to be scarred for life if you don't let him go to that birthday party at the house where you don't know the parents. But sometimes your parenting decisions might be more about reducing your own stress than doing what's best for your child.

THE NEWS MAKES THE WORLD SOUND SCARY

Whether you're scrolling through social media or you're tuning in to your local news station, you'll likely see stories about natural disasters, violence, and diseases that are spreading out of control. Perhaps you'll even see a story about a child being kidnapped or a mass shooting. Hearing stories of tragedies and atrocities can cause you to feel like the world is falling apart.

A 2014 survey by the Robert Wood Johnson Foundation found that 40 percent of Americans get stressed out by reading, listening to, or watching the news. Ultimately, anxiety that stems from the news changes the way some people parent. After the Sandy Hook Elementary School shooting, one mother I worked with enrolled her children in private school because "public schools just aren't safe anymore." Another family spent hours every week researching their homeschooling options because they didn't want to keep "putting their kids at risk."

Statistically, your child is at a much higher risk of getting killed in a car accident on the way to school than in a school shooting. But it's no wonder these parents were fearful. Despite the decrease in violent crime over the past few decades, media outlets make it sound like the world is more dangerous than it's ever been.

IT'S HARD TO RECOGNIZE WHAT'S REALLY DANGEROUS

In 2008, Lenore Skenazy allowed her nine-year-old son to take the New York City subway home on his own. Equipped with a little money and a MetroCard, he made it back unscathed.

When she wrote an article about this for the *New York Sun,* outraged parents accused her of putting her son in danger. Soon she was dubbed the "World's Worst Mom" and media outlets, psychologists, and parenting experts from around the world were weighing in on her ability to parent.

The backlash led her to start the "Free Range Kid Movement," which advocates that parents give kids more freedom. She argues that today's kids are safer and more competent than most parents give them credit for.

Skenazy isn't the only parent to make headlines for giving a child too much freedom. In 2014, a South Carolina mother was arrested for leaving her nine-year-old daughter at a park while she went to work at a nearby fast-food restaurant. Countless headlines involve similar stories of children walking alone or being left alone in vehicles.

Such headlines raise a lot of questions about safety issues and best parenting practices. While it's clearly unsafe to leave a toddler alone in a sweltering car, what about leaving a seven-year-old in a car on a fifty-degree day while a parent runs into a gas station for two minutes?

There's so much advice out there about raising healthy kids. It can be overwhelming. While one website warns that lakes could be filled with brain-eating amoebas, another health website cautions that putting a hairband on your wrist could lead to a life-threatening infection. Even though those types of risks are minuscule, hearing extreme cautionary tales may cause you to second-guess your parenting choices.

You're among the first generation of parents who can research anything in a matter of seconds—which can be a blessing and a curse. You no longer have to depend on the medical dictionary's one-paragraph answer about your child's strange rash. Now you can search hundreds of pages of information, speculation, and personal horror stories. Within a matter of minutes, you might grow convinced that the little patch of red skin may actually be a form of deadly skin cancer.

A never-ending supply of parenting opinions, fear-mongering, and sensationalism can easily cause you to become a parenting hypochondriac.

Parenting out of Fear Causes Kids to Become Anxious About the World

The goal of Anna and her militant style of parenting was to maintain complete control over everything at all times. She micromanaged her children's activities down to the smallest details. And she didn't see how overparenting was likely to stifle their development.

Even if you aren't running a boot camp, there may be some ways that you are parenting out of fear. Your attempts to manage your emotions could lead to some unproductive parenting strategies if you're not careful.

PARENTING OUT OF FEAR LEADS TO POOR PARENTING CHOICES

When you parent out of fear, you won't be able to make the best decisions for your child. Here are the most common things parents do when fear dictates their parenting strategies:

1. **They're overprotective.** Parents inhibit their child's activities when they're afraid. They limit their child's ability to create, explore, and experience a rich childhood.
2. **They're intrusive.** They often micromanage everything and insert their opinions, even when it's unnecessary.
3. **They avoid discomfort.** They make parenting decisions based on what choice will be the least anxiety provoking, rather than what's best for their children in the long term.

April, a former client who had originally started counseling to deal with her anxiety, exhibited all three of these unhealthy habits. She had a traumatic experience as a child—her younger brother drowned in a river—and now that she was a mother, she was terrified her children might drown too.

To keep them safe, she hovered over them and never allowed them to go near beaches, lakes, or pools. She figured if they never had access to deep water, they couldn't possibly meet the same fate as her younger brother.

One day, while visiting friends, her seven-year-old wandered outside when he was supposed to be playing in his friend's room. Somehow he ended up in a neighbor's pool and he was unable to swim. Fortunately, the neighbor heard him splashing around in the water and ran out to save him. But April was retraumatized by the incident.

Her first instinct was to become more overprotective of her children. It took some time before she could recognize that her attempts to keep her children away from water were actually placing them at a high risk of drowning. If she wanted to keep them safe, she needed to teach them how to swim.

Unfortunately, there are many parents out there like April. They put their energy in the wrong places. Rather than teaching safety skills, they avoid anything that might pose a hazard. But you can't keep kids out of harm's way forever. It's better to equip your child to deal with danger than assume you can always protect him from hazards.

FEAR IS CONTAGIOUS

I keep a variety of toys in my therapy office that, unbeknownst to kids, are actually tools that help me assess, diagnosis, and treat their issues. Young children can't verbalize their unhealthy thinking patterns or describe their core beliefs, but they can show me how they view the world through their imaginary play.

The toy farmhouse and various small animal figures—pigs, sheep, cows, and horses—are popular items. But there are also dinosaurs who look menacing and wolves who appear to be on the prowl.

Kids who view the world as a relatively safe place build fences around the predators. They might say things like "The T. rex will live in this area because the mean animals have to be locked up."

Those who think the world is a scary place put fences around the farm animals. A child might say something like "Little piglet, I have to keep you inside this fence because I don't want you to get eaten by the bad animals." Then the predators are allowed to roam free.

This imaginary scene gives me a glimpse into their core beliefs. Do they believe the world is an inherently good place, with a few "bad things" that need to be locked up? Or do they believe the world is a scary place and the few good things in it have to be locked away from the outside world? Whichever it is, kids develop those beliefs about the world based on their own experiences and what they've learned from their parents.

Psychologists have known for a long time that parents' fears are passed down to their children. Parents with anxiety disorders tend to have kids with anxiety disorders.

For decades, most researchers thought that anxiety must be passed on through genetics only. But a 2010 study of identical twins conducted by the John Hopkins University School of Medicine showed that's not the case. Anxiety can be a learned behavior.

Overprotective parents hover over their kids in an attempt to keep them safe. But kids who aren't exposed to adversity don't gain the resilience they need to become healthy, responsible adults. Ultimately, parents' attempts to control their own anxiety lead children to become overly dependent on them.

Overprotective parenting is one of the reasons why there are so many boomerang kids—college graduates and twentysomethings who move back into their childhood bedrooms. A 2012 Pew Research survey found that 24 percent of eighteen- to thirty-four-year-olds in the United States return home to live with their parents at one point or another.

The stampede back to Mom and Dad's house isn't always due to the poor economy, high rents, and low-paying jobs. In fact, a 2015 study published in the *Journal of Marriage and Family* found that instead of financial issues, the main reason young people return to live with Mom and Dad is that they can't handle the emotional distress associated with independent living.

Researchers have found that many young adults aren't equipped to deal with the transition from adolescence to adulthood. Getting a job, graduating from college, and paying their own bills proves to be too much for them.

Some of them fall prey to unhealthy coping skills, like problem drinking. Others develop mental health problems, like depression and anxiety disorders.

Being unprepared for the realities of adulthood certainly isn't unique to the United States. A 2015 survey in the UK found that young adults don't "feel" grown up until the age of twenty-nine. Living at home, playing computer games, and watching cartoons were the main reasons they said they didn't feel grown up.

When kids are raised to believe they need constant protection from the scary world, they don't learn skills to handle real-life problems. So it's understandable that many of them look for the safe confines of their childhood home.

What to Do Instead

Anna, as you will recall, was so busy making sure Zoey followed her strict regimen of healthy choices she lost sight of the bigger picture. She needed to stop and examine what skills she needed to teach and what steps she needed to take to help her child grow up to become a mentally strong adult.

In sports and on the battlefield, it's said that the best defense is a good offense. That's true with parenting too. If you want to raise your children to be safe and healthy, don't focus all your energy on eliminating problems. Instead invest time into teaching them the skills they need to keep themselves safe.

THINK ABOUT WHAT YOU SURVIVED AS A CHILD

It's incredible how fast our notion about what's dangerous shifts. Something that was common a few decades ago could land parents in jail now.

Seat belts and car seats haven't been mandatory for that long. But imagine letting your toddler crawl around in your moving vehicle now?

Most of today's parents would be terrified if their teen took the car for a drive without a cell phone. After all, how would your teen reach you in the event of an emergency? It's as if we forget that most of us didn't yet own cell phones when we were kids, yet we somehow survived.

Take a few minutes to think about all the things your parents allowed you to do when you were a kid that would either land them in jail or at least warrant a call to Child Protective Services today. Many of the things that never raised an eyebrow in the past would be considered child endangerment or neglect today.

From playing on rusty swing sets to riding a bike without a helmet, recalling what you lived through can put today's overly safety-conscious world into proper perspective. Think about how many things your parents let you do that you'd never imagine allowing your child to do.

CALCULATE THE RISKS YOUR CHILD FACES

Your level of fear has nothing to do with the actual level of risk. So even though something might feel scary doesn't mean it is.

So how do you decide when your child can stay home alone? Or how do you make a decision about when to let your child go places with his friends without a chaperone? Ask yourself these questions:

- **What would I say to a trusted friend?** If another parent asked you, "Should I let my child do this?" you'd be less emotionally reactive and more logical in your response. So try to give yourself the same advice you'd give to another parent.
- **What are the facts?** Educate yourself about whatever facts you can find on a particular topic. Learn about the actual level of danger and the statistical risk involved.
- **What are the risks of not letting my child do this?** Almost anything you allow your child to do comes with a certain amount of risk. But it's important to consider what type of risk is involved in not letting your child do something too. There may be social consequences, missed learning opportunities, and fewer chances for your child to develop the skills he needs to become a responsible adult when you say no too often.

When your heart leaps into your throat when your child says he wants to try out for football or you cringe at the thought of him going on an overnight camping adventure, ask yourself, "What's the real level of risk my child faces?"

FOCUS ON SAFETY BUT DON'T OVERDO IT

Teach your child the steps he can take to keep himself safe. Wearing a helmet when he rides a bike, putting on sunscreen when he's at the beach, and avoiding too much sugar are lessons you should be teaching your child.

But the way you go about teaching your child makes a big difference. Just because you're afraid of something doesn't mean you should incite panic in your child to "teach him a lesson."

That's exactly what a Missouri family did in 2015 when they orchestrated a fake kidnapping to teach their child about "stranger danger." They arranged for a friend to lure the six-year-old into a truck and kidnap him. For hours, the poor child was told he would never see his family again. Fortunately, the adults were eventually arrested.

Clearly, making the child think his life was in danger crossed the line and the "lesson" they meant to teach him was lost. This is an extreme example, and there are much healthier ways to teach children about the potential dangers of the world.

While you may never go this far to teach your child lessons about safety, examine the strategies you use to encourage your child to be safe. Showing a young child graphic images to teach him the consequences of not wearing a helmet or threatening your child with exaggerated "worst-case scenarios" to convince him not to chew his fingernails aren't the best ways to teach him safety.

Instead offer facts about safety issues and establish rules that promote good health, such as "Wear a helmet when riding your bicycle and wash your hands before you eat."

When explaining potential threats, focus on how your child can be safe. Rather than saying, "Stay near me in the store so you don't get kidnapped," ask, "What would you do if you couldn't find me in a store?" Use role-playing and hypothetical situations such as this one:

Parent: What would you do if a stranger asked for your help looking for his puppy?

Child: I'd say I'm not allowed to do that.

Parent: What if he said he just needed you to get in the car for a minute and he'd drop you right back off?

Child: I'd tell him my parents don't let me get in the car with strangers.

Parent: Then what would you do?

Child: I'd just keep walking.

Parent: What if he followed you?

Child: I'd start to run.

Parent: Would you ever yell to someone to help you?

Child: Yeah, if he wouldn't leave, I'd yell, "Help," really loud.

Keep in mind that many of the threats we focus on aren't very probable. For example, only about 115 kids are kidnapped by a stranger each year in the United States. Compare that to the 203,900 kids who are abducted by family members each year and you'll see your child is much more likely to be abducted by someone he knows, rather than by a stranger in the stereotypically imagined scenario.

How to Teach Kids to Face Fears

Anna's militant approach to parenting wasn't allowing Zoey the freedom to develop her own sense of identity. Anna was fortunate that the only way Zoey was asserting her independence was by dyeing her hair. She could have rebelled in a much more dangerous way. Anna had to loosen the reins so Zoey could learn to become a little more independent.

Make sure you're equipping your child with the valuable life skills she needs to make good choices. Sometimes, the best life lessons are taught by backing off and giving kids the freedom to stand on their own.

INCREASE COURAGE, DON'T DECREASE FEAR

Parents who let fear dictate their choices hold their kids back because they don't want their children to be uncomfortable. A mother may decide not to send her child on an overnight camping trip because she thinks, "He'll be too afraid." Or a father may think, "I shouldn't sign my daughter up for softball because she'll be nervous about not knowing anyone else on the team."

A 2012 study published in the *Journal of Family Psychology* shows anxious parents are horrible at recognizing what causes their children to feel anxious. They make incorrect assumptions about how their children will react to difficult situations. They expect their children to avoid certain challenges and they make more negative predictions about how their children are going to perform.

So a parent may order a shy child's meal for her because it is anxiety provoking for the child to speak to the server. Or if a child is nervous about riding on the escalator, the family may always choose to take the stairs instead.

But those accommodations send the wrong message. They teach your child to believe she's incapable of doing the things that scare her. And the more accommodations you make to decrease your child's fear, the fewer chances he'll have to practice being brave. And the less likely he is to conquer those fears.

The last thing you want is for your child to grow up thinking you don't believe in her abilities. Teach your child that she's capable by insisting, "You can do this."

GIVE YOUR CHILD HEALTHY MESSAGES ABOUT FEAR

There are many "inspirational" posters and famous quotes about conquering all of your fears. But those messages are unhealthy. Fear is a natural, healthy emotion that will keep your child safe.

It's good to have some fear. If his friend dares him to jump off a cliff or step into the street into oncoming traffic, you want him to recognize that his fear serves as a warning that danger exists.

Teach your child that fear helps him. When his heart beats fast and his palms grow sweaty, he's ready to deal with a scary situation. If he were being chased by a hungry lion, the adrenaline rush would help him escape.

But he may experience a false alarm sometimes—times when his fear spikes even though he isn't in any real danger. When he's about to step onstage for a spelling bee, his anxiety might skyrocket in the same way it would if he were dangling off the edge of a cliff—his body might react as if he were in a life or death situation.

Tell him to ask himself, "Is this a real alarm or a false alarm?" when he feels afraid. When it's a false alarm, encourage him to face his fears, one small step at a time. With each successful experience, he'll gain confidence in his ability to face his fears when he's not in any actual danger.

CREATE A FEAR LADDER

Exposure is the best way to desensitize kids to their fears. Help him identify specific fears he wants to conquer, and then think about ways he can face those fears incrementally. It may take lots of steps to help your child reach his goal, but if you go slow and do it one step at a time, he'll gain confidence in his ability to tackle the next step.

If your child sleeps in your bed because he's scared to sleep alone, create a fear ladder. List his goal at the top. Then identify small steps he can take to reach that goal. It might look something like this:

- Sleep on a mattress on the floor next to Mom and Dad's bed
- Move the mattress next to Mom and Dad's doorway
- Mom stays in my room with me until I fall asleep in my own bed
- Mom tucks me in and I sleep in my room with the night-light on

Don't make any assumptions about what the "next step" might be. Talk to your child about it because what seems less scary to you might not necessarily seem less scary to him.

You want him to experience a little discomfort, and with practice, his fear will decrease. Then you can move on to the next step. Over time he'll gain confidence in his ability to face his fears one step at a time.

Teach Preschoolers the Basics About Fear

Most preschoolers experience a variety of irrational fears like monsters under the bed or strange creatures in the woods. Yet they usually don't fear things parents warn them about—like running in parking lots. They struggle to make sense of real versus imaginary and they don't yet have a clear understanding of cause and effect.

You're not going to talk your child out of feeling afraid. But you can help him fight fear by evoking positive emotions. So if your three-year-old is convinced there are scary creatures in the closet, take a flashlight into the closet and read a fun book together. He'll start to associate the closet with positive emotions rather than scary ones.

Or if he's scared to get shots, make going to the doctor a more pleasant experience. Play at the playground before you go and get a special treat afterward. He'll begin to think "shot days" are "fun days."

Teach your child to identify when he feels scared. Say things like "I understand you are scared when the lights are off and you're in your room alone." Just knowing you understand his fear can help alleviate some of his anxieties.

Teach School-Age Kids to Face Their Fears

School-age kids also need reassurance that it's normal to feel afraid. When your child says she is afraid to perform at her dance recital, don't minimize her feelings by saying, "Oh, you'll be fine" or "It's not a big deal. There are only going to be ten people in the audience." Instead say, "Yes, it *is* scary sometimes to perform in front of people. But I know you can do it."

Push your child to face her fears one small step at a time. If she's shy about talking to new people, coach her on how to make eye contact and how to greet someone. Or insist that she order her own drink in a restaurant. Show her that you believe she's brave enough to do it and that you'll be there to support her efforts.

Read stories about brave characters and talk about courage. Additionally, look for real-life stories of bravery. Share your own stories of courage too.

Share the steps you took to face your fears. Say something like "I had to give a presentation in front of everyone at work today. I was really nervous. My heart started to beat fast and my hands got shaky! But I just told myself I could do it and I needed to be brave. And I stood up there in front of everyone, even though I was scared, and I think I did a good job facing my fears."

If your child has a favorite superhero or a favorite character from a movie, book, or TV show, ask questions like "What would that character do right now if he felt scared?" This can help your child find a little extra courage when he needs it most.

Teach Teens to Tolerate Fear

Areas of the brain develop at different rates, so while certain parts of your teen's brain mature, other parts lag behind. That can give your teen an interesting outlook on risk taking.

Teens wildly overestimate certain risks, yet seem to be immune to others. So don't be surprised if your teen is too afraid to ask a date to the prom yet doesn't think twice about riding his bicycle down the middle of the road.

Have conversations with your teen about risk, especially social risks that involve potential rejection or embarrassment. Make sure your teen knows that although those emotions are uncomfortable, they're tolerable.

Normalize your teen's uncomfortable feelings. Share stories of when you've felt embarrassed or when you were rejected. But be careful to avoid comparing yourself by saying, "Oh yeah, you think that's bad? When I was your age . . ." Instead talk about how you dealt with the painful emotions.

Address the life lessons that can be learned from getting turned down by someone or being cut from a team. Explain that avoiding social risks could lead to living a small life. Meeting someone new and trying something different could be the key to living life to its fullest.

Too often, teens avoid trying new things or putting themselves out there because they doubt their ability to handle discomfort. Teach your teen that being turned down is proof that he's trying. Encourage him to step outside his comfort zone—one small step at a time—each day.

Teens often seek reassurance from others that things will be okay because hearing those words decreases their anxiety. Since you can't always be there to calm your teen down or offer a pep talk, teach him to coach himself. When he says he's nervous about something, don't automatically offer reassuring words. Instead say, "What could you tell yourself right now to help you gain some courage?"

A teen who is able to remind himself, "I'll be okay," or "All I can do is my best," will be better equipped to deal with whatever challenges he faces on his own. Knowing how to be his own coach will help him become more independent and less reliant on you when he's afraid.

At the same time, make sure you talk to your teen about safety risks. Car accidents are the number one cause of death in teens. But that statistic might not necessarily deter your teen from speeding. But if you tell him he'll be at risk of losing his license, paying a fine, and losing the car, he might be more likely to think twice about speeding. So make sure you explain immediate consequences, potential long-term risks, and any other costs that might seem to resonate most with your teen.

Brave Kids Grow Up to Take Calculated Risks

Savannah was one of the first foster children to move in with Steve and me. She'd only been staying with us for a few weeks when her guardian came over to talk about plans for the summer. School was almost over and we wanted to ensure she had plenty of social interaction during the summer months since she didn't have many friends. As we brainstormed, her guardian mentioned the possibility of signing her up for a week-long summer camp.

Without a moment's hesitation, Savannah said she'd do anything to go to summer camp. She'd never been to a camp before, but as an outdoor enthusiast, she'd dreamed of sleeping in a cabin, paddling a canoe, and singing songs around a campfire.

Despite her excitement, the thought of sending her away for a week gave me a pit in my stomach. She had a short temper, she used baby talk whenever she was nervous, and she tried to dominate the conversation when she was with a group of kids. What if the campers didn't accept those quirks? And what if she didn't like it there? I didn't want to send her far away to a place where she didn't know anyone.

Over the next few hours, Savannah talked excitedly about going to camp. And the more excited she became, the more nervous I grew that she'd be disappointed in the experience.

After she went to bed, I turned to Steve and asked, "Do you think she's going to be okay at camp? What if she gets scared there?" To which he reminded me, "Remember when she moved in here with us? Two complete strangers? If she can do that she can handle a week at camp."

Of course, he was absolutely right. She was a tough kid who had been through many difficult circumstances. Going to summer camp for a week paled in comparison.

That's the same advice I would have given to a family in my therapy office—let your child go have fun. But because I felt anxious since it was my own foster child, it was harder to see that sending her to camp was the right choice. My fear clouded my judgment.

What makes this story even more ridiculous to admit is that I know firsthand how beneficial summer camp is for kids in foster care. When the foster kids I worked with in my therapy office went to camp, it was usually the highlight of their year. But most of them never get to go to camp because it's too expensive for foster families.

So when Lincoln passed away, his family and I requested that in lieu of flowers, people donate money to a fund that helps send foster kids to camp. Over the years, we've used the donations to send dozens of kids to camp. And year after year, I heard stories about the positive impact a week at summer camp had on many of those kids.

And yet here I was a few years later, doubting whether Savannah should go to camp because I was afraid other kids might be mean to her! It was ridiculous.

She went to camp a few weeks later and had a blast. She got to be a "regular kid" who learned archery and performed skits with the other campers. I truly believe that going away with kids who knew nothing about her really benefited her.

When you find yourself fearful about something your child wants to experience, just like my experience with Savannah, know that feeling nervous is part of parenting. And just because you feel afraid doesn't mean you should prevent your child from having whatever that experience might be.

If you allow fear to dictate your choices, you'll inadvertently teach your child that she should avoid anything that feels scary; you'll teach her that she is not capable of being brave. Those messages are damaging and unhealthy.

Mentally strong people don't fear taking calculated risks. It's essential to teach your child to face her fears head-on when it's going to serve her well.

Your child will be better equipped to reach her greatest potential when she has confidence in her ability to do things that feel scary. Moving out of the house, applying for a job, and challenging herself to become better can be scary. But if you've raised your child to believe she's capable of dealing with her fears, she'll be ready to tackle whatever challenges come her way.

Troubleshooting and Common Traps

If there are certain things that evoke irrational fear in you, don't expose your child to them. For example, if you're terrified of going to the dentist, don't go to your child's first few appointments with him. Have your partner, a grandparent, or another trusted adult do it.

Otherwise your fear will influence your child. He'll grow up thinking the dentist's office is a scary place. Even if you don't say you're afraid, he'll pick up on your distress. Your body language, tone of voice, and behavior will clue him into how you're feeling.

When it comes to teaching kids to face their fears, one common trap many parents fall into is trying to force their child to do so. But that can backfire and cause your child to become more fearful than ever. You can encourage him, cheer on his efforts, and even reward him for trying hard. But making him do something that he's terrified of doing won't help.

Parenting out of fear can be a hard habit to break. You may need to make some major changes to the way you discipline your child or the way you approach certain problems. But just as it's important to teach your child to face his fears one step at a time, it's important to be a good role model and show your child that you can be brave, even in the face of uncertainty.

Finally, rest assured that there isn't a right or wrong answer to many of your parenting questions. There isn't a magic age where a child should be allowed to be home alone and there isn't a clear way to make sure your child's friends are always going to be a good influence. So while many websites and parent bloggers might offer you absolute suggestions, it's a judgment call you'll have to make for yourself and for your child.

WHAT'S HELPFUL

- Teaching your child to acknowledge and label fear
- Helping your child recognize real alarms versus false alarms
- Coaching your child to face her fears
- Remembering the risks you survived as a child
- Teaching your child safety lessons
- Creating a fear ladder and teaching your child to face fears one step at a time
- Increasing positive emotions
- Encouraging your child to coach himself
- Calculating the risks your child actually faces

WHAT'S NOT HELPFUL

- Focusing on how to reduce your anxiety rather than thinking about your child's needs
- Accommodating your child's attempts to avoid anxiety-provoking situations
- Minimizing your child's fears
- Thinking about the short-term rather than the long-term goals
- Protecting your child from discomfort
- Using scare tactics
- Creating rigid rules in an attempt to keep your anxiety in check
- Exposing your child to your irrational fears

They Don't Give
Their Child Power
over Them

Clarissa was a sixteen-year-old honor student and a talented athlete. She lived in a middle-class neighborhood with her parents, Alan and Jenna. To anyone on the outside, they appeared to be the ideal family. But they had a secret.

Whenever Clarissa's parents said no to her, Clarissa said, "Fine. I'll go cut myself." The first few times she made threats to harm herself, her parents told her to stop saying such horrible things. So Clarissa decided to show them she was serious.

One night, when her parents refused to let her go out with friends, she sliced her arm with a razor. The next morning, Jenna saw the thin cuts that looked like stripes down her daughter's arm. She wasn't sure how to respond. She called Alan into the room, and in disgust, he told Clarissa to wear long sleeves until the cuts healed.

They hoped her behavior was a onetime incident that she'd regret. But they were wrong.

The following weekend Clarissa informed her parents she was going to a party. Before they could chime in, she headed for the door and said, "I'll be back whenever I want. Don't try to make me come home early because you'll regret it." That's when Alan and Jenna realized they needed help.

The first thing Jenna said when they walked into my office was "I feel like we're being held hostage." She was terrified that if they didn't do what their daughter wanted, she might hurt herself again.

Sadly, self-injury is a fairly common behavior among teens. But usually it stems from an inability to cope with stress. It's rare for a teen to use threats of self-injury as a weapon against parents. So this was an unusual case.

The problems were:

1. **Alan and Jenna had lost their power.** Clarissa was using threats of self-harm to get her way and her parents didn't know how to stop it.
2. **Clarissa's safety was a concern.** Her threats of self-harm and cutting needed to be addressed in a helpful manner.

My recommendations included:

1. **Enroll Clarissa in therapy.** I planned to support Alan and Jenna's efforts, so it was important for Clarissa to have her own separate therapist to talk to.
2. **Create a discipline plan.** Alan and Jenna needed to create clear rules and consequences. They had to work together to follow through with consequences, even if Clarissa made threats.
3. **Establish a safety plan.** They needed to know how to deal with Clarissa's self-injury in a helpful and productive manner. That meant taking her self-injury seriously but not allowing it to deter them from healthy parenting.

They agreed not to allow Clarissa to leave the house if she made any threats to hurt herself. Keeping her in the house was a safety measure, however, not a punishment.

They explained to Clarissa that threats of self-harm would no longer get her what she wanted. Instead she had to follow their rules.

If she threatened to hurt herself, they would monitor her at home. If they feared for her safety, they would take her to the hospital for a psychiatric evaluation.

In the meantime, they removed all sharp objects from Clarissa's room. They even took the razor out of the shower; she would need to ask for it if she wanted to shave her legs.

Over the next few months, Clarissa's parents worked hard to create clear rules. They gave Clarissa a strict curfew and they paid close attention to where she was going and what she was doing. They took away privileges when she broke the rules, and to their surprise, they were met with very little resistance.

Once Clarissa knew that they had taken back their power, she listened to them. And she stopped using threats of self-injury as a weapon. She realized it would no longer be an effective way to get what she wanted.

Does Your Child Have Too Much Power?

There's a big difference between empowering your child to make healthy choices and giving him too much power in your family. Sometimes, it's hard to know when that line has been crossed. Do you answer any of the following points affirmatively?

- ○ My child has the power to make me change my mind about my parenting decisions.
- ○ I struggle to enforce the rules I set for my child.
- ○ I give my child an equal vote in the choices I make for my family.
- ○ I seek my child's opinion on adult-related decisions.
- ○ I bribe my child to get him to comply.
- ○ I'd rather be my child's friend than an authority figure.
- ○ I sometimes ignore behavior problems because I know it won't do any good to speak up.

- ○ I often get into power struggles with my child.
- ○ My child rarely asks permission. Instead she tells me what she's going to do.
- ○ I sometimes tell my child to keep secrets from my partner.

Why Parents Give Kids Power over Them

Initially, Alan and Jenna insisted that Clarissa had always been well behaved and they never had a single problem until she started to cut herself. But with a little more reflection, they realized that she had been slowly gaining more power in the family over the past few years.

She had become bossy and demanding. But because she was a good student and a leader on the athletic field, they thought she deserved to be treated like an adult. They granted her extra freedom and let her make many of her own decisions.

They had been giving her power over them for a while—just in a more subtle fashion. When they'd tell her to be home by 10 P.M., she'd respond by saying, "Let's make it eleven." Since she was "such a good kid," they'd usually give in. It wasn't until Clarissa cut herself that they realized how many rules they'd been bending for her.

While you might not be able to relate completely to this story, Clarissa's example sheds light on how well-meaning parents may slowly give up their power. Then they wake up one morning and find themselves in a dangerous situation.

Threats of self-harm aren't the only way a child can gain power over you—in fact, those types of threats are relatively rare. But anytime you let your child have a negative influence over the way you think, feel, or behave, you give her power over you.

THE SHIFT IN FAMILY HIERARCHY

When a friend invited me over for coffee one Saturday morning recently, I was reminded how family hierarchy has shifted over the past couple of decades. When I got to her house at 8 A.M., she met me at the door. In a whisper she said, "The kids are still sleeping."

She tiptoed (literally) to the kitchen and in a hushed voice said, "Let's go out on the back porch with our coffee." As we sat down in the chairs overlooking her backyard, she said, "I hope the kids wake up soon so my husband can mow the lawn."

It got me thinking. When I was a kid, I don't recall anyone's parents worrying about accidentally waking up their kids on a Saturday morning at eight. In fact, it was the opposite. Parents were hauling their kids out of bed to get a jump on the day. There were chores to be done. And certainly, no one's parents waited until the kids were awake to the mow the lawn. Instead it was up to the kids to do the yard work.

Clearly, there's been a major shift in the way parents raise kids over the past few generations. During the fifties and sixties, parents believed giving kids too much affection could cause them to become emotionally damaged. They thought holding babies too much spoiled them and they emphasized obedience over nurturing.

As knowledge of brain development increased, it became clear that kids needed affection and nurturing for optimal health. Parents started to become more sensitive to kids' needs and healthy self-esteem became a top priority. And the emphasis shifted to individuality and autonomy rather than obedience.

And somewhere along the line, things got a little mixed up. The hierarchy in many families shifted and kids became more like equals rather than subordinates. As they were given fewer expectations and responsibilities, they gained more power over their parents.

The shift in power isn't all bad. Studies show authoritarian parents (those who lead like dictators) tend to raise girls who are less independent and boys who are more aggressive. Additionally, their children may be at a higher risk for psychological problems.

It's healthier for kids to know that they have a voice in their families. But sometimes the parenting pendulum swings too far in the direction of democracy and kids' opinions are overvalued.

Parents may think that they're empowering their kids by giving them tons of choices or by placing great value on their input. But there's a big difference between empowering a child and giving him too much power.

Take the 2014 incident involving Patrick Snay. The sixty-nine-year-old head of Gulliver Preparatory School filed an age discrimination suit against his employer when his contract wasn't renewed. The school came to an agreement with the man and they settled out of court.

The terms of the agreement said Snay would be paid $80,000 plus $10,000 in back pay. Additionally, the school would pay Snay's lawyer fees of $60,000.

The agreement contained a confidentiality clause that prohibited Snay and his wife from revealing the settlement terms with anyone other than their professional advisers. The Snays, however, thought they should inform their teenage daughter of the outcome.

But after hearing the news, the teenager logged into Facebook and posted, "Mama and Papa Snay won the case against Gulliver. Gulliver is now officially paying for my vacation to Europe this summer. SUCK IT."

The school filed a motion and the court ruled that this was a clear violation of the settlement. The school no longer owed Snay any money.

Court documents revealed that Snay felt his daughter suffered "quite a few psychological scars" when his contract wasn't renewed. So he and his wife felt it was important to tell her the outcome since she was aware they were going to some sort of mediation.

So while they thought they were empowering their daughter by giving her inside information, in reality, they were giving her more power than she could handle. She wasn't mature enough to maintain confidentiality.

I've worked with many parents over the years who allowed their children to weigh in on major family decisions. I've seen everything from ten-year-olds who cast the deciding vote over whether the family should move to a new city to twelve-year-olds who deny their divorced mothers permission to date! Rather than empowering their kids, they were giving them too much responsibility.

Asking your child, "Do you want water or ice water to drink?" empowers him to make a choice about what's best for him. But giving him the power to decide that the whole family is going to eat chicken nuggets and french fries every night gives him power over you.

SOME PARENTS DON'T WANT TO BE IN CHARGE

Scott sought help because he was stressed out. And a big source of his stress was his sixteen-year-old son, Ben. Ben had just dropped out of school and spent his days sleeping, smoking marijuana, and playing video games. He spent his evenings hanging out with his buddies.

Scott was concerned about Ben's future but he wasn't sure how to motivate his son to do anything. He said, "He's old enough to quit going to school but he's still just a kid. I can't kick him out."

I recommended an intensive home-based service for the family. The program involved a team of therapists who would go into the home and address the family dynamics. A therapist would assist Scott in finding ways to set limits and enforce consequences. They would also work with the school department, on either helping Ben graduate or at the very least getting his GED.

Scott agreed to discuss it with his girlfriend. Since she lived in his home, it was important to make sure she was on board with this intensive service. When he left my office, he seemed relieved to know there was a program that could give them the help they needed.

But when he returned the following week, he said he didn't want the service. Although his girlfriend agreed to it, Ben didn't.

I explained that Ben didn't have to agree. The service providers were used to dealing with family situations where teens didn't think they needed help. The intervention didn't require Ben's cooperation at all. But Scott insisted, if his son wasn't interested, he wasn't going to do it.

It was sad to know Ben was wasting his high school years sitting on the couch getting high and his father refused to stop him. Rather than empower Ben to make healthier choices, he enabled him to stay stuck in unhealthy patterns.

Here are some common reasons parents like Scott allow their children to have too much power:

- **They lack leadership skills.** Sometimes, parents are uncomfortable being in charge. They may struggle with communication skills or they may not know how to help motivate their kids to take action.
- **They lack parenting skills.** Parents who don't know how to establish rules and enforce consequences have trouble being an authority figure.
- **They lack emotional support.** When parents lack support from friends and family, they sometimes turn to their child to get their emotional needs met. Confiding in a child blurs the boundaries.
- **They lack child development knowledge.** Sometimes parents think giving their child power is healthy. They don't realize kids aren't miniature adults and having too much power isn't good for their development.

Giving Kids Too Much Power Disrupts the Family Hierarchy

Clarissa's threats of self-harm made her parents feel like they weren't able to set rules and enforce consequences. Yet her behavior clearly showed she wasn't ready for more freedom and responsibility. Once her parents gave her that power, they struggled to take it back. They couldn't really parent her until they were prepared to deal with the potential backlash they might receive for setting healthy limits.

Giving your child more power than he can handle can have serious consequences. Examine the ways in which you may already give him a little too much power in the family.

KIDS NEED RULES, NOT TO BE THE RULER

There's a good reason why kids can't vote, drive, or quit school before a certain age—they lack the skills to make major life decisions. Childhood is their opportunity to learn how to make better choices.

Kids' brains aren't fully developed yet. The parts of the brain responsible for impulse control, problem solving, emotion regulation, and decision making don't function the same as an adult's brain. So not only does your child lack the life experience necessary to make the best choices, but his brain also isn't mature enough to measure risk accurately.

When kids gain power over adults, they miss out on valuable life lessons. They incorrectly assume they already know everything. And becoming the boss without the proper training is a disaster waiting to happen.

Don't be fooled by your child's attempts to show she wants to be the boss. Misbehavior is often a test of your parenting abilities—as well as an opportunity. Your child wants to know that you're able to control the situation when he can't control himself. If you don't intervene when your child acts out, he'll doubt your leadership abilities. And he's likely to grow anxious.

I once worked with the parents of a fourteen-year-old boy named Liam who skipped school, stole from stores, and got into fights on a regular basis. The police became involved on more than one occasion.

To prevent him from going to jail—or getting himself killed—his parents sent him to a wilderness therapy school. The school specialized in teaching at-risk youth basic life skills while also addressing their emotional and behavioral problems.

To their surprise, Liam thrived at the school. In fact, he did so well the instructors sent him home after just one month. But to his parents' horror, his behavior problems resumed as soon as he returned home.

So they sent him to another residential treatment facility that specialized in treating teens with serious behavior problems. Again, Liam was a model student and he was discharged after only a short stay.

But within days of returning home, he was up to his old tricks again.

His mother concluded he must be "manipulating the system." She came into my office asking, "How do I get a treatment facility to keep him long enough for him to show his true colors? He's going to need to stay in the facility a lot longer if he's going to get some real help."

But that wasn't the whole story. Liam behaved well in residential settings because he had rules and structure. There were clear consequences for misbehavior.

His parents, on the other hand, didn't know how to enforce the rules. When he said he was going to stay out all hours of the night, they weren't sure how to stop him. When they grounded him, he'd leave the house anyway. When they took away his cell phone, he'd use the computer to communicate with his friends. They weren't giving him consequences for misbehavior and he wasn't motivated to follow their rules.

There were some deeper issues as well. Liam's parents didn't have a good relationship with him, so he wasn't interested in being respectful toward them. And he lacked faith in their ability to be in charge, so he overrode their rules by doing whatever he wanted.

It's a common problem that's become a societal issue. Children often get blamed for being the "problem" and they get sent to treatment centers or juvenile facilities. When they return home, if the environment has not changed, it's likely their behavior problems will continue.

The environment plays a major role in kids' behavior. Without the proper boundaries, they're likely to exhibit behavior problems.

FEW RULES EQUALS MANY STRUGGLES

Kids who decide when they want to go to sleep, how the family should spend their weekends, or whether they should actually have to brush their teeth experience serious problems. Giving kids too much power hurts them in several ways:

- **Lack of self-control**—Kids need parents to teach self-discipline, like how to save money and how to stick to their goals. Without proper guidance, they're likely to struggle with self-control issues into adulthood.

- **Increased risk of health problems**—Most kids choose junk food over healthy food and prefer playing video games over reading books. Research shows kids who have few rules experience higher rates of health issues, ranging from dental cavities to obesity.
- **Increased risk of mental health issues**—Kids who feel like they're in charge are more likely to develop mental health problems like depression and anxiety.
- **Lower levels of academic achievement**—Without proper structure and rules, kids are at a higher risk for academic problems.
- **Excessive screen time**—Permissive parents are five times more likely to let their children watch more than four hours of TV each day. And of course, too much screen time—whether it's TV, video games, or computer use—isn't healthy.
- **Higher rates of risky behavior**—Teens who have too much power exhibit higher rates of misconduct at school. They're also more likely to drink alcohol.

What to Do Instead

In the case of Clarissa and her threats of self-harm, Jenna and Alan had to take a firm stance. They had to step in and make it clear that they were in charge, and were willing to deal with whatever behavior problems resulted from taking back their power.

They explained to Clarissa that they were prepared to take her to the emergency room if they had to. They weren't going to allow her threats to derail them from doing what they needed to do to ensure she was making good choices.

While most parents won't ever be faced with a child who threatens self-injury, many feel like they're being "held hostage" at one time or another. A four-year-old who starts to throw a tantrum in the middle of the grocery store might have figured out that his screaming embarrasses you. And if you don't give him what he wants, he'll make sure everyone in the whole store knows he's not happy. Or your eight-year-old may have learned he can flatter you into submission when he wants to get his way.

EMPOWER YOURSELF

Changing your behavior when your child is in need is different from giving in to him because he can't control his emotions. If he's not feeling well, picking him up from school to take care of him is part of being a good parent. But giving in to him when he's throwing a tantrum teaches him unhealthy habits.

Here are some more examples of how you can empower yourself, rather than give your child power over you:

1. **Set the terms.**

   Empowering yourself: Saying, "You can eat a cookie when you're done eating all your broccoli."

   Giving away power: Agreeing to your child's conditions when he suggests, "I'll only eat my broccoli if you give me two cookies."

2. **Use rewards, not bribes.**

   Empowering yourself: Saying, "If you stay next to me the whole time we're shopping, I'll let you pick a little treat as a reward."

   Giving away power: Saying, "Here's some candy but you have to promise to be good the whole time we're in the store, okay?"

3. **Stick to limits and follow through with consequences.**

   Empowering yourself: Saying, "If you don't get into bed now, you won't be allowed to play video games all day tomorrow."

   Giving away power: Arguing about bedtime for thirty minutes without giving out any consequences, and ultimately, allowing your child to delay bedtime.

ESTABLISH A CLEAR HIERARCHY

If your boundaries have gotten a little blurred, reestablish your authority. Here are a few ways to create a clear hierarchy that separates parents from kids:

- **Separate adult conversations from kid conversations.** Your child doesn't need to know Aunt Susie is going through bankruptcy or that the neighbor had an affair. Excuse your child from the room when you're having adult conversations. Tell your child that kids don't need to know everything.
- **Allow privileges only when they're earned.** Don't allow your child to play with his electronics or go out with his friends if he hasn't earned those privileges. Just like your boss doesn't give you a paycheck unless you do the work, make sure he earns his privileges before you grant them.
- **Tell your child he needs to ask permission.** Don't let your child *tell* you he's going out with friends or *tell* you he's borrowing the car. Make it clear that he can only do those things if you grant him permission. Get him into the habit of asking permission and say no sometimes.
- **Don't ask your child for permission.** When it comes to big decisions, don't ask your child, "Is it okay with you if we move?" Ask questions like "How would you feel about moving?" but make it clear that you might do it anyway, even if he isn't on board with the decision.

REFUSE TO GET INTO POWER STRUGGLES

Arguing with your child gives away your power in a couple of different ways. For starters, if you lose your cool, you'll show your child he can manipulate your emotions by being defiant. He'll likely enjoy saying no just to watch you get angry.

Second, every minute you engage in an argument is an extra minute he can put off doing what you asked of him. He may try to lure you into a lengthy disagreement just to distract you from the task at hand.

Take this example:

Dad: It's time to turn off the TV and go clean your room.

Child: I'll do it later.

Dad: No, I said do it now!

Child: You're like a drill sergeant! All you ever do is boss me around.

Dad: Well, if you'd do your chores, I wouldn't have to keep reminding you all the time!

Child: I don't even know what you want me to do anyway. My room isn't that messy.

Dad: Yes it is! I can hardly even see the floor in there.

Every minute this father engages in a conversation with this child over whether he really acts like a drill sergeant or whether his son's room really is *that* messy is one more minute his child puts off cleaning his room. Whether your child derails you altogether, or just delays doing what he's supposed to, talking about his inactivity gives him more power.

Here's a better response:

Dad: It's time to turn off the TV and go clean your room.

Child: I'll do it later.

Dad: If you don't clean your room now, you'll lose your electronics for the day.

Child: You're like a drill sergeant. All you ever do is boss me around.

At this point, the dad could wait about five seconds to see if his son is going to get up to clean his room. If he doesn't, he can follow through with taking away his electronics. Rather than getting into a lengthy discussion, one warning (and a willingness to follow through with a consequence) sends a clear message that the dad is in charge.

Although it may seem harsh to give your child just one warning, following through with a consequence shows your child that you mean business. You'll train him to see that arguing or delaying your instructions isn't effective.

When you refuse to get into a power struggle, you teach your child that he has the power to control his behavior but he doesn't have the power to control yours. But just like you want to send the message that your child can't force *you* to do something, you also have to accept that you can't force your child to do something.

Trying to force a twelve-year-old to clean his room by repeatedly yelling, "Do it now!" won't regain your power. Instead it'll give your child power over you as you lose your cool and begin to take more drastic measures to get him to follow your commands.

USE LANGUAGE THAT ESTABLISHES YOUR HIERARCHY

Remember the eighties sitcom *The Cosby Show*? There's an episode that portrays how your language speaks volumes about your parental authority. In the episode, Cliff Huxtable's (i.e., Bill Cosby) teenage daughter Vanessa says the kids at school are picking on her because she told them that her family paid $11,000 for a painting. The other kids started chiding Vanessa that she must think she's better than everyone, it turns into a physical fight with the other girls, and she comes home from school distraught. She tells her parents, "This wouldn't have happened if we weren't so rich!" Cliff responds, "Let me get something straight, okay? Your mother and I are rich. You have nothing."

As the parents, you're in charge. The fact that you have a job and pay the bills means you own everything in your house, even if your child bought it with her own money. Your child can earn privileges and earn money from you, but only if and when you grant her those privileges.

While it's good to use the inclusive "we" and "us" sometimes to reflect your family's attempts to be "all for one and one for all," your language should also reflect the fact that you are the one in charge. Rather than saying, "We'll talk about it," when your child asks to extend his curfew by an hour, try saying, "You can explain your reasons and then your father and I will discuss it."

TAKE YOUR CHILD'S FEEDBACK WITH A GRAIN OF SALT

Giving your child too much power may not always be obvious on the outside. Your child's comments and opinions may affect your head and your heart in unhealthy ways, which could ultimately give them too much power in your life. Here's an example: Your child says, "You're the worst mom ever!"

> **Thoughts:** You start recalling all the parenting mistakes you ever made and second-guess some of your decisions. Ultimately, your child's comments cause you to conclude you must be a crummy parent.

> **Feelings:** You feel ashamed and guilty.

> **Behavior:** The next time he asks for something, you buy it for him in an effort to look like a better parent in his eyes.

With that, you allow your child's insult to have an unhealthy influence on your behavior. Here's another example: Your teen says, "You're way too old to understand Snapchat."

> **Thoughts:** You think about how many things your teen knows how to do with electronics that you don't understand. You decide there's no use in even trying to find out what your teen is doing online because you'll never understand anyway.

Feelings: Embarrassed and discouraged.

Behavior: You stop attempting to monitor what your teen is doing online.

Accepting your teen's feedback at face value could cause you to give up trying to make sure he is safe online. Remember that kids often have ulterior motives when they express strong opinions, and ultimately, you don't need your child's approval.

How to Teach Kids They Have Healthy but Limited Power

In the case of Clarissa and her self-injury, Alan and Jenna had to stick to their limits whether she liked it or not. They needed to show her she wasn't in charge when it came to certain family decisions.

There is a tough balance to strike to both empower your child while making sure you aren't giving them power over you. Teach him that he can earn new privileges and extra responsibilities, but only if you grant them.

ACKNOWLEDGE YOUR CHILD'S SECRET WEAPONS

If your child sees she can't gain power fair and square, she'll likely try to use a few secret weapons to attempt to win the battle. And often those secret weapons are dirty tricks meant to guilt, embarrass, or horrify you into resignation.

When I was a kid, my sister's secret weapon involved trying to annoy my parents until they caved. She can't carry a tune in a bucket, and she used this to her advantage. When she wanted something, and my parents said no, she sang really loud. And she'd keep singing, sometimes for hours, not stopping until all of us were ready to give her whatever she wanted.

Over the years I've worked with kids with much more sophisticated secret weapons, like the four-year-old who held his breath when he was angry. He passed out once, which terrified his parents. After that, they started giving in to him long before he turned blue and he learned that depriving himself of oxygen was a great way to get whatever he wanted.

There was also a ten-year-old I saw who threatened to go on a hunger strike if he didn't get to eat peanut-butter-and-jelly sandwiches for each meal. When he refused to eat dinner one night, his mother panicked. Worried he'd starve to death, she fed him peanut butter and jelly.

Here are some other common dirty tricks your child might use to try to gain power over you:

- Call you names
- Pretend she doesn't care about consequences
- Yell and scream
- Whine and beg
- Try to embarrass you in public
- Make threats
- Say mean things like "I hate you" or "I'm going to go live with Grandma"
- Get physically aggressive
- Make promises like "If you just let me this once, I'll never ask for anything again"
- Retaliate when you say no
- Use guilt trips

When your child uses inappropriate ways to gain power, point it out. Say, "I know you're upset that I won't let you go to your friend's house and you're trying to make me feel bad so I'll change my mind. But that's not going to work with me."

Teach your child that he is allowed to respectfully disagree with you. If he thinks his bedtime is too early or he thinks it's not fair that you won't buy him a puppy, tell him how he can state his case.

For example, he could make a list of the top ten reasons he should be allowed to have a puppy or he could write you a letter about why he should be allowed to stay up later. Be willing to hear what he has to say, if he expresses his opinion in an appropriate manner.

Make it clear, however, that just because he argues his case in an appropriate manner doesn't mean you're going to change your mind. Ultimately, the decision is up to you and your adult wisdom to do what's best.

Teach Preschoolers to Focus on Their Own Behavior

As preschoolers start to develop more independence, they tend to assert their demands in some fairly unreasonable ways. It's normal for them to throw tantrums when they don't get their way and you're likely to hear, "You're not the boss of me!" at least once in a while.

Make it clear that your preschooler is in control of *his* behavior and you're in control of yours. If he chooses to scream, beg, or throw a colossal tantrum, stick to your rules. Show him that his misbehavior won't earn him what he wants.

Keep in mind that sometimes, preschoolers misbehave because they want attention. So repeatedly saying, "Stop that" or "Don't do that," could actually reinforce misbehavior. Looking the other way and pretending you aren't affected by annoying behaviors like whining or screeching shows your child that his behavior won't be rewarded.

It's important, however, to start explaining to your preschooler that his behavior influences you but doesn't control you. Try saying, "I feel sad when you say mean things" or "I feel angry when you don't listen."

Avoid blaming your preschooler for your emotions or your behavior. Saying things like "You *make* me so mad" sends the message that he has the power to force you to feel something. The subtle difference in language affects your child's core beliefs about how much power he has.

Teach School-Age Kids to Stay out of Adult Conversation

One of the easiest ways to identify where your child sees himself in the family hierarchy is by looking at how he conducts himself when you're engaged in adult conversation. If he thinks it's okay to interrupt you while you're talking, there's a good chance he thinks he's your equal, or perhaps even your superior.

Of course, there will be occasional times when all children interrupt. He might yell out to you from the other room or he might ask if you've seen his cleats as he's running out the door to practice, but unless your child has an impulse control problem, like ADHD, those instances should be few and far between.

In addition to interrupting, kids who see themselves as having equal power are compelled to weigh in on adult conversations. Whether you're talking about how you might remodel the bathroom or what kind of car you want to buy, offering unsolicited advice about what you *should* do isn't a good sign.

When your child butts in to offer suggestions on an adult matter, address it firmly. Say, "This isn't a decision for you to make."

Make it clear that adults have the knowledge and wisdom to make the best decisions. And his job is to follow your rules and not worry about the choices you're going to make for the family. Invite him to weigh in on small choices, like "Should we frost Grandma's cake with yellow or blue frosting?" but make it clear that he doesn't get an equal vote on big decisions.

Teach Teens to Use Empowered Language

The teen years are an important time to assess how your child sees herself. While you don't want her to have a victim mentality like we discussed in chapter one, you also don't want your teen thinking she's the queen of the world. So while it's healthy for her to recognize that she has some power in life, it's equally important that she know the limits of her power.

The language your teen uses is very indicative of her underlying beliefs. If she says things like "My teacher *makes me* read too many books" or "You *make me* clean my room!" remind her that those things are choices. While there will be consequences for not doing them, no one is physically forcing her.

Point out that she's in control over her choices. Her teacher doesn't force her to read all those books. Instead she chooses to meet her teacher's expectations so she can succeed. Although it's a subtle distinction, it's a very important one.

Be on the lookout for language that indicates she thinks she has too much power. If she says things like "You *have* to drive me to the movies Friday night," remind her that if you decide to drive her, that will be your choice.

Kids Who Are Given Just the Right Amount of Power Become Powerful Adults

Makenzie was a nine-year-old girl who was placed with Steve and me because she exhibited "parentified" behavior. Both of her birth parents had serious substance abuse problems. And as the oldest of three children, Makenzie cared for her younger siblings when her parents were under the influence of drugs and alcohol.

When Child Protective Services removed the children from their home, they placed all three of them in the same foster home, before Steve and I met them. Even though Makenzie didn't need to care for her siblings once she lived with competent foster parents, she struggled to stop looking after them.

She bossed them around, argued with them, and often interfered when her first foster parents tried to discipline them.

As a result, the state made the difficult decision to remove her from that foster home, leaving her two siblings. And that's how she came to stay with us.

She continued to have regular visitation with her siblings. And over time, she accepted her role as an older sister, not as a parent. She learned that she could still read to her younger siblings and teach them how to play games, but she no longer had to be in charge of their well-being. She began to trust that her siblings' foster parents could take care of them.

She also developed friends her own age and, for the first time, had the opportunity to play and have fun. It was incredible to watch her be able to be a kid for the first time.

Eventually, she returned to her previous foster home and was reunited with her younger siblings. But it took some hard work for her to trust that her foster parents had everything handled.

When you give your child just the right amount of power, he'll feel empowered to grow and learn. But he won't feel anxious and scared about having to be in charge. He'll grow up seeing that you are the trusty leader who will guide him along the way and he'll grow to trust in his own decision-making skills.

Mentally strong people don't give away their power. By not allowing your child to have power over you, you serve as a role model of mental strength. She'll see that she can't control you, but she can control herself.

Empowering your child to make some of her own decisions, without trying to have power over you, will help her become a mentally strong adult. Whether she's faced with a mean boss or a rude romantic partner, she'll recognize that much like you, she doesn't have to give anyone power over the way she thinks, feels, and behaves.

Troubleshooting and Common Traps

It's important for the adults in the home to back one another up. If you allow your child to break the rules, but your partner enforces them, you'll be setting up an unhealthy family dynamic. Keep the family hierarchy clear by showing that the adults are in charge.

Sometimes parents ask a child to keep a secret from the other parent. While it may seem innocent to tell your child, "Don't tell Dad how much money we spent" or "Let's tell Mom you went to bed on time," those secrets upset the balance of power, not to mention it's bad for your relationship. Even if the two of you don't agree, present a united front to your child.

In unhealthy divorces or separations, power issues can sometimes be a problem. Asking a child to be a "messenger" to the other parent or to behave like a "spy" sets up a dysfunctional family dynamic. It's important for kids to be able to focus on childlike activities and for adults to take care of things like custody issues and legal problems.

Another common issue arises in those desperate situations when you need your child to behave, now. Perhaps you're on a plane and your child is screaming because you won't give him another snack after he's already eaten several. You don't want the other passengers to have to listen to him screech for two hours. What do you do?

In those rare situations, it's okay to give in for the greater good of those around you. But if your child does this regularly—like on your morning commute on the bus—you may have to let him scream a few times. Once he sees his tantrums don't work, he'll give up trying.

It's important not to abuse your power, however. If it's a decision that doesn't really matter—your child says he doesn't feel comfortable going on the roller coaster, for example—don't pressure him into doing it. Respect his opinion and reinforce to him that he doesn't need to go along with the crowd.

WHAT'S HELPFUL

- Avoiding power struggles
- Setting clear limits
- Following through with consequences

- Staying calm
- Refusing to comply with manipulative behavior
- Preventing your child's participation in adult-only conversations
- Teaching your child empowerment language

WHAT'S NOT HELPFUL

- Getting sucked into debates that allow your child to delay following your directions
- Giving in to manipulative behavior
- Allowing your child to bring out the worst in you
- Letting your child weigh in on adult decisions
- Not creating a clear family hierarchy

They Don't
Expect Perfection

While most ninth-grade students were celebrating any grade above a C on their earth science exams, Kylie cried if she got an A-minus. And even though being her lab partner guaranteed an A, no one ever wanted to because she became verbally abusive toward anyone who wasn't performing to her standards.

Science wasn't the only class in which she had problems. She cried about her "bad grades" in the other subjects too. She often argued with her English teacher and begged him to reconsider when she didn't get an A on her essays.

The other students usually just rolled their eyes when Kylie was "crying again," but Kylie didn't seem to notice. Her objective wasn't to have a fulfilling social life—her goal was to have a 4.0 GPA.

When her requests to see the guidance counselor became almost daily—either because she wanted advice on how to improve her grades or because she was trying to convince the guidance office that the school's grading system was unfair—the counselor suggested Kylie seek therapy.

That's how she landed in my office with her mother, Nadine. I asked Kylie and Nadine why they thought the guidance counselor recommended therapy. Nadine said, "Kylie knows she can get a 4.0 GPA but she's struggling to get there and that's frustrating to her."

Oddly, Nadine didn't seem concerned about the fact that Kylie was having emotional problems. Instead she seemed more worried about her grades. "I keep telling her not to waste time crying. Instead she should be focusing that energy on bringing her grades up," Nadine explained.

"We might hire a tutor to edit Kylie's English papers before she hands them in so we can help get her grade up. No respectable college wants to admit a kid who can't get an A in English," she said. Kylie nodded and said, "I think a tutor would help my grade a lot."

Nadine asked, "Have you seen instances where hiring a tutor has helped students get all A's?" After listening to the two of them strategize about how to get a perfect GPA, it was clear they had different definitions "of the problem" than I did. That also meant they had very different ideas about solutions. In my eyes, the problems were:

1. **Kylie felt pressure to get straight A's.** If she got anything less than a perfect grade, she felt like a complete failure. Even though she had excellent grades, she thought she wasn't good enough.
2. **Kylie lacked the emotional skills to deal with disappointment.** She cried whenever she got a grade she didn't like. She required a lot of emotional support from the guidance counselor and she was having trouble maintaining friendships.

I recommended:

1. **Therapy for Nadine.** Nadine appeared to be the driving force behind Kylie's quest to get a 4.0. And until she stopped putting so much pressure on Kylie, Kylie was likely to continue seeking perfection.
2. **Therapy for Kylie that would help her develop a kinder inner dialogue.** Beating herself up when she didn't get a perfect grade wasn't helpful. Learning to take a more self-compassionate approach could help her bounce back from disappointment better.
3. **Social and emotional skills training for Kylie.** Crying every day

in school when she wasn't happy with her grades, taking frustration out on her peers, and demanding to visit the guidance counselor daily impacted her social life. Dealing with her inner turmoil productively could help her maintain her composure better.

I explained to Kylie and Nadine that my job as a therapist was to help her be as emotionally healthy and mentally strong as possible. If their goal was to hire tutors and take more drastic measures to improve Kylie's grades, I couldn't help. I didn't think seeking a 4.0 GPA was a healthy goal for her given the consequences it was causing in her life.

We talked about the pros and cons of their current approach as well as the pros and cons of my recommended approach. Initially, Nadine was concerned that shifting the focus from improving Kylie's grades to helping Kylie cope with her current grades would mean she was settling for being a "mediocre" student.

She worried that a mediocre student wouldn't get into a top college and wouldn't be awarded scholarships. While these were valid concerns, the quest for perfection came with a price. Kylie could experience serious mental health problems. Or she might get so burned out by the time she finished high school that she wouldn't be able to go to college.

I suggested they think about my recommendations and let me know if they decided to address Kylie's emotional well-being. They left my office on the fence and I wasn't sure I'd hear from them again.

But a couple of weeks later Nadine called asking to set up an appointment. She said things had gotten worse in the past few weeks. Kylie was having trouble sleeping and she was irritable all the time. And she felt they needed help.

Nadine agreed to seek therapy for herself so she could learn how to help Kylie without demanding perfection. While she worked on changing her expectations of her daughter, I worked with Kylie on her expectations of herself.

She started by learning some breathing techniques to help calm herself down when she received a grade below an A-plus. I wanted to help her avoid having meltdowns in school since it was causing serious social problems.

The bulk of her treatment focused on changing her core beliefs. Rather than tell herself, "I'm a loser for making these mistakes" or "I'll never succeed if I don't get A's all the time," she learned to create a more forgiving inner monologue. In the meantime, Nadine learned to stop emphasizing perfection.

Kylie and Nadine learned that striving for excellence was healthy, but trying to be perfect wasn't. When Nadine stopped putting so much pressure on her, Kylie was able to see that she didn't have to be flawless to gain approval.

Do You Expect Perfection?

Good parents want their children to succeed. But sometimes the pursuit of excellence goes too far. Do you respond positively to any of the following statements?

In your personal life:

- I procrastinate when I'm afraid I can't complete something perfectly.
- When I complete a project, I focus on the small errors or tiny imperfections that drive me crazy.
- Either I do something well or I don't do it at all.
- I'm really critical of any mistakes that I make.
- I am willing to sacrifice whatever I need to achieve my goals.

In your parenting life:

- I want my child to fulfill the dreams I wasn't able to fulfill.
- I have trouble watching my child do something if she doesn't do it my way.
- Some of my self-worth depends on my child's achievements.
- I only want my child to participate in activities when she excels at them.
- I criticize my child more than I praise him.

Why Parents Expect Perfection

On one end of the spectrum are the types of parents who believe everyone deserves a trophy regardless of who wins the game. On the other end are the parents who are never satisfied with their child's performance—even if he is named MVP.

Nadine was one of those parents who were never truly satisfied. But she thought she was doing Kylie a favor by telling her she needed to get a 4.0 to get into college. She assumed that her "high standards" were just what Kylie needed to stay motivated. She didn't understand that demanding perfection was doing more harm than good.

TIGER MOMS THINK DEMANDING PERFECTION LEADS TO PERFECT KIDS

Amy Chua, the author of *Battle Hymn of the Tiger Mother,* famously said, "Chinese parents demand perfect grades because they believe their child can get them. If their child doesn't get them, the Chinese parent assumes it's because the child didn't work hard enough."

According to Chua, if a Western child receives an A-minus on a test, his parents praise him for a job well done. If a Chinese child gets an A-minus, his parents ask what went wrong.

In her quest to raise perfect kids, Chua never allowed her children to go on playdates, perform in school plays, or play computer games. Instead they were expected to be straight-A students who played the piano and the violin.

In an article in the *Wall Street Journal,* she said some of her Western friends thought they were being strict when they made their children practice their instruments thirty minutes to an hour every day. "For a Chinese mother, the first hour is the easy part. It's hours two and three that get tough," Chua said.

If a Chinese child ever got a B-minus (which Chua notes would never happen), "the devastated Chinese mother would then get dozens, maybe hundreds of practice tests and work through them with her child for as long as it takes to get the grade up to an A."

Chua didn't take into account that her children were missing out on valuable life experience that may have been pivotal to their future success. Negotiating conflict (which often arises during playdates) is essential to career success. And how could her kids learn how to bounce back from failure if she never allowed them to fail?

Certainly, Chua's mentality isn't limited just to Chinese parents. There are plenty of other parents who have adopted the idea that expecting perfection somehow molds kids into perfect people.

STAGE MOMS AND SPORTS DADS LIVE VICARIOUSLY THROUGH THEIR KIDS

Competition-crazed parenting extends beyond academics. Stage moms turn their daughters into ballet superstars and pageant queens and sports dads push their kids to excel on the courts and on athletic fields. Their demand for perfection rarely has anything do with their children's needs. Instead it's about healing the parents' wounds.

Sports dads who never made it to the pro leagues may hold out hope that their child will achieve the greatness that they never did. And even though only one percent of high school athletes in America receive a scholarship to a division one school, sports dads are convinced their kids will beat the odds. And they believe their child will beat even greater odds by playing on a pro team.

And if their child isn't playing to the level of perfection, some of them insist on leveling the playing field. On the milder end of the high-pressure parenting world, you have a father who delays his son's start in kindergarten. He hopes being a year older than the other kids will also mean he's bigger, which could help him dominate on the football field.

On the other end of the spectrum, you'll find parents like Dr. Cito, a pediatric dentist from Albuquerque, New Mexico, who sharpened a buckle on his son's football helmet in an effort to give him an unfair competitive advantage. The helmet cut several players, and at least one required stitches. Officials said the helmet was "sharp enough to shred a magazine cover." He was sentenced to forty-eight hours in jail, a year on probation, and four hundred hours of community service.

Fortunately, most parents don't go to those sorts of extremes. But many go so far as to help their kids travel all over the country to play sports. Or they encourage their children to practice late into the evening or allow them to play through injuries, all because they want them to excel.

It's not just sports dads who are desperate to help their kids advance. Stage moms are known for dirty tricks too.

Some of their shenanigans aren't new. Take, for instance, Judy Garland, the actress who played Dorothy in *The Wizard of Oz*. Her mother reportedly gave her pills to give her energy and pills to help her sleep while forcing her to perform in shows as a child.

Today's digital world, however, has given a new meaning to the phrase "all the world's a stage." And many stage moms are turning to the Internet to make their children famous.

Take, for example, "The CeCe Show." CeCe is a young child who has been performing since the age of 3. Her mother captures her antics on social media. CeCe has attracted hundreds of thousands of followers and earns thousands of dollars for promoting products and doing paid appearances.

In an interview with *Cosmopolitan* magazine, CeCe's mother said she tells CeCe she has to perform whether she feels like it or not because "it's her job." She went on to say, "My biggest thing is to get CeCe on TV and known to the world, not just on social media." Certainly, there are many other parents out there who are just as intent on making their kids become stars.

Experts say the reason parents get so involved with ensuring their child appears perfect or performs flawlessly is that they view their children as extensions of themselves. And pushing their child to do the things they weren't able to do helps fulfill their unrealized dreams.

A study at Utrecht University in the Netherlands found that living vicariously through kids is actually healing for parents. When parents experience unresolved regret and disappointment from their past, basking in their children's glory helps them feel pride and fulfillment. But unfortunately, even though it can make parents feel positively, it's harmful to the kids.

IT'S HARD TO KNOW HOW HIGH TO SET THE BAR

As a parent, it's crucial to motivate your child to do his best. It's your job to believe in him even when he doesn't believe in himself. And to encourage him to keep going when he doesn't think he can take one more step.

But it can be hard to know just how much you should expect from your child. And if you're uncertain, you may create ridiculously high expectations without recognizing your child's limits.

It's tempting to look around at other kids to get a sense of what's "normal." But sometimes that approach can backfire.

Just because your friend says her child is completely toilet trained by age two doesn't mean your three-year-old who still wears diapers is delayed.

But if you listened to other parents talk about their kids, or you see what they post on Facebook, you might start to panic when your seven-year-old isn't doing long division and your twelve-year-old hasn't been scouted by any college recruiters, because it can seem like everyone else's kids are ahead of your child.

Comparing your child to kids around him may cause you to expect more than he's capable of delivering. That will leave both of you frustrated when he can't meet your expectations.

All kids are different. And many environmental, biological, and interpersonal factors affect a child's development. Anything from a child's gender to a parent's income may influence when a child hits certain developmental milestones. It's important to know "what's normal" for kids your child's age, and it's also essential to keep in mind that you know your child best. He may be advanced in math and behind in reading. Or he may be the best soccer player in the whole school but still not be able to tie his cleats. If you lose sight of your child's strengths and weaknesses, it's easy to set the bar too high.

Expecting Perfection Is Bad for a Child's Mental Health

Nadine thought it was great that Kylie expected so much from herself. She didn't recognize that crying during class and feeling stressed out all the time were actually taking a serious toll on Kylie's high school career.

Many parents, like Nadine, subscribe to the old adage "A diamond is a chunk of coal that did well under pressure." They think putting pressure on their child will make him shine. But rather than encouraging him to do his best, they pressure him to be perfect. And in the long run, that approach backfires.

TRYING TO APPEAR PERFECT COULD CAUSE YOU TO IGNORE PROBLEMS

Perfectionist parents don't just want their kids to be perfect, they also demand perfection from themselves. Their need to hold everything together, even when there are signs things are falling apart, can have serious consequences for themselves and their children.

That was the case with Christina Hopkinson. In an article in the *Daily Mail,* she describes how her competitive nature caused her to strive to be the best at everything she did. Whether it was academics or sports, by all accounts, she was a high achiever.

She viewed every obstacle, including pregnancy, as a challenge where she could excel. When her baby was delivered via emergency C-section, he received perfect Apgar scores. Hopkinson viewed this as evidence that she was able to have a perfect child. As soon as she brought him home from the hospital, she prided herself on being able to cook lunch and make tea for guests, and she imagined how people must have envied her impressive ability to bounce back from major abdominal surgery.

She told everyone, including the community midwives, things were going very well in her role as a new mother. She didn't ask any questions and instead focused on her need to appear perfect. Believing she was "breastfeeding beautifully," the midwives reduced the frequency of their visits. But things weren't going well. Hopkinson noticed her son appeared listless but she resisted the urge to take him to the doctor. She feared she'd look like a paranoid or inept parent.

When the midwives returned five days later, they discovered her baby had lost 25 percent of his body weight. He was rushed to the hospital with neonatal hypernatremia, a condition that could have been fatal. He was dehydrated and the sodium levels in his blood were dangerously high.

Fortunately, after an eight-day hospital stay, her baby was healthy enough to return home. Hopkinson says the incident changed her outlook on life. She admits, had it not been for that experience, "I still would have been congratulating myself and taking credit for his utter gorgeousness, instead of realizing that there is so much—almost everything—beyond our control."

Like Hopkinson, many parents want to gain admiration from others for having the "perfect family" or the "perfect life." And to the detriment of their children, they view problems, disabilities, illness, or failure as a sign of weakness.

It's as if admitting they are human, by taking a nap or catching the flu, would reduce them to the level of mere mortals in the eyes of others. Often, that fear of being seen as "weak" prevents people from taking care of themselves.

Rather than address problems, they ignore them in hopes they'll go away. Instead of acknowledging their weaknesses they try to cover them up. They deny their pain and they refuse to ask for help. But in reality, they're not mentally strong. They're just acting tough in an attempt to gain approval from others.

KIDS PAY THE PRICE FOR NOT MEASURING UP

When parents expect kids to be perfect, they are at risk of developing what's called socially prescribed perfectionism—the belief that others will only value them if they are perfect all the time. They grow to believe that any little mistake could make it impossible for others to love them.

But from the outside, it's hard to see their pain. They hide their fears and insecurities well because they've even perfected the art of disguising their inner turmoil.

Socially prescribed perfectionism has been linked to a variety of problems, including:

- **Mental health problems**—Kids who strive to be perfect are at a much higher risk of mental health problems like depression, anxiety, and anorexia. They're good at masking their symptoms, however, so often their problems go untreated.
- **Self-defeating behavior**—Studies have linked perfectionism to binge eating, procrastination, and interpersonal conflict. Ironically, a perfectionist's desire to succeed often causes them to sabotage their own goals.
- **Chronic dissatisfaction**—Perfectionism isn't the key to success. Kids who feel like they can't ever live up to other people's expectations live tormented lives. They turn into adults who—despite their accomplishments—never feel satisfied.

Most disturbing of all, studies have found that kids who feel like they don't measure up are more likely to kill themselves. In a 2013 study published in the *Archives of Suicide Research,* researchers interviewed the parents of twelve- to twenty-five-year-old males who had committed suicide. More than 70 percent of parents said their sons had placed exceedingly high demands and expectations on themselves.

Suicide clusters in affluent communities are also cropping up and researchers suspect it's due to the pressure placed on kids to excel. In Silicon Valley, the adolescent suicide rate has soared to five times the national average. The Centers for Disease Control and Prevention has referred to it as a chronic health issue.

It's similar to what we saw in 2014, when Fairfax, Virginia, experienced a sharp increase in teen suicide. Investigators concluded that the high expectations of students, parental pressure to succeed, and parental denial of mental health problems, were among the risk factors.

University of California economists Garey and Valerie Ramey refer to today's competitive culture as "the rug rat race." With more kids going to college and fewer slots available in elite schools, there is heightened rivalry among parents. The constant need to gain a competitive edge, by spending more hours on college preparatory activities, might be making kids feel as though they're never going to meet their parents' expectations.

So if kids who excel in affluent private schools feel like failures, imagine how kids with learning disabilities feel? A study from the University of British Columbia on adolescent suicide found that 89 percent of suicide notes contained spelling errors. The researchers concluded that many of these teens likely had learning disabilities and perhaps felt as though they couldn't measure up to their peers.

Whether your child is a candidate for Harvard or he requires special education, expecting him to perform above his ability could have deadly consequences. But sadly, most parents of children who died by suicide never thought it could happen to them.

What to Do Instead

Kylie, who could not tolerate anything less than an A-plus, had to learn that a less than satisfactory grade wasn't the end of the world. If she wasn't satisfied with a B, she could strive to do better. But beating herself up and telling herself she'd failed wasn't helpful.

Her mother had to send new messages about achievement and failure. Before Kylie could forgive herself for mistakes, she needed to know that her mother was going to accept her even if she failed to live up to her expectations.

Periodically review your expectations of your child. Are you challenging him to do his best or pressuring him to be perfect?

LOOK FOR SIGNS YOU'RE PUTTING TOO MUCH PRESSURE ON YOUR CHILD

It can be hard to recognize when you're "that parent." Perhaps you get overly excited when you're watching your child's baseball games. Or maybe you insist on meeting with school administrators when your child doesn't get picked to compete in the spelling bee.

The signs that you are putting too much pressure on your child might also be a little more subtle. Here are five warning signs to look out for:

1. **You criticize more than you praise.** Focusing too much on what's wrong, without ever pointing out what your child is doing right, can cause her to feel like a failure.

2. **You compare your child to other children.** Saying things like "Well, Johnny practices four hours a day" or "Your sister never failed a math test," puts him in constant competition and doesn't take his individuality into account.

3. **You treat every situation like it's life-altering.** Once-in-a-lifetime opportunities are rare during childhood. So if you find yourself making statements like "You need to get an A on this exam if you want to be considered for the advanced class" or "You need to do really well in tonight's game if you want to be picked for all-stars," take a step back. Remind yourself that there are many opportunities for your child to shine.

4. **You lose your cool frequently.** If you're irritable and frustrated that your child isn't performing as well as you'd like, you might be feeling the squeeze too. Losing your temper may be a sign that your expectations are too high.

5. **You micromanage your child's activities.** High-pressure parents often become control freaks. If you tend to hover over your child to make sure he's doing everything "right," you might be pressuring him to be perfect.

As your child grows and matures, your expectations should grow along with him. But there may be times when your expectations outpace his ability to keep up. So keep a watchful eye out for warning signs that you're setting the bar impossibly high.

SEND HEALTHY MESSAGES ABOUT ACHIEVEMENT AND FAILURE

When I worked in a junior high school as a therapist, report-card day was always interesting. While some kids would poke their heads into my office on their way home to announce, "I got four A's, Ms. Morin!" others would stop by seeking a pep talk before they faced their parents with their less than stellar grades.

On one particular report-card day, Simon, one of my newer clients, stopped by my office. He was crying because he got two B's and he said, "I might have to go live with my dad now."

Simon's parents had divorced when he was eight and they'd been in a bitter custody battle for years. The judge recently granted his mother primary residence. But she had made it clear to Simon that he'd only be able to stay with her if the judge thought she was doing a good job raising him. And that meant he had to be a top honor student.

Poor Simon was convinced he needed perfect grades to remain living with his mother. And now he was terrified he wasn't doing a good enough job.

After Simon left my office, I called his mother. I was expecting her to say that she didn't mean to give Simon that message. But instead she confirmed that she'd told Simon he needed to get straight A's. He got all A's when he lived with his father, so she was afraid any slip would signal that she was a less capable parent.

She agreed to speak with me in my office the following week. She acknowledged she would normally be happy with a few B's on Simon's report card, but she was concerned about how it would be viewed by the judge.

I explained that telling Simon he had to get straight A's to keep living with her put him under an enormous amount of pressure. It wasn't good for him to think his living situation could be at stake every time he failed a test or bombed a homework assignment.

Initially, she wasn't happy with my comments. She asked, "Well, how is that going to make me look if his grades keep slipping?" So I asked, "How's it going to look if you put so much pressure on him to perform perfectly that he develops mental health problems?"

I explained that I've never seen a custody situation where a child had to move because he got two B's on his report card. But I have seen cases where one parent puts so much pressure on a child that he wanted to move in with the other parent.

She insisted Simon's grade would come into play during their next court hearing. So I advised her to speak with her lawyer to gain more information.

But I also explained that even if it were true that a B would put Simon's living situation in jeopardy, telling Simon wasn't helpful. Instead, her best option was to encourage him to excel and help him do his best. If he had to move in with his father, it would be because the judge thought his father's house was a better environment, not because Simon failed.

She agreed to stop telling Simon that he had to get all A's. Instead, she'd tell him the courts were evaluating *her* performance by making sure she was helping him do his best in school.

Of course, Simon had already heard her previous message that he had to get all A's. So for the next few weeks, he held his breath. He feared at any moment he'd be given the news he had to move back to his father's house. But to his relief, it didn't happen.

In fact, he stayed with his mother for the rest of the time I worked with him. And he was able to relax the way he viewed his achievement.

The new message from his mother—and the lack of immediate court action—gave him some peace of mind. He was able to spend more time thinking about when he was going to get his braces off and which position he was going to play in baseball rather than worry that his imperfect grades would cause him to have to move.

Implying that "something" bad will happen if he isn't perfect can be harmful. Saying things like "You won't get recruited on a football scholarship if you aren't perfect in tonight's game" or "Tonight's recital is your one big shot; you can't afford to make a single mistake," sends the wrong message to kids.

Pressure doesn't always come from parents. Teachers, coaches, or other mentors may tell your child he only has "one shot" to make it in life, and if he blows it, he'll never succeed. I've overheard teachers telling students, "If you don't do well on your SATs today, you won't get into college." But in reality, kids can retake their SATs if they don't do well. And the SATs are only one factor that influences college admissions officers' decisions. So it's critical to consider all the people who may be putting undue pressure on your child.

No matter what's at stake—and usually there isn't as much as you might think—send the message that you want your child to do his best. Clearly, mistakes happen sometimes. So rather than insist he never mess up, give him the message that he's mentally strong enough to bounce back when he doesn't perform up to his own expectations.

STRIVE FOR EXCELLENCE, NOT PERFECTION

Studies consistently show that kids perform to their parents' expectations academically as long as parents have reasonable expectations. If your expectations are too far out of reach, your child will likely give up. And when he does accomplish something admirable, he'll struggle to enjoy his success because he'll be thinking about how to do better in the next game or how to maintain his title as champion.

If your child strives for excellence—as opposed to perfection—his mistakes won't demolish his self-worth. Here are three ways you can help your child strive for excellence:

- **Ask yourself whose need this expectation serves.** Do you want him to be the star player on the team because it will make you feel good? Do you want him to get good grades so you'll feel like a good parent? Make sure your expectations are good for your child, not you.
- **Focus on effort, not the outcome.** Say, "I expect you to sit down and study for one hour" rather than "I expect you to get an A on your test." Make it clear that persistence and practice will help him do better.
- **Back off when your child shows signs he's overwhelmed.** While it's helpful to encourage your child to push through a struggle when he's willing to try, insisting he keep going after he's mentally checked out isn't helpful. If he says he hates soccer or he doesn't want to play the piano anymore, it could be a sign you're pushing him too hard.

PROVIDE A PRAISE-AND-CRITICISM SANDWICH

Criticizing your child too much isn't healthy. It'll harm your relationship and decrease your child's motivation.

Balance out criticism by offering your child praise, criticism, and then praise again—making a praise-and-criticism sandwich.

Here are a few examples of how you can point out the good, say what you expect him to do better, and finish on a positive note:

- "Nice job putting your clothes away. Your shelves are still a little messy but I like the way you made the bed so neatly."
- "You really hustled in the game today. But I noticed you weren't paying attention once the coach put you in the outfield. I think we should work on keeping your head in the game no matter which

position you play. But I could tell you were determined to hit the ball every time you got up to bat."

- "You put a lot of effort into this project. It looks like you spelled this word wrong, though. But everything else looks really good."

Point out the good first, to give your child a sense of accomplishment and help her see what she's done well. Then tell her what needs improvement so she can become better. Follow up with a little more praise to keep her motivated.

Don't overuse the praise-and-criticism sandwich, however. Give your child praise without any criticism sometimes. Otherwise she will feel as though you're always paying attention to the negative, even when she does something well.

How to Teach Kids to Do Their Best

In the case of Nadine and Kylie's quest for a 4.0 GPA, the key to letting go of perfectionism involved reducing the pressure on Kylie. She had to focus on doing her best rather than being perfect.

If your child wants to be the best at everything he does, he may never feel competent. Teach him to focus on all the things he can control—like his effort and attitude—while putting less emphasis on gaining a perfect outcome.

LOOK FOR SHADES OF GRAY

Be on the lookout for signs that your child may be developing a bit of a perfectionist mentality. One telltale sign that is easy to spot is all-or-nothing thinking.

Budding perfectionists see themselves as complete winners or total losers. They conclude that one simple error makes their performance a dismal failure. Here are some of the types of things you might hear if your child experiences some all-or-nothing thinking:

- "I failed my math test. I got two answers wrong!"
- "I got out of sync for a few steps right in the middle of the dance recital. I must have looked like the worst dancer ever."
- "That game was a disaster. I missed both of the goals I tried to make."
- "There's no sense in playing the saxophone anymore. I didn't get picked for the jazz band."
- "I messed up so much during my tryout for the school musical that they gave me the part of an extra. I'm going to give up singing."

When you hear your child say something indicative of all-or-nothing thinking, point out that most things aren't black or white. Help him find shades of gray.

Ask questions like "Is it possible you did a great job even though you made one mistake?" or say, "Just because you didn't make the team this year doesn't mean you won't next year. You have a whole year to practice."

Be aware of the language that you're role-modeling for your child as well. Avoid declaring her math meet a "total victory" and don't tell her that her gymnastics performance was a "complete success." Those types of labels can fuel all-or-nothing thinking.

Similarly, avoid all-or-nothing language when talking about things in your own life. If you fumble one question during a job interview, don't walk through the door declaring you're terrible at interviews. Instead, talk about the good as well as the bad. Say something more balanced, like "I think I answered their question about my past job experiences well, but I drew a complete blank when they asked me about my greatest weakness."

Teach Your Preschooler to Keep Trying

Children don't come out of the womb perfectionists. If they did, they might never learn anything. Imagine a toddler refusing to try walking because he was afraid he'd fail? Or what if, after his first fall, he declared himself a failure and never tried again?

Thankfully, young children don't think like that. Instead they're determined to learn new things and get better, but they don't expect to be perfect.

That's especially true with preschoolers. They want to keep up with the big kids, even though they lack the necessary motor skills, coordination, attention span, and many other tools.

It's a prime time for parents to start pushing kids too hard and too fast. And ultimately, for no real reason. Studies show the age at which your child learned to walk, for example, isn't linked to improved motor skills or higher intelligence. In fact, whether your child began walking at nine months or twenty months, he'll likely have the same motor skills as other children by the time he starts school.

So while it can be tempting to make sure your child is an early reader or that he can do addition long before his peers, remember that high achievement isn't everything. Unless he possesses other, softer skills, like how to calm himself down when he's angry and how to resolve conflict peacefully, his early success may not take him too far.

So resist the urge to want your child to be advanced in everything he does. Instead concentrate on building a healthy relationship and having fun. Praise his efforts, even when he makes mistakes, and encourage him when he sticks to a tough task.

Teach Your School-Age Child It's Okay to Focus on Fun Sometimes

A competitive spirit can be healthy, but sometimes school-age kids take their need to be number one a little too far. One fun but simple way to test your child's competitive nature is to play the balloon game.

Blow up a balloon and ask your child to play pass. Take turns bopping the balloon back and forth. But call out random point values like "It bounced off the chair before you hit it! That's ten points," and "Oh, it hit the ceiling. That's minus one thousand points!" Make sure your point valuations are random and absurd. If she argues, you can even say, "That's minus twenty-two points for arguing." Don't keep a final tally. Instead just make a ridiculous game.

If your child laughs and plays along, it's a good sign. If she insists, "That's not fair" and she quits, it might be time to consider if your household might be putting too much emphasis on winning. And of course, if you have trouble playing a game "just for fun" without any real score, you can probably guess where your child inherited her competitive spirit.

Some kids' personalities make them more competitive than others. But it's good to keep an eye on how your child is doing. You want her to have the drive to do her best, but you don't want her to feel as though she has to be perfect at all costs.

When it comes to goal setting, ask your child what she thinks is reasonable for herself. Does she expect to get an A on her social studies test or does she think she'll be lucky if she passes?

Encourage her to do slightly better than she expects. If she says she thinks she can get a B, ask her, "What could you to do to increase the chances that you'll get a B-plus?" Perhaps studying more or asking the teacher for extra help could raise her grade.

But at the same time, make sure you talk about the fact that she can't completely control her grade. While she can control how much effort she puts in, she can't control how hard the teacher makes the test.

Teach Your Teen That Imperfections Aren't Bad

Sometimes teens think their imperfections, problems, or past mistakes make them less worthy as human beings. When I'm working with a teen who insists she can't possibly be lovable with her "unsightly stomach" or "inability to do math," I do the "river rock exercise."

I keep a container full of medium-size river rocks in my office. I'll often ask the teen to pick a rock that she'd like to keep. Most teens sort through the collection and then finally pick their rock. Then I ask, "What made you pick that one?"

I usually get a response like "Well, it had this weird crack along the edge that made it look kind of neat," or "I wanted this red one that has splotches of white mixed in." Then I'll say something like "So even though the rock isn't perfect—it has bumps and scars and uneven colors—you still like it?" At the point, they usually get where I'm going with the conversation and they'll smile. It lends itself to a lengthy discussion about how your imperfections don't make you bad, they make you unique. And other people can still love you anyway.

Show him he can handle being imperfect. Sometimes that might involve challenging him to make a mistake on purpose. For parents who struggle with perfectionism, the idea that you should encourage your teen to mess up can be nerve-racking. But it could be instrumental in helping him see falling short of perfection isn't the end of the world.

If your teen is a perfectionist in the classroom, encourage him to make a mistake in his work. Whether he puts the wrong answer on a math problem, or he includes a typo in his English paper, help him see that the world won't end. While that may seem like an outrageous idea, encouraging your child to mess up once in a while could change the entire course of his life. When he sees that the sky didn't fall and the earth continued to rotate on its axis, despite his purposeful error, he might be more willing to let himself off the hook when he struggles with the idea that he has to be perfect all the time.

Show him that he's strong enough to deal with making a

mistake—as well as the consequences that stem from mistakes. Tolerating being imperfect will build your teen's confidence in his ability to handle feeling uncomfortable.

Kids with Realistic Expectations Grow Up Celebrating Other People's Success

Olivia was a ten-year-old girl in foster care whom I met when her foster parents had a family emergency out of state. She stayed with me for a couple of weeks until they returned.

Prior to their departure, Olivia's foster parents let me know that like many kids in the foster-care system, her overcompliance was likely a survival skill. Perhaps she didn't get abused when she was "good." But now she was trying her best to appear to be the perfect kid because she was terrified that if she messed up, her foster parents would find a "better" kid.

Over the next couple of weeks, Olivia's eagerness to please was evident. She would ask things like "Can I sweep your floor?" or "Do you want me to vacuum for you?" She never complained about anything. In fact, she always said things like "I don't mind" whenever she was asked to do something.

After that visit, I became Olivia's regular respite care provider. Whenever her foster parents needed to go out of town or go somewhere that Olivia couldn't, she'd stay with me. And it was amazing to watch her transformation over the years.

She believed she had been taken away from her parents because she was bad. And she thought if she wasn't perfect, she'd never get adopted. But over time, her foster family—who eventually adopted her—showed her that they loved her even when she messed up. When she grew secure about not having to be flawless to be loved, she grew independent and assertive.

When your child believes she's good enough, even when she's not perfect, she'll be willing to do things in which she might fail. She'll be able to handle mistakes and she'll be equipped to bounce back from failure. Mentally strong people don't resent other people's success. But if you expect your child to be perfect, she'll always look around and find people who are smarter, wealthier, more attractive, and more successful, and she'll never measure up. When you set realistic expectations, however, she'll set realistic expectations for herself. She'll establish her own definition of success. She'll be able to celebrate alongside others when they meet their goals because she won't compare herself to other people.

Troubleshooting and Common Traps

A parent's expectation of perfection might not be limited to sports or grades. Some parents expect their child's behavior to be perfect. One parent might expect his four-year-old to sit still during a lengthy restaurant meal while another one may question why his eight-year-old can't get along with his brother in the backseat during car rides.

Remember that your child is supposed to break the rules sometimes. He's supposed to act out. And he's going to make mistakes.

A common trap many parents fall into when it comes to a child's behavior is expecting too much too fast. This can be especially true in regard to reward systems.

A father may tell his daughter she can earn a hundred dollars if she does all of her chores all month. But that might be too lofty of a goal and she may give up early. It's better to reward your child's small steps toward success by paying her for each chore she completes. Giving her an all-or-nothing challenge can lead her to think the effort she put in wasn't worth anything.

It's also important to manage your response when your child isn't perfect. Don't get carried away by your fears. If he gets a bad grade on a science test, it likely won't ruin his life. I've never heard an adult say, "My entire life changed course because I failed one biology test in the tenth grade."

So rather than teach your child to avoid failure, teach her that she's mentally strong enough to deal with not being perfect. Help her see that she is still a lovable, wonderful, imperfect individual.

WHAT'S HELPFUL

- Giving praise, criticism, and then praise again
- Striving for excellence, not perfection
- Telling your child stories about your failures
- Asking your child what he expects from himself
- Encouraging a perfectionist to make a little mistake on purpose
- Looking for signs you're putting too much pressure on your child
- Doing activities for fun sometimes, without any competition

WHAT'S NOT HELPFUL

- Threatening your child with the bad things that could happen if her performance isn't perfect
- Comparing your child to other kids
- Criticizing your child too much
- Dwelling on your child's mistakes
- Role-modeling "all-or-nothing" thinking
- Expecting perfection from yourself

They Don't Let
Their Child Avoid
Responsibility

Martha and Jim called my office requesting the "soonest-available appointment." When they came to their first session a few days later, Martha said, "We finally got our son to move out of the house and we don't want him to come back. We need your help."

"I know it sounds mean, but he's really tough to live with," Jim explained. After high school, their son Chris didn't want to go to college because he preferred to get a job. But he never actually looked for work. Instead he spent the next seven years playing video games and hanging out with his friends. Although he'd sometimes say he was looking for a job, his parents were confident he never put in any effort.

So when he finally landed a job as a waiter, at the age of twenty-five, they were thrilled. And as soon as he mentioned he might get an apartment with a friend, they began helping him pack. They were relieved he was going to become independent, and even more excited he was finally going to be out of their basement.

Martha said, "He's a slob. I'd come home from work and find dirty dishes in the sink and dirty clothes on the bathroom floor. When I'd tell him he needed to clean up after himself, he'd get mad."

"We'd argue about money too. He'd ask for us to pay for concert tickets or to give him money so he could go out with his friends. And sometimes we'd give it to him just to get him out of the house," Jim said.

Now they were free from daily conflict. But it wasn't the end of their problems.

Chris wasn't earning enough money to be truly independent. And he was asking Jim and Martha for money every month. To make sure he could keep his apartment, they were handing over cash. But their generosity was taking a toll on their bank account and they weren't sure what to do.

When I asked about their son's ability to manage money, they acknowledged that Chris wasn't financially savvy. They weren't sure if he could balance a checkbook, create a budget, or set aside money for savings. They also weren't sure how much money he was earning. Whenever they asked him, he said it was none of their business and they didn't press him any further.

When I suggested that it was their business if they were going to be giving him money every month, they agreed. But since he wasn't interested in sharing that information, they felt like there wasn't anything they could do.

But one thing was for sure—as long as they were enabling him, he wasn't going to change on his own. If they wanted him to become financially stable, they were the ones who were going to have to change.

The problems they were facing included:

1. **They were depleting their savings.** The money they sent to Chris came out of their savings account. If they continued sending him money, they were going to go broke.
2. **They didn't want Chris to move home.** They thought it was healthiest for everyone if Chris didn't move back in. But they didn't want him to be homeless.

I recommended they establish these ground rules with Chris:

1. **He had to share information about his income.** If they were going to give him money every month, they needed to know how much money he was earning.
2. **He had to work with them on creating a budget.** Creating a budget was the first step in helping him manage his own money.
3. **He had to learn how to manage his finances.** Scheduling a weekly meeting to pay bills, balance his checkbook, and address the budget were steps that could teach Chris to take control over his finances.
4. **He would only receive a certain amount of money each month from them.** If Jim and Martha decided to give Chris a little money to cover his bills, they needed to establish a clear dollar amount. They also needed to set firm limits and refuse to give him extra money if he ran out.

Jim predicted that Chris would refuse to follow these rules. And if he and Martha didn't give him money, he thought Chris would be evicted from his apartment. Then he'd have to move back home and quit his job because it was too far to commute. He worried Chris would then live with them forever.

I reminded him that if Chris chose not to work with them on his finances, it would be his choice. And if he couldn't pay his bills, it would be a direct result of his choices; and if he got evicted, they'd be under no obligation to allow him to move back in.

Jim agreed they wouldn't be "legally obligated" to let Chris move back in, but he felt like it was their moral obligation. He thought Chris wasn't as smart as most other young adults. I assured them, if Chris was smart enough to graduate from high school, and he was able to hold down a job, he could learn to manage his money. Assuming he was incapable of paying his bills would only give him an excuse to be irresponsible for the rest of his life.

Martha and Jim agreed to talk it over for the week. And when they returned the following week, they were both on board with the plan. Jim said he'd spent a lot of time thinking about it, and ultimately he decided he needed to help his son become more independent. He felt bad that he hadn't taught Chris money-management skills earlier in life, but he knew if he didn't teach him now, he might never learn.

The following week they told Chris about the new plan. When he heard their rules, he said, "It's like you don't even care that I won't have enough money to eat!" and he hung up the phone. He didn't talk to them for a couple of days. But then he called asking for money.

They held firm and said they'd need to meet to talk about finances first. He called them "controlling" and hung up again. But by the next week, he called and said he'd do whatever they wanted as long as they gave him money because his half of the rent was due.

They agreed to meet at his apartment and they reviewed his finances together. Chris had no idea how much money he earned or how much his bills were. So Martha and Jim helped him figure it out.

Then they helped him establish a budget and they discovered he fell short of earning enough to pay his bills. So Martha and Jim agreed to cover his car payment as long as he continued to practice living within his budget and continued working with them on learning financial skills.

Martha and Jim only came to two more appointments. They said they felt less stressed and were more hopeful about the future—and their son's future. They were confident they were finally on the right path toward teaching him to be responsible enough to live independently.

Do You Give Your Child Enough Responsibility?

While it's important to avoid treating your child like a miniature adult, it's equally important to avoid treating him like he's an incompetent kid. So while you may be tempted to let him "just be a kid," make sure you're raising him to become a responsible adult too. Do you respond yes to any of the following points?

○ I do things for my child that he's capable of doing for himself.
○ I don't give my child many chores.

○ I give my child frequent reminders about the things he's supposed to be doing.

○ My child gets to keep his privileges, regardless of whether he earns them.

○ I don't invest much time in teaching my child life skills, like how to do laundry or balance a checkbook.

○ I have trouble recognizing how much responsibility my child can safely handle.

○ I excuse my child's mistakes or forgetfulness quite often.

○ I spend more time helping my child "be a kid" than teaching her to be accountable.

Why Parents Let Kids Avoid Responsibility

When Chris was young, Martha and Jim had concluded he wasn't as smart as his older brother. They had lower expectations for Chris and they never taught him the life skills he needed to become responsible.

Fortunately, they were able to start teaching him some life skills as an adult. It's much easier to do this when a child is young, but for one reason or another, many parents don't make the act of teaching responsibility a priority.

While you may never raise a child who expects you to financially support him for life, you may be limiting his potential by allowing him to avoid certain responsibilities.

PARENTS CAN'T SEE THE FOREST FOR THE TREES

Sometimes parents are so focused on the outcome that they forget to look at the life lessons their children are learning along the way. Take, for example, the disturbing trend of lawsuits that parents bring against teachers.

Rather than hold their teens accountable when they cheat, have too many absences, or fail classes, some parents have started suing school departments. And sometimes, under the threat of a lawsuit or pressure from the schoolboard, teachers change grades or dismiss the disciplinary action. Although suing schools when a child's rights are violated isn't a new concept, the idea that a "bad grade" violates a child's rights seems to be catching on.

Even if a teacher's grading system is "unfair," should parents really sue the teacher? Learning how to deal with unfair practices can be a great life skill. And when children see their parents and other adult role models deal with unfair life circumstances, they learn that these are part of life. At one point or another, your child will likely encounter an unreasonable boss or an unfair supervisor, but that doesn't mean he needs to sue them.

Along the same lines, some parents worry less about a child becoming responsible than about whether she has a competitive advantage. So they focus all their energy on ensuring that their children's transcripts will appeal to college admissions officers.

And clearly, writing "I make my bed every day" on a college application isn't likely to get a child into an Ivy League school. So instead of making sure their children know how to fold laundry or change their sheets, parents sign them up for activities that will pad their résumés— like playing the cello, earning a varsity letter, and leading the math team to victory.

In fact, most of today's parents don't give their children any chores at all. According to a 2014 Braun Research survey, even though 82 percent of adults said they had regular chores growing up, only 28 percent said they ask their children to do any.

That means a whopping 72 percent of kids aren't lifting a finger at home! While some parents say their children are too busy to do chores, others say they just want their kids to have fun. But either way, kids without chores are missing out on learning vital skills that will prepare them for the future. After all, part of having a successful relationship someday requires an understanding of how to contribute to family life.

TEACHING KIDS TO BE RESPONSIBLE TAKES A CONCERTED EFFORT

Sometimes, it's hard to know where your responsibility ends and your child's begins. Perhaps you think your job is to maintain the house. And when your child's room is a mess, you feel it's your responsibility to clean it up, because after all, his room is part of your house.

Or maybe you feel it's your responsibility to make sure your child has everything he needs to perform well at school and in his activities. So when he forgets to pack his soccer cleats, you deliver them before practice. After all, you don't want to look like an irresponsible parent when your child is the only one who doesn't have his uniform.

When it comes to household responsibilities, it's usually faster to just do the work yourself. Teaching your child how to do laundry or how to cook meals takes a fair amount of time. And mistakes—like when he tosses a red shirt in with a load of white clothes—could be costly. So to save themselves time, money, and hassle, many parents opt to do household tasks themselves.

And when you do decide to teach your child how to do certain chores, there's a good chance you'll have to teach him more than once. You may need to spend a fair amount of time coaching him to mow the lawn without leaving strips of tall grass in between rows or teaching him how to prepare a meal fit for the family to eat. For many busy parents, it can feel like there aren't enough hours in the day to teach a child to become responsible.

PARENTS FIND IT HARD TO LET GO

Tania sought therapy because she was feeling depressed. One day, in the middle of one of her appointments, her cell phone rang. Tania said, "It's my son. Excuse me for just a minute."

She answered the phone and started talking in a soft voice, as if she were talking to a three-year-old. "Well, just heat up some french fries and hot dogs for dinner tonight, okay? Tomorrow you can come over for dinner and I'll make lasagna," she said.

When she hung up the phone, Tania explained, "Whenever my son's wife is out of town, he calls me for help. He wanted to know what he should cook the kids for dinner tonight." She thought it was cute that he still asked for her help about such basic things.

She said, "I was always afraid they'd grow up and leave me. I'm so glad they still need their mama."

That led to a conversation about how much of Tania's purpose in life derived from taking care of her kids. As a stay-at-home mother, she had always done everything for them. And now that her thirty-year-old son didn't know what to cook his own kids for dinner, in a twisted way she felt pride.

Answering that phone call from her son in my office that day sped up her therapy process. The focus of her treatment shifted to helping her establish meaning and purpose in life as an empty-nester, and doing it in a way that was healthy.

Like many parents, Tania had trouble dealing with the grief involved in letting her children grow up. To protect herself from sadness, she remained overly involved in their lives. While having her kids still depend on her gave her some temporary pleasure, it wasn't enough to help her feel like she was living a fulfilling life.

During one of my first jobs as a social worker, I had a clinical supervisor who used to say, "You raise kids until they're twelve. After that, your role shifts from the driver to the passenger." That doesn't mean kids don't need you during their teen years. But it does mean that rather than doing things for them, they should be taking over many responsibilities on their own.

Letting Kids Shirk Responsibility Enables Them to Stay Immature

My clients Martha and Jim learned the hard way that letting Chris be irresponsible was a bad idea. Even though he was technically an adult, he wasn't ready for the adult world. He lacked the skills needed to be independent and they felt like they were paying the price—literally.

So while you might think making your ten-year-old's bed for him every day isn't a big deal or you might assume filling out your teen's college scholarship forms is actually helping him, in the end, you could be doing more harm than good. Kids won't learn the skills they need to reach their greatest potential if you don't make them responsible for their own lives.

IRRESPONSIBLE KIDS BECOME IRRESPONSIBLE ADULTS

When animals are born and raised in captivity they aren't usually released into the wild. Biologists say letting these animals fend for themselves is cruel, because they lack the life skills they need to survive on their own.

But that's what many parents do to their kids. They do everything for their children and their kids grow up unprepared for the rigors of adulthood. They lack the skills necessary to succeed in college, the military, or a job. That's why we're seeing another disturbing trend—parents becoming overly involved in their adult children's employment. In a 2007 survey conducted by Michigan State University, 32 percent of large companies report they hear from employees' parents.

While 31 percent of hiring managers say they've seen parents submit their children's résumés for them, 4 percent say they've experienced parents attend interviews with their adult children, and 9 percent say parents have tried negotiating their child's salary.

Some HR departments report getting phone calls from parents when their employees receive disciplinary action. Just like in middle school, young adults are complaining to Mom and Dad when they get in trouble. And parents are getting involved and trying to ensure that their children aren't held responsible when they mess up in the office.

If you don't think your child is able to get his own job, or you think he can't deal with workplace issues on his own, that's a big problem. This is not to say she might not need your help. She may have questions about how to negotiate her salary or she may want you to read over her résumé. Offering your words of wisdom can be helpful. But that's different than taking over and doing things for your child.

If you've always rescued your child from facing his own battles and sheltered him from responsibility, he'll lack the experience and confidence he needs to get by in the real world. Your child's future boss—or partner, for that matter—isn't interested in someone who still relies on his parents financially, physically, and emotionally.

What to Do Instead

Martha and Jim wanted their son Chris to be more responsible. But rather than empower him to be more responsible, their behavior was breeding his irresponsibility. If they hadn't changed their behavior, they might have stayed stuck in that unhealthy situation forever. If they wanted Chris to change, they had to make sure he was learning how to help himself. That meant they had to become teachers, rather than enablers.

Your attempts to safeguard your child from responsibility will do him a disservice. Commit to creating a plan that will help him gain the skills he needs to become a responsible adult.

EXPECT YOUR CHILD TO BE RESPONSIBLE

Most parents underestimate what their children are capable of doing. But if you step in and do things for your child, he won't learn how to do them for himself.

Give your child opportunities to practice doing things on her own. Although it takes longer to let her help you with something, think of it as an investment. The more time you put into teaching her how to do something now, the less time you'll have to spend doing it for her later.

Here are a few examples of how you can help increase your child's sense of responsibility:

- Rather than make his snack for him, show him where you keep the fruit. Talk about why you wash grapes or why you're cutting up apples. The next time he asks for a snack, give him more responsibility—ask him to get the fruit or supervise him while he washes it.
- Instead of asking your child, "Did you pack your water bottle and your uniform for the game tonight?" ask, "What do you need to pack for tonight's game?"
- Don't do your child's science-fair project with her the night before it is due. Instead say, "It looks like your science-fair project is due in two weeks. What can you do to make sure it gets done on time?" You may want to help her develop a plan to get it done on time.

As your child grows older and more mature, continue to allow her to show you that she can be responsible. When she makes a mistake, you'll know she needs even more opportunities to practice.

HOLD YOUR CHILD ACCOUNTABLE

Every morning, Mandy had to wake up her thirteen-year-old son, Ryan, at least six times. The first few times, she politely told him to get up. But when he refused to budge, she resorted to yelling and shaking him. When he finally managed to drag himself out of bed, he was incredibly slow at getting himself ready.

Ryan missed the bus at least a couple of days each week. And each time he missed it, Mandy drove him to school—which caused her to be late for work. "I can't let him stay home just because he missed the bus. He'd love that!" she said.

They lived too far away for Ryan to walk to school safely. So I suggested she charge him for the time and gas money she spent driving him to school.

The problem was, Ryan didn't have any money. He didn't do chores, so he didn't earn an allowance. Fortunately, Mandy agreed to make some changes.

If Ryan missed the bus, he'd have to do chores until he earned enough money to pay her back. He wouldn't be allowed to have any of his privileges, including video games, until those chores were done.

So the next time Ryan missed the bus, Mandy gave him a ride and told him the "fare" was fifteen dollars. That evening, she gave him a list of chores, each with a dollar value assigned. He'd need to complete all the chores on the list to pay her back.

She informed him he wasn't allowed to use his electronics or go anywhere with friends until his chores were done. To her surprise, Ryan completed every chore on his list that night. The next day, he got out of bed the first time she woke him up and he made it to the bus stop with a few minutes to spare.

Mandy was thrilled that the consequence was effective. She was aware, however, that Ryan might slip back into his old behaviors at some point. But this time she was prepared to hold him accountable for his behavior.

Be on the lookout for ways in which you may be inadvertently rewarding your child's irresponsible behavior. Here are a few examples:

- A ten-year-old girl always says she doesn't have any homework. Then, at bedtime, she remembers an assignment she needs to do. Her parents allow her to stay up until she gets it done.
- A twelve-year-old boy "forgets" to do a major homework assignment until the night before it's due. He knows his mother will help him throw something together so he doesn't get a bad grade.
- A fourteen-year-old boy didn't practice piano all week and he knows his teacher will be upset. So he convinces his mother to tell her he hasn't been feeling well so she won't be upset.

When your child is irresponsible, make sure there is a negative consequence that will teach him to be more responsible next time. If you don't hold him accountable, he won't learn. Here are some examples of consequences that teach kids to become more responsible:

- A girl loses articles of clothing during soccer season. After she leaves two sweatshirts in the locker room (which were never found), her parents make her buy replacement articles of clothing with her own money.
- A boy forgets to put on his bike helmet when he takes his bike for a ride. His parents take away his bike for the rest of the day.
- A girl never pays attention when the theater director announces the date and time of their next rehearsal. Her parents leave it up to her to call and ask. And her parents establish a rule that says they need twenty-four hours' notice about when she will need a ride to a rehearsal.

LET REPEAT OFFENDERS FACE NATURAL CONSEQUENCES

There are times when you might not need to go out of your way to give your child a consequence. Instead you can sit back and allow him to face the natural consequences of his behavior. This can be especially helpful when your child is a "repeat offender."

Here are a few examples:

- A child forgets to pack his basketball sneakers in his backpack. His mother refuses to deliver them to the school since this is the third time he's forgotten. Without his sneakers, he's not allowed to participate in practice.
- A child insists he doesn't have any homework. Rather than double-check his assignment book, his parents allow him to go to school the next day without finishing his work. He has to stay in during recess because his math assignment isn't done.
- A child wants to spend all of his allowance money during the first few minutes the family is at an amusement park. His parents allow him to do it. Then he doesn't have any money to spend for the rest of the day.

Show empathy, rather than anger, when allowing your child to face a natural consequence. Say, "I know you're sad you won't be able to participate in practice. But hopefully next time you'll remember to bring your sneakers so you can play with the team."

Natural consequences are most appropriate for children ages eight and over. Younger children often lack the ability to understand that the consequence is a direct result of their behavior.

Before you allow for natural consequences, make sure that the consequence is likely going to teach your child a lesson. While one child may be upset if he has to stay in for recess, another child might not mind at all. So consider how the consequence is likely to work for your child.

USE GRANDMA'S RULE OF DISCIPLINE

Grandma's Rule of Discipline teaches that privileges can be earned in exchange for responsible behavior. Use a positive framework so your child recognizes that he has some control over what he earns and when he earns it. So instead of saying, "You can't play outside until your room is clean," say, "You can play outside as soon as your room is clean."

That slight change in wording makes a big difference in how your child views his responsibility. Instead of thinking, "I can't have something because my parents won't let me," he's more likely to recognize, "It's up to me to decide when I earn my privileges."

That shift in attitude teaches your child that he's responsible for his choices. And the more responsible he chooses to be, the more privileges he'll earn.

Here are a few examples of effective ways to implement Grandma's Rule of Discipline:

- "When you're done with your homework, you can play on the computer."
- "When you put your toys away, we'll play a game together."
- "As soon as your chores are done, you can ride your bike."

After you've told your child what he'll gain when he's made a good choice, leave it up to him to decide on the timeline. Avoid nagging, pleading, or reminding him to do his work. If it gets too late to go outside, and he still isn't done with his chores, let him know that playing outside is no longer an option, but he can try again tomorrow.

BE A RESPONSIBLE ROLE MODEL

While it's important to *talk* to your child about daily responsibilities like cleaning the house or going to work, it's even more important to *show* you take responsibility seriously. Part of being a responsible adult means helping people in need and addressing problems and safety issues.

So while it may be tempting to shirk responsibility sometimes, especially when you're in a hurry, remember that your child is always watching. If she sees that you go out of your way to be responsible, even when it's inconvenient, she'll see how important it is.

Here are a few examples of how you can be a responsible role model:

- While shopping in the grocery store, a father notices liquid spilled on the floor. He tells an employee so it can be cleaned up before someone slips and falls. He explains to his child that even though they didn't spill the liquid, it's his responsibility to address the problem since he noticed it.
- A mother sees an elderly neighbor out for a walk but the woman appears confused. The mother walks over to talk to the neighbor so she can see if she needs any help. She tells her child it's important to help other people who might be in need.
- A mother notices there is a bus stop on a blind corner. Each morning, there are several kids congregating in the road and it appears to be a safety hazard. The mother contacts the school to share her concerns that the bus stop may be in an unsafe area. She explains to her child that the school administrators may want to hear about those types of safety issues so they can make changes that will keep kids safe.

Pay attention to the times when you might be tempted to say, "Someone should do something about that." Remember, you have an opportunity to be that person. Show your child that you're willing to step up to the plate and do the right thing, even when no one asks you to. Then he will be more likely to recognize he has the opportunity—or perhaps even the responsibility—to do the same in his life.

How to Teach Kids to Be Responsible

In the case of Chris and his ongoing requests for money, Martha and Jim had to lay down some ground rules. They had to find a way to teach their son the things he should have learned in grade school without treating him like a small child. But because they hadn't taught him important life skills at any early age, their job was complicated and delicate.

Consider the ways you might be letting your child avoid responsibility that she's capable of handling. Get proactive about teaching her the exercises that will help her learn responsibility sooner rather than later.

GET KIDS INVOLVED IN CHORES EARLY

Don't underestimate the power of a child who makes her bed. Researchers from the University of Minnesota found that doing chores at a young age was the biggest predictor of young adults' success. Involvement in chores was more important than a family's income, a child's IQ, or the family dynamics.

But the study found that it's critical for kids to start doing chores when they are three or four years old. Kids who didn't start doing chores until they were fifteen or sixteen weren't as likely to be successful. If your child is already a teenager, however, don't despair. Better to assign chores late than never.

Marty Rossmann, the associate professor who conducted the study, reports that chores teach responsibility that lasts a lifetime. Young children gain competence, self-reliance, and improved self-worth from doing chores, all of which likely contribute to their future success.

Kids who perform chores grow up to become adults who are well adjusted and have more empathy for others. Teaching them responsibility from a young age even improves their relationships as adults.

Your child needs to know that doing chores and behaving responsibly aren't always fun. But just because it feels boring doesn't mean he can't do it anyway. Behaving contrary to his emotions is an essential life skill.

When it comes to paying kids for chores, the research is mixed. Some studies show rewarding kids for chores decreases their motivation to do anything when they're not getting paid. But other studies show paying kids for chores provides an opportunity to teach them how to be responsible with money.

So a middle-of-the-road approach could give your child the best of both worlds. Don't pay for every chore your child does. There should be family chores that everyone does—setting the table, picking up after themselves, and doing the dishes are all part of being a good citizen.

Expecting your child to do these things without being told and without earning money is important. You want to make sure when he lives with a roommate or a partner someday, he's able to be responsible without anyone reminding him what to do.

Ensure your child recognizes a need and acts on it. If Grandma needs help getting the groceries out of the car, or a friend is struggling to carry an armload of boxes, you want him to step in and offer his services before he's told to do so. And you don't want him to expect to get paid for it. So make sure you emphasize the importance of being a good citizen who pitches in and helps without any expectation of remuneration.

Then you can give your child extra chores that he gets paid for, like mowing the lawn or washing your car—things you might pay to have done. Just make sure you offer rules and guidance that will help him learn to save and spend his money responsibly.

ACCEPT EXPLANATIONS, BUT NOT EXCUSES

When your child messes up, look for an explanation, but don't let him excuse his irresponsibility. An excuse blames other people or external circumstances. An explanation assumes personal responsibility. Here's an example:

An excuse: I failed the test because my teacher didn't explain things well enough. She didn't even tell us what we should study.

An explanation: I failed the test because I didn't understand the material. I studied the wrong things.

Even if the test was hard, or the teacher didn't teach the information clearly, she still had choices. She could have asked for help when she didn't understand. Teach her to take responsibility for her behavior so she can improve her chances of success.

When your child makes excuses, point it out. Say, "That sounds like an excuse. What could you have done to prevent it from happening?" or "What was your role in that?" Help your child see that offering excuses won't reduce her responsibility.

Teach Preschoolers to Be Helpers

A truly responsible child will need to be able to recognize when she should step in and help out without anyone telling her. Although it seems like a complicated skill to learn, you can actually start teaching it during the preschool years. One simple way to do so is by referring to your child as a "helper."

A 2014 study by the University of California, San Diego, found that three- to six-year-olds were more motivated to help others when they were given the option to "be a helper." When told they could choose to help others, however, they were less likely to pitch in. (Similarly, a 2011 study by Stanford University found that adults who see themselves as voters—rather than someone who votes—are more likely to cast a ballot.)

When kids view themselves as helpers, they're ready to jump in and assist wherever they're needed. So say things to your child like "Let's see how we can be helpers today," or "You're a really good helper." You may shape your child's view of himself as a capable, independent person who can assist other people.

Although your preschooler isn't able to do complex household chores, you can teach her to be a helper by involving her in the tasks you're doing. Let her help you wash the dishes and mop the floors. When you're running errands or shopping, give her little jobs to do and point out that she's "a good little helper."

Here are some chores you can assign to your preschooler:

- Make the bed
- Put her toys away
- Match socks
- Put away some of her laundry
- Dust
- Sweep the floor
- Empty small trash cans, like those in the bedroom or bathroom

Teach School-Age Kids to Connect the Dots

Whenever possible, point out the direct link between your child's behavior and the outcome. Help your child connect the dots by saying things like "Let's connect the dots. You studied really hard and all that work helped you get that good grade," or "Your soccer skills have really improved because of all that practicing you've been doing in the backyard every night."

If he puts in a lot of effort, but still fails, assure him that his hard work didn't go to waste. Say things like "All that practice could prepare you to make the team next year," or "Studying hard can help you learn more, even if you don't always get a good grade."

When your child realizes his choices influence the outcome,

he'll accept more personal responsibility for his decisions. As he grows older, he'll see how he has a fair amount of control over the likelihood that he'll reach his goals.

In addition to connecting the dots, help him be more responsible by assigning him chores such as:

- Mop the floors
- Cook simple foods, like a grilled cheese sandwich
- Peel vegetables
- Put laundry away
- Pack his own lunch
- Clean the bathroom
- Vacuum the carpets

Teach Teens to Look at the Big Picture

By the time your child becomes a teen, you only have a few more years before she enters the adult world. So it's essential to step back and look at the big picture together.

Just because your teen has good grades and excels in sports doesn't mean she's equipped to become a responsible adult. Think about all the life skills your child needs to learn. In addition to knowing how to do household tasks, like the laundry, she needs interpersonal skills, relationship skills, communication skills, etc.

Don't overlook simple things that you might assume your teen already knows how to do. I run into teens every day who refuse to make a phone call. They're so used to texting that they're clueless about telephone etiquette. And there are likely going to be times your teen is going to need to talk to a live human being on the phone. So let her schedule an appointment for herself or let her make a call to a business when she has a question about a product or service.

Look at each day as an opportunity to help your child gain more life skills that will help her succeed. When she breaks the rules or doesn't follow through with her responsibilities, consider it as feedback to you that she needs more practice making better decisions.

In addition, your teen should be able to do all the household chores you do. You may want to rotate chores so she gets an opportunity to try doing everything at one point or another. Here are some chores you can assign to your teen:

- Cook meals
- Change bedsheets
- Babysit younger siblings
- Wash the car
- Mow the lawn
- Do the dishes
- Pick up items from the store
- Wash windows
- Weed the garden
- Rake the lawn

Responsible Kids Grow Up Knowing How to Bounce Back from Failure

Veronica brought her fourteen-year-old son, Zack, to therapy because she was concerned he might have ADHD. She said Zack was forgetful, disorganized, and downright lazy. It's a common issue I see in my therapy office—frustrated parents who just can't understand why their child isn't motivated to do any work. But after talking with them for a while, the problem was pretty clear.

Veronica had concluded that Zack was an irresponsible kid. So she constantly reminded him to do everything. She'd say, "Zack, don't forget to pack your water bottle for the game," or "Remember, you're going to need to study for that science test tonight."

Since she always reminded him to do everything, Zack never worried about managing his time. He waited until his mother told him what to do. And even then he usually just did the bare minimum.

He wasn't learning how to think for himself. Instead he was just following orders. No wonder he was forgetful and disorganized. Fortunately, a few changes to Veronica's parenting helped him start to become more responsible.

Since Veronica had always prevented Zack from facing consequences, by nagging and reminding him what to do, he'd never experienced any of the ramifications of his behavior. Once she stepped out of the way and allowed him to experience natural consequences, he became much more responsible.

Give your child difficult tasks, even though he will fail sometimes. With practice, he'll learn how to recover from failure and he'll discover that he can handle more responsibility than he might give himself credit for.

Hold him accountable for his behavior. Over time, he'll learn how to hold himself accountable. And he'll learn to bounce back from failure and try again.

Mentally strong people don't give up after the first failure. But your child needs practice failing so he can learn to rebound from failure. Teaching him to be responsible is the best way to help him discover how to deal with challenges and how to do better when he fails.

Troubleshooting and Common Traps

Sometimes parents get caught up in assigning chores based on traditional gender roles. Girls wash dishes and boys clean the garage. Make sure your child's skills aren't restricted in this way.

Another common problem is inconsistency. Sometimes parents find that on days when they have more energy they're able to follow through to ensure their child is doing his chores or they're more involved in coaching their child to be responsible.

But on days where they're tired or stressed out, they're less likely to follow through. Your child won't learn unless you send a consistent message. The more consistent you're able to be with teaching responsibility now, the less time you'll have to spend addressing problems later.

Frustration over responsibilities often stems from unclear expectations. Telling your child to "clean his room" or "do his chores" isn't helpful. Make sure he knows exactly what you mean and what you expect from him.

If your child is a repeat offender, don't lose your cool. Lecturing him won't help. Avoid saying things like "How do you keep forgetting to bring your sneakers? There aren't many things you even need to bring to school and you always forget that one simple thing!"

Instead problem-solve together. Say, "This is the third time you've forgotten to pack your sneakers. What could we do to help you remember?" Whether your child needs a checklist by the door or a calendar on his tablet, help him find a way to become more responsible and work together to make it happen.

WHAT'S HELPFUL

- Expecting your child to behave responsibly
- Giving consequences when your child doesn't behave responsibly
- Allowing for natural consequences when your child repeats the same mistakes
- Using Grandma's Rule of Discipline
- Referring to your child as a "helper"
- Assigning chores at an early age
- Granting privileges only when they are earned
- Holding your child accountable

WHAT'S NOT HELPFUL

- Nagging, pleading, and lecturing your child
- Bailing your child out repeatedly when he is irresponsible
- Allowing your child to make excuses for his choices
- Emphasizing organized activities over teaching your child responsibility
- Doing too much for your child
- Not following through with consequences

They Don't Shield
Their Child from Pain

Since her divorce five years ago, Julie had retained primary custody of her three children, ages ten, fourteen, and sixteen. Her ex-husband, Michael, lived nearby and he usually visited their children a few times per week. But since he only had a one-bedroom apartment, the kids never spent the night at his house.

In fact, they rarely even went to his apartment. Instead Michael visited them at Julie's house, which was the same home he lived in when they were married. Julie agreed it was easier that way since his apartment was so small and the kids had their video games, bicycles, and other belongings at her house.

When Julie and Michael were married, he traveled for work. So even though they were divorced, things weren't all that different for the kids. They saw Michael almost as much now as when he actually lived in the home.

Julie felt bad that Michael lived alone, so she invited him to dinner every Sunday night. She knew he wasn't a very good cook, so she always sent him home with leftovers.

Michael spent the holidays at Julie's home too. She thought it was important for the kids' sake that they celebrate Christmas and birthdays as a family. She bought the gifts but always told the kids they were from "Mom and Dad."

Julie had dated a few men over the years but none of her relationships were ever serious—until now. She and her current boyfriend, David, had been together for about six months and Julie could see a future with him.

But there was a problem. When Michael and David saw one another, Michael was rude. He said mean things to David and made sarcastic comments about him to Julie and their children.

To spare David from Michael's insults, Julie started going to David's home when Michael came over to visit the kids. And lately, that was feeling like a real inconvenience.

Christmas was only two months away and Julie was anxious. She wanted to invite David to her home to spend the holiday with her and her children. But she knew Michael would want to come over.

She sought therapy to help her deal with her stress. Trying to figure out how to spend Christmas and who to spend it with was incredibly troubling. "I'm afraid I'm going to have a nervous breakdown before the holidays even get here," she said.

She was clear that she had moved on and had no desire to spend any time with Michael. I asked her why it was so important to spend the holidays with Michael and she said, "Because the kids want us to all be together like a family."

Inviting both David and Michael to her home would be tense and awkward. But she felt like if Michael didn't come, the kids would be sad. And she didn't want to ruin their holiday. But at the same time she wanted to spend Christmas with David. She felt stuck.

The problems Julie was experiencing were:

1. **She was delaying grief.** Although she'd made the decision to get a divorce, she didn't want her children to experience the pain that accompanied it. She thought she was minimizing the damage to her kids, but really she was just delaying the inevitable.
2. **Her choices were harming her current relationships.** Julie wasn't able to move forward. Her ongoing contact with Michael interfered with her ability to have a healthy relationship with David.

My recommendations:

1. **Create some separation from Michael.** While some parents do maintain a close friendship after getting divorced, it was clear that Julie and Michael weren't able to do it. She needed to establish some healthy boundaries with her ex-husband.
2. **Allow the family time to grieve.** Even though it had been years since their divorce, they had never separated their lives. Creating that separation now meant everyone would need time to grieve.

It took Julie a couple of weeks to grasp how her decision to stay close to Michael temporarily shielded her children from the pain. She decided that it was time to set clearer boundaries with Michael so she could move on with her life.

So for the first time, she told Michael he wasn't welcome in her home on Christmas. She decided not to have David come to her home either. She didn't want her children to blame David for their father's absence.

She spent that Christmas with the kids without Michael. They decided to create a few new traditions for themselves. Julie said it was a strange experience and the kids were sad that Michael wasn't there. But she explained to them that it was time to have separate holiday celebrations. The children visited with Michael later that evening at his home.

In the coming weeks, Julie started setting more limits with Michael. She told him that he needed to visit with their children in his own space—at least for the most part. And that he would no longer be coming over to her home every Sunday for dinner.

She even changed the locks on the doors and didn't give Michael a key. That meant he could no longer just walk in or show up whenever he wanted but would have to ring the doorbell like a guest.

Michael wasn't happy with the changes. He told her to "stop being ridiculous." But Julie understood his angry reactions were his attempts to push back against the changes she was making. She held firm to her decision and made it clear that they had to live separate lives.

Julie noticed her kids seemed saddened by the changes. And we discussed how their reaction was normal. For the first time ever, they were starting to grieve the fact that their family was no longer intact.

And grief was part of their healing process. They wouldn't be able to fully embrace the consequences of the divorce until they were allowed to be sad and angry and to experience all the other emotions that were stirred up by these altered family circumstances.

Over time, Julie saw that the changes were positive for everyone. She felt like her life was finally able to move forward. And she thought her children were developing a new sense of "normal" in their lives as they started to heal.

Do You Shield Your Child from Pain?

It's healthy to help your child avoid unnecessary pain sometimes. But some parents go too far and become so overprotective that they prevent kids from experiencing struggles that could help them grow stronger. Do any of these statements sound familiar?

- ○ I avoid telling my child the truth because I want to protect him from the pain.
- ○ I put a lot of effort into making sure my child doesn't get his feelings hurt.
- ○ I don't think my child can handle too much hardship.
- ○ I sometimes let my child win at a game because I don't want her to feel bad.
- ○ I stay focused on what will make my child happy right now, regardless of the long-term consequences.
- ○ If I think my child may get rejected, I discourage him from putting himself out there.
- ○ I go to great lengths to prohibit my child from taking risks.
- ○ I don't think kids should have to deal with any type of emotional pain.
- ○ I want to protect my child from real-world problems as long as possible.

Why Parents Shield Kids from Pain

Julie divorced Michael because she thought it was in her best interest—and the best interest of the children—for them to go their separate ways. But at the same time she didn't want to see her kids endure the pain of divorce. So she thought she was doing the right thing by maintaining a close relationship with Michael. But Michael couldn't stand to see her in a new relationship. And it was clear that she wasn't doing anyone any favors by trying to shield the children from the pain of their divorce.

Examine times when you shield your child from pain. Consider whether that pain could actually be helpful to them in some way.

HAPPINESS IS ALL THE RAGE

When I ask parents what they want for their kids, the most common answer I hear is "I just want my child to be happy." Whether a child is struggling with depression, learning disabilities, health problems, or serious behavior problems, almost every parent I meet wants their child to enjoy life.

Clearly, the happiness trend isn't limited to my office space. A quick online search yields over a half-million articles on the subject of raising happy kids. Articles like "7 Ways to Raise Happy Kids" and "10 Ways to Raise a Happy Child" tout the "secret" strategies to making sure your child always has a smile on her face.

And while it's good to be concerned about your child's happiness—research shows happy people enjoy benefits ranging from higher incomes to better relationships—happiness shouldn't be your short-term goal.

Letting your child skip out on his chores provides short-term pleasure. But it won't teach him responsibility. And an irresponsible person isn't likely to live an especially happy life.

Buying your child whatever he wants will make him happy today. But if he never knows what it's like to have to wait to get what he wants, he'll never appreciate anything he has. You have to let your child experience some pain in life if you want him to become a truly happy person. Yet many parents just can't bear the thought of letting their child suffer. So they step in and help their kids avoid anything that might cause them discomfort.

Helping kids avoid danger and dodge serious pain is healthy. But sometimes it's easy to take things too far.

Here are a few examples of parents taking things too far by shielding their kids from everyday realities, which can lead to unhealthy habits or behaviors:

- **Lying or withholding information:** A mother tells her daughter that the doctor said her weight is healthy, even though the doctor said the child is overweight.
- **Manipulating the outcome:** A father lets his son beat him at chess so he won't feel bad if he loses.
- **Setting strict limits:** A parent who worries their child may get hurt playing sports might never let her try out for a team.
- **Enabling:** A mother who doesn't want her teenage son to have to endure nicotine withdrawal buys cigarettes for him.
- **Doing things for kids:** A mother cleans the garage, even though it is her son's chore, because she doesn't want him to have to do it.
- **Distracting:** A parent races from one activity to the next to keep the children from feeling sad after their dog died.

KIDS SHOULDN'T BE EXPOSED TO MORE PAIN

When foster children move into our home, it's tempting to try to prevent them from any further suffering. Children who have been abused, neglected, and separated from their families shouldn't have to deal with tough homework assignments or being cut from the baseball team. But sheltering kids from the everyday stresses of life does not make up for the hardships they've endured.

In fact, kids who have endured extremely difficult circumstances often need to gain confidence in their ability to deal with life's everyday problems. That was the case with our ten-year-old foster child, Marissa. She hadn't been able to protect her younger siblings from being abused by their stepfather. And she felt like she was a bad kid who couldn't do anything right.

But by allowing her to face little struggles every day, like squabbles with friends and challenging homework assignments, she realized she had good problem-solving skills. She recognized that she could speak up when there were kids being bullied and that she could advocate for herself when she didn't understand her work.

Successfully tackling those minor inconveniences helped shift her core belief about herself. With enough success, she was able to see that she was a competent person who had the ability to make a difference in the world.

When a child experiences a painful event, it can be instinctual to try to overcompensate. After a divorce or the loss of a family member, a parent may say, "He's been through so much already. I don't want him to have to deal with anything else." But you can't prevent your child from experiencing all of life's inevitable hardships. And becoming overprotective sends the wrong message. It will teach your child that she's too fragile to deal with the realities of life, which will affect how she thinks about herself and the world.

Shielding Kids from Pain Teaches Them They Can't Handle Discomfort

Julie's attempts to shield her children from grief didn't help them in the long term. They were going to have to face the fact that their parents weren't together at some point. So while it was important for her to take steps to minimize the pain, shielding the kids only delayed their grief.

It's hard to tell sometimes when your efforts to shield kids from pain cross the line. In the short term, you might feel like you've done the right thing. Your child may seem happy and healthy—but in the long term, he may suffer serious consequences.

KIDS CAN HANDLE MORE THAN YOU THINK

Addie was an eight-year-old girl with a lot of anxiety. Although her mother said she'd always been a bit anxious, lately her anxiety had skyrocketed. She was chewing on her fingers, she couldn't concentrate in class, and she didn't want to sleep in her own room at night.

I worked with Addie for several weeks to learn more about what types of things were making her anxious. I ruled out the usual suspects like bullies and nightmares. But it was clear that there was something specific on her mind.

Finally, after several weeks, she said, "I heard my parents talking and they said my dad has diabetes." I asked her what she knew about diabetes and she said, "You die from it. That's why it's called *die*-a-betes." She began to cry and said, "I don't want my dad to die."

We invited Addie's mom to join the session and she confirmed her husband's diagnosis. But they hadn't told Addie because they were afraid she'd worry. They thought it was just too much for her to handle. But obviously, Addie had figured it out, and without any information, she assumed the worst. And this poor child had spent the past few weeks thinking her father might die at any given moment.

Her treatment involved educating her on the facts about diabetes. Once she began to believe it wasn't going to lead to sudden death, she relaxed.

Parents often underestimate exactly how much kids can handle. Kids are smart and they'll figure things out even when you don't tell them. Despite your best intentions, your attempts to protect your child from pain might backfire.

If your child finds out you aren't telling her what's really going on, she may think she's in even more danger than you're letting on. A child who hears about a shooting from the other kids at school may begin to think he's at a high risk of being shot too. Unless he knows the facts and the safety measures being put into place, his imagination may run wild.

PAIN ISN'T THE ENEMY

Ava was a six-year-old child who had been coming to therapy to address some behavioral issues. I'd only been seeing her for a few weeks when I got a call from her mother.

She said their cat had been sick and Ava's father took it to the vet. The vet's exam revealed some serious health problems, and they decided the most humane thing to do was to have it put to sleep right away.

When Ava's father returned home without the cat, Ava asked, "Where's Fluffy?" Her mother jumped in to say, "Well, the vet thought Fluffy was so cute he wanted to keep her at his office for a while." Upon hearing the news, Ava got really angry, saying the vet shouldn't be allowed to keep their pet.

And now her mother wasn't sure what to do. She knew she'd gotten herself into a bind. But she had blurted out a made-up story because she wanted to spare Ava the pain.

I told her she should tell Ava the truth with an explanation of why she lied. She was hesitant at first because she thought it would be too upsetting. So we talked about how shielding Ava from the pain wasn't a long-term plan. Eventually, she was going to have to find out anyway.

When they came in the next week, Ava explained to me what happened to her cat. Together, with her mother, we talked about grief and how she could take care of her sad feelings.

Just like Ava's mother, many parents make excuses and lie to protect their kids. But lying sends them the wrong message. Ultimately, it causes kids even more heartache when they know they've been deceived.

Be honest with your child. And if you lied already, tell the truth. And then be there for her so you can help her deal with her painful feelings.

Sadly, kids who never gain the skills they need to deal with pain often spend their entire lives trying to escape their painful feelings. They may run from one activity to the next, filling their time, or they may seek unhealthy coping strategies that will only give them temporary relief.

KIDS LEARN THROUGH EXPERIENCE

When I first began teaching college classes, like the entire faculty, I was given training in how to identify mental health problems in students. As a mental health professional, I was impressed that the school took so much care in ensuring all faculty members were provided with tools and resources to help students who were overwhelmed by the demands of college.

But it only took a week or two to realize why the school took that problem so seriously. Every week students stayed after class to talk, and rarely did they ever have questions about their grades. Instead they were struggling with roommate issues. Or they didn't know how to handle the stress of college life. The list went on and on.

I was only thirty at the time, so I hadn't been out of college *all* that long. But I don't ever recall hearing about students seeking emotional support from their professors when I was in school. But I've since learned that the issue wasn't limited to that particular college. Declining resilience among college students is an epidemic.

In 2015, the *Chronicle of Higher Education,* a national newspaper for university faculty, published an article titled "An Epidemic of Anguish." Dan Jones, the past president of the Association for University and College Counseling Center Directors, said today's college students "haven't developed skills in how to soothe themselves, because their parents have solved all their problems and removed the obstacles. They don't seem to have as much grit as previous generations."

Research supports the idea that today's college students are struggling more than ever when it comes to dealing with the rigors of real-world pain. In a 2015 survey of first-year college students, half of the students reported feeling stressed most or all of the time. They reported struggling with anxiety, loneliness, and depression. Sixty percent said they wished they had gotten more emotional preparation for college. Eighty-eight percent said more emphasis was placed on being ready academically. Many of the students weren't sure how to deal with their distress. More than one in five said they turned to drugs or alcohol. And not surprisingly, those who struggled the most had lower GPAs.

It's quite likely that the vast majority of these young adults were shielded from struggles for most of their lives. Kids who don't practice dealing with emotional challenges will struggle with everyday life well into adulthood.

Your child won't become a great guitar player by listening to the radio. And he can read all the books in the world on how to be a good basketball player, but those books won't get him into the NBA. If he wants to get good at something—such as dealing with distress—he needs to practice.

Your child is going to face tough circumstances at certain times throughout his life. Unemployment, financial problems, divorce, and the loss of a loved one are a few of the hardships he might face at one time or another. If he doesn't practice dealing with pain now, he's not going to be equipped to handle it later.

What to Do Instead

When Julie finally decided to make changes in her relationship with Michael, she realized she had to let her kids face the pain. That meant allowing them to be sad when their father wasn't in their home and angry that they weren't going to spend holidays together as a family anymore.

It was essential that everyone have time to grieve the loss of their family. Recognizing that their parents would go on with their lives separately meant the kids had to adjust to the changes.

Instead of preventing your child from experiencing pain, equip him with the skills he needs to deal with it successfully. Then your child will be able to turn painful periods of his life into opportunities to build mental muscle. Rather than just tolerating pain, he'll learn from his pain.

EXAMINE YOUR BELIEFS ABOUT PAIN

Whether it's physical or emotional, your beliefs about pain might cause you to spare your child at all costs. Here are some beliefs that could make it difficult for you:

- Pain is intolerable.
- Kids can't cope with pain.
- Pain is harmful.
- Children shouldn't have to endure any type of pain.

When parents hold these beliefs, they shield kids from as much pain as possible. But each time they shelter their child from minor irritations and everyday problems, the less practice she has coping with discomfort. In turn, she is less equipped to deal with pain. And the parent becomes even more protective. It's a harmful, self-perpetuating cycle.

Studies show letting your child experience some pain can be helpful in several ways:

- **Pain helps your child recognize pleasure.** If your child never feels pain, she won't recognize pleasure. To really appreciate the pleasure end of the spectrum, you have to experience pain sometimes.
- **Pain can help your child form social bonds.** Children who have endured painful experiences relate to one another especially well. Whether both your child and his friend have lost their pets, or both felt afraid during a tornado warning, tough times and shared experiences help kids grow closer with one another.
- **Relief from pain boosts pleasure.** While pain isn't pleasurable, the relief from it can be. Whether your child breathes a sign of relief after a nerve-racking performance or makes the soccer team after being cut the last two years in a row, she'll feel happier than if she'd never encountered any pain at all.
- **Rewards are more enjoyable when you've tolerated pain.** Your child will enjoy that sports drink more when he's hustled in practice or he'll appreciate his allowance more when he worked hard to mow the lawn. Pain heightens the senses and it makes rewards seem even more pleasurable than usual.
- **Pain captures your attention.** Similar to the way yoga or meditation helps people live in the moment, pain also helps kids

become very aware of what is going on right now. Being mindful is a skill, and sometimes pain helps people become aware of what it feels like to be in the here and now.

DISTRACT YOUR CHILD FROM ACUTE PAIN

There are definitely times when you need to spare your child from pain. If he's standing on the edge of a cliff, you wouldn't hope he learns his lesson if he falls, right? But if your four-year-old wants to play with a dog who bites or your teenager wants to go to an unsupervised party where there is likely to be alcohol, by all means step in and protect him.

But there will also be times when you can't protect your child completely. If he has a horrible backache or he's terrified while sitting in the dentist's office awaiting a root canal, telling him to "deal with it" isn't helpful. In times of acute pain, provide a distraction to help him endure it. Talk about something unrelated, read a book together, or give your child a task to take his mind off the pain. Similarly, if your child is going through emotional pain—like her best friend just moved away—taking her for a special outing could grant her some temporary relief.

Just make sure you use it as a life lesson. Explain to your child, "I wanted to help you feel better so I hoped that talking about your vacation would give you a little bit of relief." Go on to explain that distraction can be a good way to deal with intense pain, though we shouldn't distract ourselves all the time. Otherwise your child may be tempted to avoid problems regularly because it's too stressful to address them.

Reinforce to your child, "This is hard, but I know you're tough enough to handle it." Send a clear message that you have confidence in his ability to deal with difficult circumstances.

TELL KIDS WHAT THEY NEED TO KNOW

A recent op-ed in the *Washington Post* called "How Should Parents Discuss Major World Catastrophes with Their Children?" described one mother's attempt to shield her eight-year-old daughter from world events. The author of the piece, Sarah Maraniss Vander Schaaff, said she hid newspapers, turned off the TV, and didn't listen to the radio because she didn't want her daughter to know bad things happen.

But one day, her daughter got a glimpse of a TV show talking about Malaysia Airlines Flight 370, the plane that disappeared en route to Beijing. Suddenly Sarah had to explain what the news program was about. Talking to her daughter about the realities of the world caused her to think, "Some piece of the protective layer I had imagined I'd created around her has forever been torn open. I can't patch it, and now she knows I made it."

When kids are never warned that there are bad things in the world, they go from believing life is full of rainbows and puppy dogs to knowing that evil exists in an instant. That's a big leap. It's best to give your child a mildly censored view of the world rather than keeping her in the dark.

The fact is, today's world is a scary place. And while your six-year-old doesn't need to know all the gory details of the latest terrorist attack and your eight-year-old doesn't need to know you're awaiting Grandma's test results to see if her biopsy was cancerous, shielding your child from all of life's realities could leave her a bit too naive.

In general, don't allow children under seven to watch the news. Hearing about natural disasters, crime, and world crises can be too upsetting, and often there are graphic pictures and videos that could be too much for children to handle.

But that doesn't mean you can't give your child any information at all. He may hear about the news from other people. And that's why it's important to give children age-appropriate information when they ask questions.

Older children are likely to hear about what's happening in the news from friends or on the computer. So it's helpful to provide some basic facts. Here's how you can talk to kids about painful events:

- **A family illness**—If someone in the family has a serious illness, your child will likely catch on that something is wrong. If it's an illness that may take a toll on someone's appearance, it's especially important to tell a child what is going on. Name the illness and talk about the steps that are being taken to treat it.

- **Death**—Young children don't understand that death is permanent, so a five-year-old may seem to accept that his loved one is gone one minute and then ask when he'll see him again the next. Avoid using phrases like "Grandma went to sleep" or "She passed away." Instead say things like "Grandma's body stopped working and we're not going to see her again. But we can still love her and remember her." When talking to an older child or a teenager, be honest and direct by saying, "I'm sorry to tell you this, but Grandma died today. The doctors said there was nothing they could do." Be prepared to answer tough questions about death and what happens to people after they die.

- **Terrorism**—Use language that your child will understand by saying something like "Some bad people hurt other people." Emphasize the measures people are taking to ensure your safety by saying things like "There are lots of people who work hard to keep us safe." Unless your child is a teen, avoid talking too much about religious or political motives.

- **Natural disasters**—Whether it was a flood, a tornado, or a wildfire, provide a brief explanation of what happened. Don't provide unnecessary details, but make sure your child is aware of the basics. Discuss what steps are being taken to address the problem, such as "Firefighters are working really hard right now to help people."

- **An upcoming event**—If an upcoming event will be upsetting to your child, don't give him too much advance notice. Knowing he's going to have painful surgery next month might make him so anxious he has trouble functioning now. Give him a little bit of

advance notice—perhaps a week or a day—and talk about all the
steps everyone is going to take to help him.

One of the best ways to help your child deal with a painful event is
to remind him that there are good people in the world working to keep
others safe. Mr. Rogers famously said, "When I was a boy and I would
see scary things in the news, my mother would say to me, 'Look for the
helpers. You will always find people who are helping.'" That's some pretty
sound advice. Point out to your child that there are police officers, gov-
ernment officials, emergency crews, doctors, and others who are helping
to protect and ease people's pain. And make sure to talk about everyday
citizens who are pitching in and doing their part too.

As we discussed in chapter seven, you can empower your child by making him a "helper." Just like being a helper can teach him to be responsible, it can also help him cope with tough times. Get him involved in
making the situation better. Tell him he can write thank-you notes to the
workers. Or look for one thing he could do with you to help other people,
like donating clothes or money to people in need.

ACKNOWLEDGE THE PAIN

When I was six years old, I fell and hurt my arm. I started to cry and ran
into the house holding on to my wrist. As my mother examined the damage, a family friend who happened to be at our house said, "Now stop, it
doesn't hurt that bad."

It did hurt that bad, but I stopped crying. I didn't want to look like a
wimp in front of her and her kids. So I forced myself to fight back any
more tears. Even after they left, I decided to put on a brave face and denied being in any pain.

Over the next couple of days, the pain got worse, but I refused to complain. By the third day, I couldn't move my wrist at all. Despite my attempts
to conceal the problem, my mother noticed my right wrist had grown use-

less when I was attempting to shovel some peas into my mouth with my left hand. She brought me to the doctor, and X-rays showed it was broken. My mother felt terrible and I remember her asking, "How could I have let her go around with a broken wrist for three days without even knowing?"

It wasn't my mother's fault that she didn't know my wrist was broken. Her well-intentioned friend's comments had caused me to hide my injury. She'd dismissed my pain, and as a young child, I thought she knew more than I did.

Denying your child's pain—emotional or physical—isn't helpful. Discouraging sad or painful feelings won't make them go away, just as the pain in my own wrist persisted. Instead it might just teach your child those feelings aren't okay.

Try saying things like "I can see that really hurts," or "I know you're in a lot of pain right now," even when your child's reaction seems a bit out of proportion to the circumstances. Then support her efforts to deal with the pain in a productive manner.

If your child's behavior becomes socially inappropriate, don't reward him with lots of attention. If he trips while you're in the grocery store, and he's screaming and rolling around the floor, calmly say, "It looks like you need a break for a few minutes in the car." When he calms down, take him back into the store and finish your shopping without doting on him too much. Doing so may reinforce to your child that saying he's in pain—emotional or physical—is a good way to capture your attention or help him escape something he doesn't want to do.

It's also important that you don't lie about something that is likely going to hurt. Saying, "This shot won't hurt a bit," will damage your credibility. If it's going to hurt, a better message is to say, "It will probably hurt but I know you can do it."

When something is going to be painful, send the message that it's important to do it anyway. Say things like "Going to your friend's going-away party will probably be pretty sad. But it's okay to be sad and it's important that you go see her before she leaves."

Teach Kids to Deal with Pain

In the case of divorced mother Julie, she had worked hard to keep her kids happy. Although she felt guilty and didn't want them to suffer, the truth is, they needed opportunities to learn about pain. Giving your child the coping skills to get through tough times will allow her to build important mental muscle.

TEACH YOUR CHILD TO RECOGNIZE WHEN PAIN IS A FRIEND AND WHEN IT'S AN ENEMY

There's a big difference between pushing through the pain when your legs are tired and trying to run on a broken ankle. The same can be said for emotional pain. There are times when it makes sense to keep going despite the pain, and times when it's essential to take a break or get some help.

Talk to your child about how emotions can be helpful or hurtful. Here are some examples:

- **Fear**—Fear can be a friend when it stops a child from doing something dangerous, like jumping off a bridge. It can be an enemy when it tries to prevent him from doing something good, like asking the teacher a question.
- **Sadness**—Feeling sad can be a good reminder that you need to honor a memory. So drawing a picture of a pet who died could be helpful to a child's healing. But sadness can be harmful when it causes her to become withdrawn.
- **Anger**—Feeling angry could be a sign that someone is being treated poorly. When a child feels mad he might stand up for a friend who is being picked on. But anger can become an enemy when it causes him to hurt other people.

When you notice your child dealing with emotional turmoil, talk about it. Ask, "Do you think your fear is your friend or your enemy right now?" Discuss various strategies for dealing with his feelings in a meaningful way.

Sometimes the concept that painful feelings can be helpful can be hard for kids to grasp. But with regular conversations, your child will learn how difficult circumstances and tough emotions can help him.

TAKE CARE OF EMOTIONAL WOUNDS

Joshua was an angry thirteen-year-old boy who was referred to counseling because he kept getting into fights at school. He lashed out at other kids almost every day and his teachers were concerned about his mental health. Consequences, like detentions and suspensions, weren't deterring his aggression.

Unlike most boys fitting that description, however, Joshua was actually quite pleasant in my office. He was polite and respectful.

After several weeks of getting to know him, he mentioned—almost as if in passing—that he'd had a younger brother. This was news to me. When I had asked him and his parents about their family, they said he had an older sister, but they never said anything about a brother. So I asked him about it. Joshua revealed that when he was seven, his five-year-old brother was killed in a terrible accident. He was quick to add, "It was sad but I'm okay."

As I got to know him better, I learned that he never talked about his brother. He said, "It makes my parents too sad to hear his name, so we just don't talk about it." In fact, after his brother died, the family had packed up, moved to a new city, and continued on almost as though his brother had never existed.

It was no wonder Joshua lashed out at other kids sometimes. He'd never had the opportunity to deal with his grief and his hurt was turning into anger.

I met with Joshua's parents and brought up the sensitive subject of their youngest child. Both of them appeared surprised Joshua had told me what happened. His mother said, "We assumed it was too tough for him to talk about, so we never bring up the subject. We thought giving him a fresh start in a new school, where no one knew what happened, would help him stop thinking about it."

But of course, Joshua did think about it. He missed his brother. And he'd never had a chance to talk about it.

I told his parents I thought his unresolved grief was a big part of his aggressive behavior. I recommended they enroll him in a grief support group so he could talk about his feelings with other kids his age. In the meantime, I recommended they attend some therapy sessions with him so they could all start to address their feelings. And fortunately, they agreed.

Joshua had to heal the underlying pain that was behind his destructive behavior. And slowly, over time, his aggressive behavior vanished.

Teach your child that there's a big difference between being strong and acting tough. Kids who act tough may say things like "That didn't hurt" or "I don't care" in an attempt to mask their pain. But tolerating pain isn't enough.

Kids can learn from their pain. But before they can learn from it, they have to acknowledge it. Whether your child's feelings are hurt because her friend said something mean or she's feeling bad because she didn't get picked to be on the baseball team, encourage her to admit when she's hurting.

Talk to your child about the importance of caring for wounds—both physical and emotional. If she had a cut on her arm, she'd need to clean it out and keep it from becoming infected. If it was a really deep cut, she might need to get stitches. Similarly, emotional wounds need tending. And if an emotional wound is really deep, she might need to see a doctor.

You can't control all of the painful experiences your child will endure in her life and you can't shield her from all pain. So rather than try to prevent her from encountering hardship, give her the tools she needs to deal with pain in a healthy manner.

HELP YOUR CHILD EXPRESS PAIN

One of the best ways to deal with emotional pain is to talk about it. Encourage your child to speak up when he's struggling.

If he's not comfortable talking to anyone, writing in a journal can help him sort out his feelings and deal with his pain. There are several journaling activities that can help kids begin to make sense of their emotions:

- **Art journal**—Young children who struggle with writing can benefit from drawing pictures. Set aside a few minutes before bed every night and tell your child to draw a picture about his day. This can teach him to start making sense of what he did and how he feels.
- **Private journal**—Kids can benefit from writing about their thoughts and feelings every day. Some kids do fine with a blank notebook, but others need a simple prompt. You can buy a journal that says, "This is what I did today," or "This is how I feel." Talk to your child ahead of time about whether she wants you to read it together or if she prefers to keep it private.
- **Parent-child journals**—Journaling back and forth can be a good way to share your feelings. It can be especially helpful for older kids who feel a little uncomfortable talking about their feelings face-to-face. Writing in a journal and giving it to you can be a good way for them to share some of their more private concerns. And you can write back with tips on how to deal with feelings and problems, or to simply show that you're listening.

Teach Preschoolers to Face Challenges

It can be a natural tendency for kids to avoid difficult circumstances when given a choice. Providing encouragement can help your preschooler become more willing to do things, even when it's hard.

Be a good role model by pointing out times when you're willing to keep working despite the pain. Say things like "I'm really tired and I'm going to keep jogging anyway" or "I'm a little afraid of going down this slide but I know I'll be safe, so I'm going to be brave."

Praise your preschooler's willingness to endure slight pain as well. Say things like "I know it's frustrating when those pieces don't fit together but I like how you keep trying" or "It can be scary to ask a friend to play with you but you did it anyway!"

Facing tough times and difficult challenges head-on can help your preschooler gain confidence in himself. Just make sure that you help him face those challenges one small step at a time so he can experience success. If you tell him to do things that are too hard or too painful, he'll doubt himself and he may be less likely to tackle those challenges in the future.

Teach School-Age Kids to Be Resilient

Your children are going to face hardship, pain, and problems in their lives. That's inevitable. But you can take steps to decrease the toll those things take on them.

Imagine your child has a resilience piggy bank. You have endless opportunities to put coins into his bank by helping him gain the skills and tools he needs to deal with hardship. Every time he has a painful experience, it's like a coin is being withdrawn. As long as he still has lots of coins in his bank, he can afford to deal with withdrawals. Rejection, failure, and grief won't hurt so much when you've made regular positive deposits.

The best way to make deposits into your child's bank is by helping him feel competent. Kids who feel competent are better equipped to deal with adversity. Explore your child's interests and help develop his talents.

Helping other people can be a good way to foster resilience as well. A child who reads to younger children or one who helps an elderly neighbor with yard work will see that he has the ability to make a difference in the world, which can be the key to bouncing back from difficult events.

Teach Teens to Learn from Pain

Your teen may not feel comfortable talking to you all the time—and that's okay. In fact, it could be a sign she is gaining some healthy independence.

But it is important for your teen to be able to talk to other healthy adults. Make a list of trustworthy people she feels comfortable talking to. Try to come up with at least three to five people who could serve as good resources when she's going through a tough time. That could include coaches, grandparents, aunts and uncles, neighbors, family friends, or anyone else who could offer a supportive ear.

Make sure your teen knows that processing painful events with other people can help her see things from a different perspective, which could help her learn from her hardship. Losing a friend, getting dumped by her first love, or not making the team can become experiences that help her grow stronger.

Talk to your teen about how painful events can turn into important life lessons. Share what you learned from hardships you've experienced. Perhaps financial problems taught you to become better with your money. Or maybe the loss of a family member taught you to cherish your time with loved ones.

Most importantly, talk to your teen about how most people are stronger than they think. Assure her that it's normal to have self-doubt and to question her ability to endure painful experiences. But in the end, pain is part of life, and getting through hard times can help people grow stronger.

Kids Who Grow from Pain Become Adults Who Are Comfortable in Their Own Skin

Overcoming hardship may actually benefit kids. In a 2016 study conducted at Kent State University, researchers examined what happened to kids who grew up with parents who were struggling with chronic physical pain. Many of these kids grew up in homes where a parent's health issues weren't visible. Crohn's disease, fibromyalgia, and chronic back pain aren't easily observed by others, which made these kids' situations particularly challenging.

When they interviewed young adults about their childhood experiences, the researchers discovered that the emotional pain they experienced while growing up helped them in several ways:

- **Expanded understanding**—Their experiences helped them to look at the world a little differently. They described being more empathetic and having a better understanding of how some things in the world are out of anyone's control.
- **Stronger character**—They reported more compassion, forgiveness, determination, and motivation because of their experiences.
- **Aided development of important skills**—They learned practical skills, like money management and time management, as well as coping skills.
- **Instilled commitment to live well**—Their parents' illnesses taught them the value of self-care. They recognized the importance of eating well and avoiding unhealthy habits like smoking.
- **Nurtured spirituality**—Many of them reported they had a strong faith and they used prayer to help them get through tough times.

Your child won't grow stronger unless he has opportunities to carry some proverbial weight. Let him endure a little bit of pain and hardship so that he can develop the skills he needs to get through life.

You can't spare your child from pain and you can't go through all of life's challenges with him. He'll have to experience some pain on his own. When you give him the skills he needs to grow from that pain, he'll be able to draw from his inner strength.

Mentally strong people don't fear alone time. They're comfortable with who they are and they're confident they can stand on their own two feet, no matter what life throws their way. When faced with tough times, they are able to dig deep to find the tools they need, not just to endure pain, but also to learn from it.

Troubleshooting and Common Traps

Sometimes parents don't feel comfortable showing their children when they're in pain. They refuse to cry in front of their kids or they deny that they're sad.

This can be confusing to kids. They may grow up thinking it's bad to show emotion or that they're weak for feeling pain. So it's important to be a good role model. It's okay to show your child when you're in pain sometimes. Just make sure you're role-modeling healthy ways to deal with your emotional wounds.

Another common trap that many parents fall into is feeling like they have to have all the answers. When tragic events strike, it's okay to tell your child you don't know what will happen next. Or that you aren't sure why something occurred.

And don't be too hard on yourself when you make mistakes. When it comes to deciding when to let your child face certain challenges or how much pain to let her endure, there aren't any clear right or wrong answers. It's a judgment call on your part.

There may be times you think you've given your child more than he can handle. Or times when you think you shielded him a bit too much. Just remember you can always continue to monitor the situations your child faces and make further adjustments accordingly.

WHAT'S HELPFUL

- Distracting your child from acute pain
- Being honest with your child when something is going to hurt
- Acknowledging your child's pain
- Encouraging your child to keep a journal
- Building your child's resiliency bank account
- Helping your child learn from painful experiences
- Examining your beliefs about pain
- Providing age-appropriate information about the realities of the world
- Teaching your child to recognize when pain is a friend and when it is an enemy

WHAT'S NOT HELPFUL

- Minimizing or denying your child's pain
- Lying to spare your child's pain
- Encouraging your child to act tough
- Expecting your child to handle hardship without enough support
- Masking your pain
- Preventing your child from facing tough times

They Don't Feel
Responsible for Their
Child's Emotions

Jeremy and Suzanne accompanied their twelve-year-old daughter, Grace, to her first therapy appointment. Grace was referred to counseling because she was having social problems at school. When I asked her why she thought her guidance counselor wanted her to see me, she said, "Because the other kids at school are mean." When I asked her what they did that was mean, she said, "I don't know. They just are."

Suzanne chimed in and asked, "Honey, do you want to tell her about what that girl did on the bus?" Grace immediately crossed her arms, stuck out her bottom lip, and said, "No!" When I asked her mother to fill me in on the details, Suzanne said, "Well, if Grace doesn't want to talk about it, we won't discuss it."

That statement alone gave me an inkling into why Grace might be struggling. So I asked a few questions about her friends and social interactions. Jeremy said, "The other kids sometimes say Grace is a crybaby." He explained that since Grace was an only child, sharing and compromising weren't her strong suits.

Jeremy acknowledged that Grace could sometimes be a little demanding when things didn't go the way she wanted. Upon hearing him say that, Grace glared at him and said, "That's not true!" At that point, Suzanne offered to take her out into the waiting room for a few minutes so Jeremy could talk to me privately.

Once they were out of earshot, Jeremy explained, "Grace is a sensitive child and the school doesn't seem to understand that. And her friends just don't seem to 'get her' either. That's hard for Grace."

Grace sought solace with the school nurse when she thought the other kids were being mean or unfair. The nurse used to allow Grace to call Jeremy or Suzanne so they could console her. But most recently, the nurse started telling Grace to return to class or go back out for recess to "work it out" with her friends.

Upset by the response, they purchased a cell phone so that she could secretly call or text them from the bathroom when she needed to talk. When she was having a really bad day, they'd pick her up early so she could come home and "relax."

"I can always tell when Grace needs to come home, so I call the school and have her dismissed early. She's usually upset when she gets in the car, so I take her out for ice cream and we talk about what's upsetting her. As soon as she has a chance to talk about it, she calms right down," Jeremy explained.

When he finished offering his insights, Grace and her mother joined us again. It appeared the problems were:

1. **Grace lacked emotional and social skills.** Grace didn't know how to deal with being sad, angry, or disappointed. She lacked proper coping skills and it was affecting her relationships.
2. **Grace's parents were rescuing her from discomfort.** Grace's parents had labeled her "sensitive." They thought it was their job to protect her as much as possible from feeling uncomfortable.

My recommendations included:

1. **Emotional regulation skills training for Grace.** Grace needed to learn age-appropriate coping skills. She also needed to gain confidence in her ability to feel a wide range of emotions.

2. **Skills training for her parents.** Grace's parents needed to change their role from "rescuer" to "coach." They had opportunities every day to teach Grace how to deal with emotions on her own.

I explained that treatment for kids often employs a two-pronged approach: Grace could work with me on learning new skills and her parents could work with me on learning how to coach her as she practiced those skills in the real world. When I recommended we start scheduling weekly appointments, Suzanne said, "Well, that's up to Grace. This is all about what Grace thinks will be helpful to her." Fortunately, Grace agreed to come back.

As I began working with the family, it became clear that Suzanne and Jeremy walked on eggshells to avoid doing anything that might set her off. If Grace didn't want to do something, they made sure she didn't have to do it. So it was understandable why she was having problems at school—the other twelve-year-olds didn't accommodate her like her parents did.

At a time when peer relationships were critical to her development, Grace's friendships were deteriorating. Her parents' willingness to rescue her from uncomfortable emotions had stunted her emotional development. She had the emotional maturity of an average four- or five-year-old.

They never viewed emotion regulation as a skill that could be learned. Once they saw that Grace could learn to manage her anger, calm herself down, and deal with being upset—just like she could learn to tie her shoe or to make her bed—they viewed their interactions differently.

Each time she was upset, they realized they could seize the opportunity to teach her how to cope with feeling uncomfortable. They began to recognize that it wasn't their responsibility to make her happy. It was Grace's responsibility to be in charge of how she felt.

With assurance that it was in her best interest, Jeremy and Suzanne agreed to stop picking her up at school when she was having a bad day. At home, they also had to start saying no, holding her accountable, and giving her consequences when she broke the rules.

It took a couple of months to teach Grace basic skills—like how to identify how she was feeling and how to express those feelings in a healthy manner.

Slowly, she learned that it was okay to feel sad or angry, but yelling, scream-ing, and pouting weren't winning her any points with the other kids.

As Grace's ability to understand her emotions improved, her empathy for others also increased. She began to recognize how others likely felt when she was bossy or when she threw a fit. Slowly but surely, Grace developed the skills she needed to create genuine friendships with the other kids.

Do You Take Ownership over Your Child's Emotions?

It's normal to want to cheer your child up when he's in a bad mood or to calm him down when he's upset. But if you always take charge of chang-ing his emotional state, he won't learn how to do it for himself. Do any of the following statements describe you?

- ○ I don't spend much time talking to my child about feelings.
- ○ If my child is bored, I think it's my job to provide entertainment.
- ○ When my child is upset, I work hard to calm him down.
- ○ I feel uncomfortable when my child is anxious, sad, or angry.
- ○ I put a lot of effort into cheering up my child whenever she's sad.
- ○ Sometimes I tiptoe around my child to avoid upsetting him.
- ○ I only feel like I'm doing a good job as a parent when my child is happy.
- ○ When my child is mad at me, I think I must have done something wrong.
- ○ I tell my child to "calm down," but I've never spent time teaching her how to calm herself down.

Why Parents Feel Responsible for Kids' Emotions

Like most parents, Jeremy and Suzanne wanted to raise a happy child. But they doubted Grace's ability to manage her emotions on her own. So they took it upon themselves to help her out every chance they got.

In the previous chapter, we discussed the importance of allowing kids to experience pain. But exposing them to painful experiences isn't enough. You also have to allow them to take responsibility for dealing with their pain in a healthy manner. Just like it's easier to do chores yourself—rather than teach your child how to do them—it's easier to regulate your child's emotions for him. But doing so can actually do more harm than good in the long run.

IT'S HARD TO HAND OVER THE REINS

Telling an infant to calm down won't stop him from crying. If you want a baby to stop crying you're likely going to need to hold him, change him, or feed him. Since he can't regulate his emotions, it's up to you to modify the environment to bring him some relief.

As your infant turns into a toddler, however, he begins to develop the ability to recognize how he's feeling. To a certain extent, he learns how to modify his environment on his own. He can ask for a drink when he's thirsty or he can take off his jacket when he's too hot. As he grows into a preschooler, he starts learning how to make internal adjustments when he can't change his environment. He deals with some emotions all by himself, without requiring immediate modifications of that environment.

If he's frustrated or scared, he can learn how to calm himself down. And if he's bored or sad, he can learn how to cope with those emotions without depending on you to do it for him. With guidance and coaching, he can recognize what skills work for him and which choices are the healthiest ways to deal with his feelings.

At least that is what happens when parents actively teach kids to monitor and regulate their emotions. But many parents struggle to hand over that responsibility to their child. They continue to take responsibility for their child's emotions long after she needs them to do so. So parents of older kids continue to modify the environment by saying things like "Don't tell Billy we ate pizza without him because he'll be upset" or "Let's not take Olivia to the store because she'll cry if we don't buy her something." As a result, their children never learn to take responsibility for their emotions. And it becomes much more challenging to teach a fourteen-year-old to calm herself as compared to a four-year-old.

PARENTS ARE UNCOMFORTABLE WITH THEIR OWN EMOTIONS

My therapy office is an emotional laboratory where I get to witness first-hand how people deal with their feelings. Tackling difficult subjects gives me insight into how families address emotional issues in their home.

Take, for example, Kevin and his eleven-year-old daughter, Rosie. Rosie was being bullied at school, and when she described the mean things kids said to her, she started to cry. But as the tears rolled down her cheeks, her father started making funny faces and saying silly things. Rosie turned to him and said, "Dad, I'm talking about something serious. Stop acting like it's a joke!" Kevin said he just wanted to "lighten the mood." Like many parents, he was uncomfortable watching his child cry and he tried to "fix it."

But Rosie didn't want to be cheered up at that moment. She needed support and validation. A distraction from her pain was only a temporary solution.

Kevin's reaction was a common one. Most parents want to reach out and help their child feel better in the moment. But doing so means parents are taking responsibility for how their child feels.

Your Child Needs to Know How to Deal with His Own Inner Turmoil

As you saw with the example of Grace, when kids don't learn how to take responsibility for their emotions, they're likely to experience emotional and behavioral issues. Grace's tantrums interfered with her friendships. The other kids didn't want to hang around her when she was crying or bossing them around.

Since her parents always catered to her when she was upset, she never had opportunities to deal with uncomfortable feelings on her own. Feeling disappointed, frustrated, angry, and sad are all part of life. But her parents constantly gave in to her so she could escape those feelings.

Every parent tries to change a child's emotional state at one time or another. But doing so too often could be harmful.

A LACK OF EMOTIONAL COMPETENCE COULD HAVE LIFELONG CONSEQUENCES

Have you ever encountered someone who flies off the handle over the littlest things? Or have you ever had a friend who acted like everyday minor inconveniences were a major tragedy? It's likely those people were never taught how to manage their emotions effectively.

When people don't learn those skills, they behave badly. They become aggressive or manipulative in an attempt to get their needs met.

Researchers at Penn State studied what happens to kids who learn prosocial skills and emotional competence at a young age versus those who don't. They spent twenty years followings kids from kindergarten through their midtwenties and they discovered a link between kindergarten social skills and early adult success.

The kids who showed more prosocial skills at age five—like sharing and getting along with others—were more likely to finish college. For every one-point increase in children's social competency score in kindergarten, they were twice as likely to obtain a college degree. They were also 46 percent more likely to have a full-time job by age twenty-five. But the kids who had the most trouble cooperating, listening, and resolving conflicts were less likely to finish high school and college. Additionally, they were more likely to have legal problems and substance abuse issues.

For every one-point decrease in social competency in kindergarten, a child had a 67 percent higher chance of being arrested in early adulthood. A one-point decrease also meant a child had a 52 percent higher rate of binge drinking and an 82 percent higher chance of being in public housing (or at least on the waiting list). With all this research, isn't it interesting that we invest so much time and money into academic skills and so little into emotional and social skills? Clearly, emotional competence might be more important than other skills we traditionally link to success and happiness.

If you wanted your child to be a great basketball player, you wouldn't invest all your time into teaching him only how to make foul shouts. After all, he could be the best foul-ball shooter in the world, but if he lacked other basic skills—like dribbling and defense—he wouldn't succeed. But that's exactly what we do to kids. We focus on academic skills and then expect them to be successful in the real world despite their complete lack of other skills.

If your child is the smartest kid in the world, but he can't tolerate feeling sad, he'll never be willing to risk failure or rejection. Or if he's a gifted athlete but he can't manage his anger, he won't be able to keep his head in the game when he thinks the other team isn't playing fair.

Kids Who Can't Control Their Emotions Try to Control Other People

During my first semester as an adjunct college instructor, only one person failed my class. He'd missed a fair amount of work and his term paper was terrible. But if he'd done well on the final exam, he could have passed.

But he didn't. He bombed the exam and his final grade for the semester fell far below passing.

Soon after I posted the grades in the online portal, I received an e-mail from him asking me to double-check his grade. He was sure he should have passed. I e-mailed him back and assured him his term-paper grade, missing homework, and dismal final exam meant he failed.

About four days later, I received another e-mail from him. By now, Christmas break was well under way and he said, "I'm really struggling to enjoy my semester break because I'm so upset about that failing grade. I can't eat and I can't sleep. Please consider giving me a passing grade."

It was my first experience with the phenomenon called grade grubbing, where students ask professors to change their grades for basically no reason at all. In this case, the student wanted me to change his grade because he was feeling distressed.

Needless to say, I didn't change his grade. It wouldn't have been fair to the other students. But it also would have been doing him a disservice. He failed a class, so he *should* feel uncomfortable. And hopefully, those uncomfortable emotions could help motivate him to do better next time.

Unfortunately, the I-can't-handle-feeling-uncomfortable-so-you-should-change-something mentality is a common problem on college campuses throughout the country these days. When college kids feel offended, they try to convince everyone else to stop offending them. Rather than knowing it's okay to feel sad or hurt or angry, they try to control other people. "Stop printing that in the news" or "Don't let my professor get away with that," all because they don't like what they hear.

Consequently, schools have had trouble defining the line between free speech and political correctness. Take, for example, the Halloween costume incident at Yale.

In 2015, school administrators sent out an e-mail reminding students to avoid wearing insensitive Halloween costumes. In response, Erika Christakis, a lecturer at one of Yale's residential campuses, sent an e-mail of her own. Her message read in part, "Is there no room anymore for a child or young person to be a little bit obnoxious . . . a little bit inappropriate or provocative or, yes, offensive?"

Students were outraged by her words. They began protesting and hundreds of them signed an open letter to her, stating she was invalidating their feelings. One student even confronted her on video, saying Christakis created an unsafe space. When Christakis disagreed, the student replied with obscenities.

A couple of months after the incident, Christakis resigned from her job. Her husband, Nicholas Christakis, stepped down from serving as head of Silliman College at Yale following the incident as well.

Ironically, the administration's attempts to be inclusive led to much controversy. Isn't it a little scary that some of our brightest and best young people at a top Ivy League college experience such distress over what costume to wear on a children's holiday?

But it's not an isolated incident. Colleges everywhere are dealing with similar issues. As more and more students claim, "My feelings are hurt and you need to change," administrators are wondering what to do. If they don't change, they risk looking insensitive. But if they do change in an attempt to spare someone's feelings, they risk stifling free speech.

I'm sure many of these young people were brought up thinking that if they felt uncomfortable, it's because someone else was violating their rights. And just like we discussed in the victim mentality chapter, many of them believe it's their duty to make sure no one says things they don't want to hear.

It's important for kids to grow up learning that just because their feelings are hurt does not mean someone else needs to change. It's okay for other people to have a different opinion from yours or to make different choices. Teach kids they need to put more effort into controlling how they feel rather than trying to control what others do. Kids need to know they are a hundred percent responsible for their emotions and that they can handle feeling bad.

If your child doesn't learn, "It's up to me to deal with my emotions," she'll try to control other people. And while being bossy, rude, and demanding may occasionally help her get what she wants, ultimately, people aren't going to like her very much. And she may turn into someone who constantly accuses others of being insensitive or politically incorrect because she can't cope with opinions contrary to her own.

KIDS WON'T UNDERSTAND THEIR EMOTIONS

When Chelsea brought her eleven-year-old son, Max, into my office, the first thing she said was "I don't know why we're here. But his doctor said we had to see you because they can't find anything wrong." Max had been missing a lot of school due to stomachaches and headaches. His doctor had run several tests and examined him from head to toe without finding anything. So he suggested it might be a mental health problem. And to his mother's surprise, the doctor was right.

After I heard more about his symptoms and the problems he was experiencing, it was evident that Max was stressed out. He was anxious and nervous all the time. He worried about everything from his grades to his grandmother's health. But he didn't understand his feelings well enough to verbalize them.

I have no doubt he really was experiencing some physical pain. There's a strong link between the mind and the body. Stress can activate physiological responses within the body that lead to stomachaches and headaches. Children who lack skills to regulate their emotions tend to report more somatic issues. A 2008 study by Vanderbilt University discovered that 67 percent of children with recurrent abdominal pain have anxiety disorders. Somatic complaints are also common among children and teens with depression.

So while antacids and pain relievers temporarily masked his pain, Max couldn't gain relief until he addressed his underlying emotional issues. When we began addressing his emotional issues, his physical health problems decreased. He had to learn how to communicate his feelings and how to deal with them in a healthy manner if he wanted to feel better physically.

Teaching your child about emotions and how to regulate his feelings makes him better able to recognize when he's feeling stressed out or especially down. Early detection can prevent future problems and assist kids in getting treatment early.

What to Do Instead

Once Grace's parents began to view themselves as coaches, they were instrumental in helping her learn how to regulate her emotions. Their hands-on coaching helped her apply the skills she was learning in therapy. When she was upset, her parents provided much-needed reminders or hints about how she could calm herself down.

Over time they decreased their support so Grace could take over being fully responsible for managing herself and her emotions. By the time she completed therapy, she fully believed she had the mental strength to manage her feelings, no matter how intense or how uncomfortable they felt.

Learning how to manage emotions and endure unpleasant feelings are skills that can be taught. Just like other skills, however, children need ongoing guidance and practice.

TEACH YOUR CHILD TO LABEL FEELINGS

If your child can't identify her emotions, she'll struggle to take responsibility for how she feels. A child who can't say, "I'm mad," is likely to communicate her anger through her behavior. Tantrums, screaming, and aggression often stem from a child's inability to tell you how she feels.

If you're like most people, you probably don't hear many feeling words in everyday conversation. Usually people are more apt to say, "He's a jerk" rather than "I felt angry." And even when people do reference feelings, they use phrases like "I had butterflies in my stomach" or "I had a lump in my throat." So unless you make a conscious effort to teach your child feeling words, it's unlikely she'll have an extensive emotional vocabulary.

Teach your child feeling words by saying things like "It looks like you're feeling angry right now" when she stomps her feet. Or say, "It looks like you're feeling really excited that we're going to the park" when she runs to get her shoes. As your child's understanding of emotions grows, use more sophisticated feeling words, like "nervous," "disappointed," "relieved," and "frustrated."

Here are some other ways to teach your child about feelings:

- **Share your feelings in everyday conversation.** Use plenty of feeling words when you're talking to your child. Say things like "I felt sad today when Grandma wasn't feeling well" or "I felt really angry when that boy pushed the girl off the swings at the playground."
- **Ask your child, "How are you feeling today?"** Create a daily

habit of asking your child how he's feeling. Choose a specific time, such as when you're eating dinner or when he's getting ready for bed, to inquire about his emotional state. See if he can explain why he's experiencing specific emotions.

- **Explore your child's emotions when he tells stories.** When your child tells you about his day, ask questions like "How did you feel when you scored the goal in the game?" or "How did you feel when your teacher said you couldn't go out for recess?" If your child struggles to name specific feelings, try saying things like "I think I would have felt angry if that happened to me!"

VALIDATE YOUR CHILD'S FEELINGS

Rushing in to fix your child's problems means *you* take responsibility for *his* emotions. Validating, on the other hand, shows you understand, but leaves it up to your child to cope with his feelings. But it's important not to dismiss your child's feelings. A statement like "I'm sorry you feel bad that we aren't going to the movies" lacks empathy.

Show you accept your child's emotions by taking your comments a step further. Say, "It's disappointing when you can't do something you really want to do. So it's understandable that you feel bad we aren't going to the movies today." Validation shows your child that it's okay to feel bad.

Here are some examples of things you can say to validate how your child feels:

- "I see you're feeling really angry because I said you can't go to your friend's house. I can see how disappointed you may feel that you have to stay here."
- "It's hard to lose a game. I'd feel sad too."
- "I can understand feeling so angry that you wanted to say something mean."
- "I think a lot of kids get nervous about the first day of school. Doing something new can be scary."

Even when you don't understand your child's emotions or they seem out of proportion to the situation, validate how she feels. Kids need to know that their feelings are okay and that you respect how they feel, even if you don't feel the same.

CORRECT THE BEHAVIOR, NOT THE EMOTION

Sometimes kids get confused about the difference between thoughts, feelings, and behavior. Here's an example:

Parent: How did you feel when your friend said you couldn't play with him?

Child: I felt like he didn't want to be friends anymore.

Parent: That sounds like what you were thinking, not what you were feeling. You thought he didn't want to be friends. How did you feel about that?

Child: Sad.

Parent: Oh, you felt sad. That makes sense. So what did you do?

Child: I got mad at him.

Parent: You felt mad too. That's a feeling. I probably would have felt mad too. What did you do when you felt mad?

Child: I walked away and said I was going to find a new friend to play with.

Parent: Walking away when you felt angry was a good choice.

Explain to your child that thoughts involve words or pictures that go on in his brain. Feelings describe his mood, like happy or sad. Behavior involves the action he chooses to take with his body.

When your child understands the differences between those three things, he'll gain a better understanding of his choices. For example, it's okay to feel angry, but it's not okay to hit someone. Similarly, feeling sad is okay, but screaming and throwing a fit isn't acceptable behavior.

Tell your child that he won't get in trouble for his feelings or for his thoughts. Instead your rules have to do with behavior.

Establish clear household rules that outline acceptable ways to express emotions. Write down your rules and keep them posted somewhere in your home. If you say, "No yelling," make sure that's a rule that you're going to be able to follow as well. If you're guilty of raising your voice, your child will follow suit and your written rule won't be effective.

Here are a few simple rules that can help kids regulate their emotions:

1. **Respect other people's physical space and their belongings.** No hitting or hurting anyone else's body and no damaging property.
2. **Use kind words when you speak to other people.** No name-calling or putdowns.
3. **Use an indoor voice.** No yelling or screaming.

While slamming doors may not be a big deal to some families, other parents won't allow it. So make sure to create a list of rules that everyone in the household is going to be able to follow. Remember, you can change and alter the rules as needed. Just make sure your child understands your expectations.

LET YOUR CHILD EXPERIENCE UNCOMFORTABLE EMOTIONS

Your job isn't to put a smile on your child's face. Instead your role should be to help your child learn how to deal with uncomfortable emotions on his own.

Here are a few uncomfortable emotions your child needs to experience:

- **Anger**—Your child needs to learn how to calm himself down when he's upset.
- **Anxiety**—It's important for your child to understand that anxiety doesn't have to prevent him from doing what he wants.
- **Guilt**—When your child says he's sorry or that he feels bad, don't rush in to say, "Oh, it's okay." Let him feel guilty so he'll be motivated to change his behavior.
- **Sadness**—Don't cheer your child up just because he's sad. Let him practice soothing himself.
- **Disappointment**—When things don't turn out the way your child wants, don't automatically try to make it up to him. Let him feel disappointed sometimes.
- **Boredom**—Just because your child complains he's bored doesn't mean you need to entertain him. There will be plenty of times in life when he'll need to tolerate boredom.
- **Frustration**—When your child is working on a difficult task, it's okay for him to feel frustrated. But that doesn't mean you need to help him or fix it.

Let your child feel a wide range of emotions and let him experience them fully. Coach him, but don't rescue him. Over time he'll gain confidence in his ability to successfully deal with his feelings on his own.

How to Teach Kids to Be Responsible for Their Feelings

While some kids are sensitive, Grace's parents used that label as a way to excuse her from dealing with discomfort. Before they could start teaching her to take responsibility for her emotions, they had to trust that she could handle uncomfortable feelings. If you treat your child as though she's fragile, she'll grow to believe she can't deal with hardship. But if you help her see she's strong enough to deal with uncomfortable feelings, she'll feel equipped to cope with those feelings on her own.

HELP YOUR CHILD IDENTIFY MOOD BOOSTERS

Your child needs to know that it's normal to feel a wide array of emotions. And when something bad happens, it's okay to feel sad. In fact, feeling sad can be part of the healing process.

But that doesn't mean your child has to stay stuck in a bad mood. He can take control over how he feels. If he wakes up on the wrong side of the bed or he had a bad day at school, he can make choices that will help him feel better.

It's tempting to behave according to how you feel. So if you're sad, you might sit home by yourself. But that behavior will only reinforce your feelings of sadness. Behaving contrary to how you feel changes your emotions. So going out with friends might cheer you up. Or going for a walk could boost your mood.

The key is to help your child discover *healthy* ways to deal with his emotions. If you don't, your child may find some not-so-healthy ways to feel better. A sad child might turn to food to comfort himself. Or a lonely teenager may seek online relationships to get attention.

Proactively teach your child healthy ways to soothe himself, calm himself down, and cheer himself up. Keep in mind that the same mood boosters don't work for everyone. Playing outside for a few minutes may help one child calm down, but coloring quietly may be the most effective tool for another child.

Here's how to work with your child to discover which tools will boost his mood:

Parent: Let's make a list of all the things you like to do when you feel happy. Tell me, when you feel really good, what do you like to do?

Child: I like to go to the beach and I like to play in the park.

Parent: Oh, those are fun things to do. What about when you're at home. Let's say you come home from school and you feel happy. What would you probably want to do?

Child: Play with the cats and talk to my friends.

Parent: And do those things keep you happy?

Child: Yes, I laugh and I have fun when I'm doing them.

Parent: Great. Let's think of some more things you might do when you feel happy.

Child: I like to go for walks outside and I like to call Grandpa and read some of the jokes in my joke book to him.

Parent: You're right! You definitely love to do both of those things.

Write all the things that your child says he likes to do when he's happy. Then, when he's in a bad mood, tell him to go pick something to do on his list. Teach him that doing one of those things when he's sad or lonely could boost his mood.

You can also make a mood booster kit. Create a small box filled with items that will remind him of the things he likes to do when he's happy—like his joke book and some art supplies. You can include things that make him smile, like a funny picture of Grandpa. With practice, he'll learn which activities help him the most and he'll begin doing those things on his own.

HELP YOUR CHILD IDENTIFY CALMING ACTIVITIES

Just like your child needs to know how to pick himself up when he's feeling down, he also needs to know how to calm himself down when he's upset. Whether your child is frustrated with a math problem or he's angry he's losing in a board game, he needs to know how to keep working toward his goals despite being upset. One of the keys to managing anger and frustration is self-awareness.

Teach your child to recognize warning signs that he's becoming upset. Talk about those physiological warning signs that could indicate he's about to explode. Perhaps his heart beats faster or maybe his face feels hot. If he can learn to recognize those warning signs, he can intervene and calm his body before he "explodes."

Ask your child, "What do you like to do when you're calm?" Coloring, playing with Play-Doh, or listening to calming music are just a few potential activities that might help calm his body and his brain.

Similar to the mood booster kit, create a "calm-down kit" by placing items in a box. When your child is anxious, overly excited, or angry, say, "Let's go get your calm-down kit." Then he can take ownership for selecting the tools that will help him manage his mood.

SHARPEN YOUR CHILD'S EMOTION REGULATION SKILLS

Dealing with uncomfortable emotions in a healthy way could be one of the most important skills you ever teach. But you can't simply *tell* your child how to manage his emotions. He'll need ongoing practice and coaching from you. As he grows older and faces new challenges and even more difficult circumstances, he'll continue to need your guidance and support.

Like any good coach, provide lots of positive praise and reinforcement. Point out your child's effort and hard work. Say things like "I really like the way you decided to go to your room for a minute to calm down when you felt upset today."

Stay consistent with your rules and consequences as well. Show your child that you're committed to helping him learn from mistakes in a supportive manner. Hold regular conversations about how he can do better in the future. Ask questions like "Instead of hitting your sister, what could you do differently next time?" Help your child identify new strategies that could help him make a better choice the next time he experiences intense emotions.

Teach Preschoolers to Calm Down

The emotion preschoolers tend to struggle with most is anger. Whether your child is mad because a friend grabbed his toy or he's upset because you said it's time to leave the playground, he's likely to show you that he's not happy by yelling, stomping, or crying.

Raise your preschooler's awareness of the warning signs that he's feeling angry by asking him to draw a picture of how he looks when he's mad. Tell him to show you what happens to his body. Perhaps his face gets red or he balls his hands into fists. When he's done, talk about how mad feelings affect our bodies and our behavior. But if he can spot those warning signs that his body is getting angry, it's his job to calm his body down.

A simple way to teach preschoolers to cool off is to help them do some breathing exercises that produce a relaxation response. Not only can slow deep breaths calm the body, but they can also decrease feelings of anger.

Here's a simple way to teach a child how to do some deep breathing:

1. Breathe in through your nose, like you're smelling a piece of pizza.
2. Then breathe out through your mouth like you're trying to cool the pizza down.
3. Repeat this exercise several times slowly to calm the body and the brain.

When you notice your child getting upset, remind him to "stop and smell the pizza." Over time he'll learn to do this on his own, with fewer reminders from you. And he'll start to understand how to calm himself down.

An alternative to this is to teach your child to take "bubble breaths." Go outside and blow some bubbles. Ask your child to show you how to breathe to create the biggest or best bubbles. Most likely he'll take in a big breath and blow out slowly.

Explain how taking "bubble breaths" can help calm his body. And when he's upset, tell him to "take some bubble breaths."

Teach School-Age Kids to Change the Channel

Thinking about an upsetting event or worrying about something that could happen in the future will keep your child stuck in a bad mood. Thinking about something more pleasant will change how he feels. It's usually not as simple as telling yourself, "Don't think about what those mean kids said today," however. In fact, the more your child tells himself not to think about it, the more he might dwell on his upsetting thoughts. Changing his behavior is the key to taking his mind off something that keeps running through his head.

Using a version of the popular "white bear experiment," I teach kids how to "change the channel" in my therapy office. You can use this exercise to teach your child as well:

1. Tell your child to think of white bears for thirty seconds. This could include anything from polar bears to stuffed animals.
2. Stay silent and let your child imagine the bears. When time is up, say stop.
3. Then tell your child to think about anything he wants for the next thirty seconds. But tell him that he cannot think about white bears.
4. Wait thirty seconds and ask him how he did. Most kids will say white bears kept creeping into their thoughts. If your child says he managed to avoid thinking about white bears, ask him how he did it.
5. Then give your child a simple task to do for thirty seconds. I hand the child a deck of cards and tell him to sort the deck by

number or suit or something along those lines. Whatever task you give your child, make sure it will be something that will require his full attention if he wants to race to accomplish it in thirty seconds.

6. When time is up, tell him to stop. Then ask him how much he thought about white bears during the task. If he's like most people, he'll probably say not at all.

The point of the exercise is to show kids firsthand how changing their behavior can change what they're thinking about. So if your child is ruminating about something that upsets him, getting his hands busy could be the key to helping him feel better. Refer to this as "changing the channel," in his brain. Just like a TV, if the station playing in his head isn't helpful, he needs to turn the channel to something more productive.

When he's had a rough day at school and he's in a bad mood, say, "How can you change the channel to make tonight a good night?" Or when he says, "I'm bored," ask, "What do you think you could do to change the channel?" Then leave it up to him to find activities that will boost his mood or help him feel better. Offer ideas or suggestions if he's struggling, but with practice, he should learn how to do these things on his own.

Just make sure you don't send the message that he needs to be in a good mood all the time. There may be times when he wants to talk about his sad feelings or when he feels sad over something that happened. Changing the channel should be reserved for those times when he's stuck or when his feelings aren't serving him well.

Teach Teens to Lengthen Their Fuse

On a bad day, your teen is likely to have a short fuse. A failed test, an argument with a friend, and being yelled at by the basketball coach could cause her to come home in a bad mood. It may take only one more minor irritation to set her off.

Teach your teen how to lengthen her fuse. Talking to a friend, listening to her favorite song, or doing some yoga might reduce her stress. Help her identify the things that could help her handle stress in a healthy way. Share the strategies that help you lengthen your fuse on a rough day too.

Discuss how to recognize when she has a short fuse. Perhaps she gets irritable when anyone talks to her. Or maybe she starts tapping her fingers loudly or pacing back and forth. Talk about the warning signs you experience when you have a short fuse.

Then explain how everyone has options when they're stressed out, tired, or having a bad day. And everyone can take steps to lengthen their fuse.

A longer fuse means she'll be less likely to say things she doesn't mean or do something she'll regret. Talk with your teen about taking responsibility for recognizing when her fuse is short. But if you notice she seems to be particularly stressed out and irritable, suggest she take steps to lengthen her fuse.

If she ends up getting angry and blowing up at someone or having a meltdown, talk about it when she's calm. Discuss whether she had any warning signs that her fuse was getting short and discuss how she might make better choices next time.

Emotionally Competent Kids Become Adults Who Expend Energy Only on Things They Can Control

Logan was a nine-year-old boy who was referred to therapy by his school because he had some serious anger problems. When he got upset, he tipped over desks or threw things around the classroom. Whenever Logan had these violent outbursts, the teacher cleared the classroom to keep the other kids safe. When it was "safe" for everyone to return, Logan was usually taken out of the room for a while. He'd either go down to the principal's office or spend some time with a one-on-one aide.

When I met Logan, he was the first one to say, "I can't control my temper. I get really mad and make bad choices." I assumed he'd heard that from adults in his life. His parents agreed that he had trouble managing his anger at home sometimes too, but they said it seemed to be worse at school.

I spent some time working with Logan and it was clear he was a bright kid who had some pretty good insight into his problems. So I asked him for some more details about his angry outbursts—like when they happened and what led up to them. Then we talked about what a big problem it was that he flipped desks over and got aggressive. It interrupted class, caused the other students to leave the room, etc. So I asked, "What do you think we could do to help this problem?"

He said, "Well, why don't I just leave the classroom instead of everyone else?" And with that, Logan created his own solution. We worked with his teacher and his principal to create a plan. Logan would be given a red pass to keep in his desk. When he felt himself getting angry, he'd place the pass on the teacher's desk to signal that he needed to leave, and then he'd walk straight down to the principal's office. An adult would keep an eye on him while he sat in the office and cooled off on his own.

Once that plan was put into place, Logan's teacher never had to clear the classroom again. Instead Logan took responsibility for his emotions. He excused himself quietly and calmed himself down. After he was calm, he returned to class.

Logan's confidence soared when he realized he could take more control over his emotions. And as we continued to work on anger management strategies, he required fewer breaks from the classroom with his red pass. He began practicing his coping skills right at his desk. And ultimately, his attitude changed. Rather than thinking he was a bad kid with anger problems, he began to believe he was a competent kid who could tame his temper.

Emotional competence will serve your child well throughout his life.

Researchers have examined the competitive advantages adults gain when they understand how their emotions impact their thoughts and behavior. They've linked emotional intelligence to improved work performance, better marriages, and improved physical and psychological health.

Mentally strong people don't waste energy on things they can't control. Wishing the circumstances were different or trying to force someone else to change isn't productive. Emotionally competent kids grow up knowing to put their energy into the right places. When they can't control their circumstances, they focus on controlling their attitudes.

Troubleshooting and Common Traps

It's hard for many parents to teach their kids about feelings because they weren't ever taught these skills themselves. So despite their best intentions, some parents give kids bad advice. The biggest misconception I see is when parents believe you have to release anger or it will somehow build up and cause you to explode. So in a well-meaning effort, they will tell their child to punch a pillow when he's angry.

But research shows encouraging your child to "let his anger out" will backfire. He's likely to become angrier and more aggressive. So a better approach is to teach your child skills to calm himself down, in a more socially appropriate manner.

Another common trap is that parents think suppressing emotions is a sign of mental strength. I had a father bring his eight-year-old son into my therapy office after the child's grandmother died. The father said, "I'm so proud of him. He's been so strong. He's only cried twice even though he and his grandma were really close."

But being strong has nothing to do with how many times your child has cried. Instead it's about being aware of your emotions and knowing how to deal with those emotions in a healthy manner.

Instead of telling your child not to show emotions, which isn't helpful, teach him how to cope with his feelings in a productive manner so he can heal.

WHAT'S HELPFUL

- Teaching your child to label emotions
- Validating your child's feelings
- Establishing rules and limits for behavior
- Helping your child discover effective mood boosters
- Identifying calming activities
- Coaching your child to manage emotions
- Teaching your child specific emotion regulation skills like breathing exercises and how to lengthen her fuse
- Correcting your child's behavior, but not the emotion

WHAT'S NOT HELPFUL

- Minimizing or dismissing your child's feelings
- Rescuing your child every time she's in distress
- Modifying your child's environment as she grows older
- Always cheering your child up when she's sad
- Constantly calming your child down when she's upset
- Entertaining your child every time she's bored
- Underestimating your child's ability to cope with uncomfortable feelings
- Encouraging aggressive ways of releasing anger

They Don't Prevent Their Child from Making Mistakes

Although fourteen-year-old Taylor got along well with her father, she was especially close to her mother, Maria. As a stay-at-home parent, Maria was devoted to helping Taylor gain every competitive advantage possible. She picked out her classes, monitored her schoolwork, and paid for tutoring during the summer months to ensure Taylor excelled academically.

When it came to athletics, Maria was also very supportive. She spent hours researching the best basketball camps and invested her energy into making sure Taylor had the resources she needed to outshine the other kids. Maria was confident she had helped pave the way for Taylor's lifelong success.

Until one night, when Taylor asked a strange question. Shortly after going to bed, she called out to Maria, who went to Taylor's doorway to see what she needed. Taylor said, "I think I have to go to the bathroom but I don't know if I should get up." At first, Maria thought she was kidding. But when Taylor insisted she was experiencing inner turmoil, Maria realized she was serious. Taylor said, "Well, I might just think I have to go to the bathroom and if I get up and turn the light on, it'll wake me up even more and then I'll have trouble sleeping. What do you think I should do?"

Still stunned, Maria said, "Well, why don't you just try to go to sleep." Taylor said, "Okay, thanks, Mom." Maria went downstairs and explained to her husband, Ken, what had just happened. Ken said, "I'm not surprised, Maria. You make every decision in her life for her. And now, at the age of fourteen, she can't make a single decision without consulting you first."

It was at that moment that Maria realized she'd been offering more than just guidance. She'd been designing Taylor's life for her right down to the tiniest details. And now her teenage daughter couldn't even decide to use the bathroom without the fear she was making a mistake.

Maria set up a counseling appointment right away and she and Taylor came into my office together. Taylor didn't share her mother's concerns, however. She said, "My mom helps me with stuff, and together, we're doing great. I don't know why she's so worried." Maria spoke up and said, "Taylor, if you can't decide whether you need to go to the bathroom on your own, clearly we aren't doing that well."

As I learned more about their situation, it became clear that the problems were:

1. **Maria prevented Taylor from making any decisions on her own.** Maria acted more like Taylor's personal assistant than her mother. She managed her schedule, organized her belongings, and made decisions on her behalf.
2. **Taylor lacked basic decision-making skills.** Taylor sought advice for her mother on everything she did and she always did whatever her mother said. She never needed to solve problems on her own.

My recommendations were:

1. **Maria needed to back off and stop micromanaging Taylor's daily life.** She had to let Taylor do things on her own, even if she thought Taylor was making a mistake.
2. **Taylor needed to learn how to make choices without her**

mother's input. For the first time, Taylor needed to develop her own opinions. And she needed to build confidence in her ability to make decisions and then bounce back from mistakes when she messed up.

Over the next few weeks, we explored all the steps Maria had been taking to prevent Taylor from making any mistakes. She corrected Taylor's homework, offered her advice on what to wear, and scheduled her time for her.

In hindsight, she realized Taylor sought her opinion before making any decisions. And she realized that without her input, Taylor had no idea how to manage her life. Now she wanted to back off, but she wasn't sure how to do it. She was afraid Taylor would be lost if she stopped offering her help.

And she was right. Cutting her off completely after making all of her decisions for her might be too tough for Taylor. So we created some ways in which she could slowly start supporting Taylor's efforts to make decisions on her own, one step at a time.

At first, Taylor struggled, even with small decisions. She'd ask questions like "Mom, should I wear this shirt or the pink one?" and Maria learned to respond by saying, "Either one is a good choice. Which one do you think is best?" Taylor's questions weren't just about eliciting her mother's opinion—she needed approval and validation before she could find the courage to make even the simplest of choices.

Maria also stopped double-checking all of Taylor's work. And for the first time ever, Taylor's grades slipped a little. As hard as it was for Maria to let that happen, she knew preventing those mistakes would cause more problems for Taylor in the end.

Fortunately, Maria was committed to backing off and teaching Taylor she could tolerate making mistakes. Slowly, Taylor learned that mistakes weren't the worst thing in the world.

As her mother cheered on her willingness to try, Taylor gained confidence in her ability to bounce back when she failed. She definitely made some blunders, but she was able to learn firsthand that she could deal with it and even learn from those mistakes.

Do You Prevent Your Child from Failing?

Many parents insist on being in the driver's seat of their children's lives. They think if they can direct every movement, they'll make sure their child never makes a mistake. Do you respond positively to any of these points?

- ○ I correct my child's homework so he doesn't get a bad grade.
- ○ I can't stand to see my child mess up.
- ○ I think it's my job to jump in before my child makes a mistake rather than allow him to suffer the consequences of messing up.
- ○ I think mistakes should be avoided at all costs.
- ○ I want to spare my child the embarrassment and hurt that come with making mistakes.
- ○ I fear if my child makes a mistake, she won't put in the effort to fix it.
- ○ If my child makes a mistake, I worry that I might be the one to suffer the consequences.
- ○ I think it's my responsibility to spare my child from the pain of failure.
- ○ If I think my child is doing something wrong, I feel compelled to jump in and show him the right way to do it.
- ○ I think preventing my child from making academic mistakes is the best way to set her up for college and life after high school.

Why Parents Prevent Kids from Making Mistakes

Maria thought she was leading Taylor toward success by preventing her from making mistakes along the way. She figured if she could help her daughter do things right the first time, she'd perform better. She assumed her high level of involvement was the best way to give Taylor a competitive edge.

And on one hand, it was working. Taylor was a successful student and athlete. But it was only because Maria was right there directing her every move.

While Maria's overinvolvement was an extreme example, many parents do similar things on a much smaller scale. Constantly shadowing a toddler, coaching your grade-school child from the sidelines, and getting overly involved in your teenager's friendships are more common examples of helicopter parenting. Consider if there are learning opportunities you may be preventing because you, like Maria, intervene before your child has a chance to make a mistake.

HELICOPTER PARENTS THINK THEY KNOW BEST

Overbearing parents used to be rare. There'd be the one embarrassing mother who'd insist on draping a sweater over his son's shoulders while he sat on the bench during the soccer game. Or there was the occasional father who would demand a meeting with the guidance counselor to talk about course schedules before allowing his high school student to choose an elective. People used to raise an eyebrow at parents who did those kinds of things.

But these days, helicopter parents are the norm. They overstep boundaries throughout their children's lives and they don't see their involvement as excessive. By definition, helicopter parents are so overprotective that they limit their children's ability to make mistakes. They micromanage their children's daily activities and work hard to make sure their children succeed.

The societal shift that has normalized helicopter parenting likely stems from several factors. Latchkey kids from the eighties may want to give their kids more support than they had when they were growing up. But their efforts to be more involved may have crossed the line into becoming overly involved.

The rise in helicopter parenting may also stem from technological advances. Parents who access the news 24/7 may feel as though the world is more dangerous than it was in the past. And although you might think cell phones give kids more freedom, we've actually seen the opposite. Parents check in with their children now more than ever.

Parents are also more child-centered than ever before and there's a bigger emphasis on college and success. As a result, many parents have made it their mission to ensure their children don't do anything that could mess up their chances for a bright future.

Helicopter parenting also seems to be contagious. Once a few parents began to hover over their children, others began to think that good parenting meant intrusive parenting. And parents felt pressure to become overly involved to ensure their children could remain competitive. And that's exactly what we see today.

When intrusive parenting was rare, all kids were making mistakes sometimes. They forgot homework assignments, their projects weren't always done on time, and they occasionally arrived late to hockey practice. But since those things happened to most kids at one time or another, it wasn't a big deal.

But once a few parents started becoming overly involved in micromanaging their children's lives, those kids gained a competitive advantage. Their parents provided them with personal concierge services that ensured they were always prepared for school and their extracurricular activities. That put pressure on the "normal parents" to help their kids stay competitive too.

PARENTS BELIEVE MISTAKES ARE BAD

Some parents think preventing kids from making mistakes teaches them the "right" way to do things without having to endure the pain of failure. And that concept makes sense sometimes. After all, you don't want to let your child put his hand on a hot stove so that he'll learn it's hot. Doing so could scar him for life. But for many parents, the notion that mistakes must be prevented carries over into every area of their children's lives. They work hard to ensure their child gets one hundreds on his homework, never forgets an assignment, and always has his uniform clean for the game.

Quite often parents developed these beliefs early, during their own childhoods. A mother who was ridiculed whenever she messed up may work hard to prevent her children from feeling that type of shame. Or a father who believes he never reached his full potential because he didn't take school seriously may adopt rigid homework rules that prevent his children from making any slipups on their assignments.

They may also make assumptions about what mistakes really mean. Rather than a mistake being something you make, it signifies who you are. So if you fail a test, it means you're stupid. Or if you don't get hired for a job, it means you're a loser. With this mind-set, it's no wonder some parents prevent kids from making mistakes. They want to spare them from suffering a serious blow to their self-esteem.

PARENTS DON'T WANT TO SUFFER THE CONSEQUENCES

I once worked with a mother who was desperate for her son to learn how to manage his anger. Seth was twelve and he had an explosive temper. Whenever his mother tried to get him to do his chores or when she took away his video games for breaking the rules, he became enraged. Sometimes he'd threaten to break things. Occasionally, he'd throw things— like his smartphone—and once he punched a door. His mother was afraid he was going to break something every time he got angry. So to prevent his destructive behavior, she pacified him whenever he got upset.

When I asked her what would happen if she didn't intervene, she said, "He'd break something." So I asked her what would happen if he broke something. She said, "Well, then I'd have to be the one to fix it." Since Seth didn't have any money and he wasn't particularly skilled at fixing things, she assumed it was her responsibility to repair any damage he made.

I challenged her to step aside when he was angry and let him break something. If he broke his belongings, let him live without them. If he damaged someone else's property, make him responsible for repairing it.

That might mean assigning him extra chores so he could earn the money to replace a broken item.

There was a good chance he would refuse to follow through with repairing something if he broke it. But it would be her job to enforce the consequence and help him learn from his mistakes.

Within the week, he broke the remote control to the TV in his bedroom. His mother had told him to clean his room, and she didn't back down when he was angry, so he threw the remote across the room and broke it.

When she refused to buy him a new remote control, Seth got upset. But after a few weeks of having to get up and walk over to the TV to change the channel, he became motivated to learn how to manage his anger for the first time. He didn't want to break things—especially his own belongings—when he got angry. Now that he had been allowed to make mistakes when he was angry, he recognized he had a problem.

Let your child make mistakes when he's under your supervision. It's better for him to learn important life lessons now rather than later in life when the consequences may be more serious. It takes self-restraint to keep from interfering when your child is about to make a mistake. Not only could a mistake be costly for him, but helping him learn from it requires patience, time, and energy.

Teaching him how to learn from his mistakes so he doesn't repeat them takes a lot longer than just preventing the mistake in the first place. But with your support, your child can turn those mistakes into a valuable life lesson.

Preventing Kids from Making Mistakes Teaches Them Mistakes Are Horrible

Taylor struggled to make simple decisions for herself because her mother had always done everything for her. She didn't see her mother's behavior as intrusive. Instead, she thought they were a team. But Taylor's lack of independence could have led to some serious trouble when she tried to live on her own.

Sometimes there are much more subtle ways a parent's misguided attempts to prevent mistakes can become problematic. Examine when your guidance may cross the line from helpful to harmful.

KIDS WHO DON'T MAKE MISTAKES MAY EXPERIENCE LIFELONG CONSEQUENCES

Several students stayed after class one day to talk about the steps involved in becoming a therapist. As our discussion drew to a close, one student hung around until everyone else left. She had her course catalog with her and she asked for my input on which classes might be most helpful to her. She highlighted the ones I suggested and took notes while I explained how certain classes might help her career.

At the end of our conversation she thanked me and asked, "If I forget something you've said, can my parents e-mail you? They may have some questions about which classes to sign me up for."

For a minute, I thought she was confused about the sign-up process. (Sometimes eighteen-year-old students temporarily forget that they're now in charge of doing their own paperwork.) I reminded her she could sign up online and wouldn't need her parents' permission. She said, "Oh, I know. But my parents will want to make the final decision to make sure I'm signing up for the right things."

I don't know this young woman's parents, but I'm guessing they had always gone to great lengths to prevent her from making mistakes in many areas of her life. And now that she was an adult, they were still taking charge. And she seemed happy to let them do it.

That's not to say they shouldn't have had any involvement in her college career—especially if they were the ones paying the bill. Refusing to pay $60,000 a year for a child to major in art history is one thing, but micromanaging her course schedule was another. The student was convinced her parents had to make decisions for her because she was afraid she'd make a mistake if left to her own devices. If you teach your child that mistakes need to be prevented—and you're the one who prevents them—she'll struggle to make decisions when you're not around. She'll be afraid to take risks and step outside her comfort zone.

Ironically, however, most helicopter parents think they're doing their kids a great service. They think they'll be sending them off to college with a competitive advantage. They also assume they've reduced their children's stress by sparing them from embarrassing and costly missteps. But studies show that parents who prevent kids from making mistakes are actually doing them harm.

Research says kids who aren't allowed to make mistakes experience:

- **Higher rates of mental health issues.** A 2014 study from the University of Mary Washington in Virginia found that college students with helicopter parents were more likely to be depressed and less satisfied with their lives.
- **Increased likelihood of being prescribed psychiatric medication.** A 2011 study conducted by researchers at the University of Tennessee at Chattanooga found that college students whose parents hovered were more likely to take medication for anxiety and depression and more likely to recreationally consume pain pills.
- **Lower executive-function capabilities.** A 2014 study from the University of Colorado discovered that people who are raised in highly structured environments, with fewer opportunities for free time, lack the skills necessary to manage themselves and their resources in a way that will help them reach their goals. They lack mental control and self-regulation skills.
- **Increased risk of physical health problems.** A 2016 study from Florida State University found that emerging adults with helicopter parents were more likely to have physical health problems. This is most likely because they lack the skills to take care of their health issues on their own. If their parents aren't there telling them what to eat, how to exercise, and when to go to sleep, they may struggle to care for their bodies.

MISTAKES ARE GREAT TEACHERS

One Monday afternoon I received a phone call from a parent in my therapy office in the junior high school. I'd been working with Mason for a few weeks to address a few social issues, but now his mother was concerned about his grades.

His midsemester progress report revealed several zeros on homework assignments. Mason's mother was confused about how this could have happened. Every night she sat down with him and helped him with his homework. She was so confident he was getting his work done that she rarely ever checked the online portal to see his grades.

I recommended she talk to the teachers—and with Mason—to get to the bottom of it. And I agreed to speak with Mason later in the day. When he came into my office for his appointment, I let him know his mother had called with concerns. He said, "Oh, I knew she'd be mad when she saw my grades." He admitted he was missing a fair amount of work. He said he forgot to bring his science book home sometimes. Without it, he couldn't do his work. He knew his mother would be angry about his irresponsibility, so he'd tell her he didn't have any science homework that night.

He also hadn't completed a major social studies project. He kept putting it off. As the due date drew nearer, he was afraid to tell his mother he'd waited until the week it was due to begin. So he just never did it because he didn't want her to get angry. He gave examples of mishaps that occurred in each subject. He said as the semester wore on, he felt like his problems were piling up and he was digging himself in deeper. But he didn't dare tell his mother he was behind on his work. He said, "She would tell me I was being irresponsible and get really mad. So I thought it was better not to talk about it."

Like many kids who have been taught "mistakes should be prevented," Mason put more energy into hiding his mistakes than learning from them. His mother had spent so much time focusing on the importance of doing everything right that he wasn't sure what to do when he did something wrong.

When kids get the message that mistakes are bad—whether they think mistakes are embarrassing or they don't want someone else to be upset—they become good at covering them up. But unless they acknowledge these mistakes, they won't ever learn from them.

What to Do Instead

Maria had prevented Taylor from making mistakes to the point that she became immobilized over making the smallest decisions for herself. To repair the situation, Maria had to back off and allow Taylor to make decisions for herself. Even when she disagreed with the choice Taylor was making, she had to allow it to happen. But she had to make sure she was giving Taylor the emotional and cognitive skills she needed to handle mistakes. As a teenager who wasn't used to any type of blunder, Taylor lacked resiliency. Her mother had to teach her to bounce back from mistakes.

Fortunately, Maria became a good role model for recovering from mistakes. She told Taylor, "I made the mistake of doing everything for you. Now I have to teach you that there are some mistakes you have to make on your own."

It's not enough to just let your child make mistakes. You have to give her the skills she needs to learn from her errors.

EXAMINE HOW YOU SEE YOUR PARENTING ROLE

Take a minute to think about your main role as a parent. If you had to sum up your duties in one sentence, what would you say?

If you see your role as more of a protector, your goal will be to help your child survive. If you see your role as more of a guide, your goal will be to help your child thrive. Parents who see themselves as protectors tend to prevent their kids from making mistakes. They don't want anything bad to happen to them. Parents who view themselves as guides know that mistakes help kids learn. They're willing to let their children make their own way through the world and they don't try to define success for them.

No matter how you see your role, there are likely times when you've prevented your child from making mistakes, either because you wanted to spare yourself pain or you wanted to spare your child. Spend some time thinking about the types of mistakes that could have been learning opportunities.

Consider how you might respond to the following scenarios:

- Your six-year-old steps out of her bedroom wearing an outfit that doesn't match. It's bright enough and bold enough that it will definitely attract some attention. Do you let her wear it to school or do you help her find something else to wear?
- Your ten-year-old proudly shows you his science-fair project. It's supposed to be a volcano but it looks like a large blob and it doesn't actually erupt. Do you let him use that project or do you help him build a better volcano?
- Your fifteen-year-old introduces her new friend to you. You've heard about this girl from other parents and she's known for being disrespectful to parents and teachers. Do you tell your teen she can't see this new friend outside of school or do you let them hang out?

You know your child best, so there isn't always a clear right answer for how to respond. But it's essential to be aware of the reasons behind your choices and to ask yourself, "Is this best for my child in the long term?"

PREVENT HARMFUL MISTAKES

Of course, not all mistakes make good teachers. There are times when you should step in and prevent your child from making mistakes that could be really harmful to himself or to other people.

Here are three types of mistakes you should prevent:

1. **Mistakes that pose a safety risk**—If your toddler is getting too close to the edge of the pool, don't let him learn his lesson the hard way. Intervene before he falls. Similarly, don't turn a blind eye when your teenager is smoking, drinking, or speeding in hopes that he'll learn his lesson. He could die from his mistakes before he ever learns.

2. **Mistakes that are harmful to other people**—If your child says he's going to announce to certain kids that they didn't get invited to his birthday party, don't let him do it. Similarly, if you see or hear that your teen is posting provocative or offensive comments on Facebook, intervene.

3. **Mistakes that won't teach your child a lesson**—If your child doesn't experience any negative consequences, he likely won't view his behavior as a mistake. But just because something turned out well doesn't mean it's a good idea. If he jumped off a bridge and didn't get hurt, he may think he should do it again. Explain that just because it turned out okay doesn't mean it was a good idea.

RESIST THE URGE TO INTERFERE

The strangest encounter I've ever had with a helicopter parent wasn't in my therapy office or even in the college where I teach. It was through my work as a writer.

I was writing an article for *Forbes*, which coincidentally was titled "10 CEOs Offer Their Best Advice for Turning Mistakes into Learning Opportunities." I reached out to several CEOs who gave me their words of wisdom. But before I finished the article, I wanted tips from a few more business owners.

So I put out a general query inviting CEOs to send me their best tips. One tip was from a young adult named Mark who said he was the CEO of a clothing company he'd started. His tip was a bit redundant compared to the others I received, so I set it aside. A few days later, I received an e-mail I'll never forget. It said, "Mark hasn't heard back from you yet about being included in your *Forbes* article. So I'm adding some more tips in case his advice wasn't what you were looking for." It was from Mark's mother.

On the one hand, this young man was trying to portray himself as a competent CEO. And at the same time his mother was sending the message that he was so incompetent that she had to go behind his back to prevent him from becoming a failure.

Although Mark's case was an extreme example, many parents do similar things with their children by correcting their homework every day. And while it's healthy to support your child's academic efforts, most parents aren't just pointing out mistakes—they're fixing them because they can't stand the thought of their children going to school with mistakes on their papers.

Fixing your child's mistakes shows that you're more concerned with her grade than with her ability to learn. And it can lead kids to believe that success is defined by their final grade or the score of the game, regardless of what they learned in the process.

The teacher doesn't want to know what *you* can do. Teachers need to know what information your child retains and understands, so don't prevent your child from going to school with a few wrong answers sometimes. Also, ask yourself, do you work best when your boss is standing over your shoulder pointing out each error you make? Or do you prefer time to review your work in privacy before sharing it with others?

While some kids need a lot of support to stay on task, most kids need a little space. And giving them a little freedom with their work can be good for your relationship. Rather than being seen as the nitpicky supervisor with big demands, you could become the supportive boss who offers guidance.

TURN MISTAKES INTO LEARNING OPPORTUNITIES

Twelve-year-old Connor kept getting into trouble at school for fighting. But his father was more concerned about the school's discipline policy than about teaching Connor how to handle conflict better. He arranged for school meetings, wrote letters, and ranted about his dislike of the principal on social media. When the school recommended Connor seek therapy, his father agreed. But his intention was to use Connor's therapy time as an opportunity to complain about the school. He asked questions like "Do you think a suspension is really fair?" And he'd tell me about a teacher's behavior and ask, "Doesn't that sound like the teacher was provoking Connor on purpose?"

He never once asked how to help Connor manage his anger better. Instead of teaching him socially appropriate ways to solve problems, Connor's father was teaching him that the school was an unfair place. It was no wonder the boy's behavior was getting worse, not better.

I see this type of thing from parents often. They put their energy into the wrong place. Rather than teach their child an important lesson, they become a fierce advocate. It can be hard to hear negative feedback about your child. But getting defensive and taking criticism personally isn't helpful. And it won't help your child learn.

I've worked with parents who have tried to convince the school administration to let their daughter into the talent show even though she messed up in the audition. And I worked with a father who went to court to fight his daughter's speeding ticket, even though she was driving twenty miles an hour over the speed limit.

While advocating for your child can be healthy, it's also important for your child to face consequences when he makes a mistake. If you constantly bail him out, you'll be doing him a disservice. Teach your child that mistakes are inevitable, and that while they may have consequences, each outcome offers an opportunity to learn.

How to Teach Kids About Mistakes

Taylor's mother, Maria, had to give Taylor skills that would help her rebound from mistakes. She had to teach her that making mistakes wasn't horrible and she could take steps to deal with them and learn from them.

With practice and guidance, Taylor learned to make healthy decisions for herself. When she made a poor choice or when her decisions didn't turn out well, she learned that it wasn't a disaster and she could continue to work toward her goals.

Teach your child that he's mentally strong enough to face his mistakes head-on. Teach him to admit his blunders and move forward as best he can.

DEBRIEF WITH YOUR CHILD

It's easy to say things like "Great job in your recital" or "Your science-fair project turned out great," and then move on with your day. But the conversations you have with kids about the events in their lives can help them learn more than the events themselves. Research shows that reviewing events sparks learning, regardless of their outcome. So it's important to invest time into making your child's choices a learning activity. This is how to make those debriefings effective:

When your child succeeds: Discuss areas where he can improve. Recognizing mistakes is key to challenging him to do better next time. But make sure you also congratulate him on what he did well. Focusing too much on his mistakes could backfire.

When your child fails: It doesn't matter whether you talk about the positive or the negative. What matters is that you talk about it. So ask your child what he learned and how he thinks he did. Although talking may be the last thing your child wants to do when he messes up, debriefing is what turns a failed venture into a learning opportunity.

Rather than point out your child's mistakes, ask him to review his performance. See if he's pleased with how he did and see if you can help him discover ways to do even better next time. Here's an example:

Parent: I could tell you tried really hard during the basketball game. How do you think you did?

Child: I think I did a good job.

Parent: What do you think you specifically did well?

Child: I got four points and I played really good defense.

Parent: I noticed you were really working hard on defense. Are there any things you want to do differently next time or things you want to work on to get even better?

Child: Well, I missed both my foul shots and I forgot one of the plays.

Parent: How do you think you could improve those things?

Child: I can practice my foul shots more in the backyard. And maybe I can go over the plays with you on a piece of paper to see if I can remember them all.

Teach your child to celebrate learning opportunities, whether he met his goal or not. Challenge him to strive for improvement no matter what, while also showing him that he should be proud of his effort, as long as he did his best.

TALK ABOUT YOUR FAILURES

Kids love to hear stories about failure and mistakes, so talk about the mistakes you made as a child or the times you messed up. Discuss how you recovered from your mistakes and why it was okay that you weren't perfect.

Whether you scored a goal for the wrong team or you were eliminated during the first round of the spelling bee, share those early memories. But make sure the story doesn't have a disastrous outcome like "and that one bad grade is why I never got accepted into Harvard." Instead say things like "I felt really bad at the time. But in the end, it wasn't a big deal" or "I realize now it wouldn't have really mattered if I had won the science fair. What mattered most was that I did my best."

And share stories of recent mistakes too. Say, "I shook hands with someone today and called him by the wrong name by mistake," or "I forgot about that meeting I wanted to go to tonight. I'm going to have to start keeping better track of my schedule." Show your child that you continue to be a work in progress and you're comfortable knowing that you won't ever be perfect.

Teach Preschoolers to Let Their Imaginations Run Wild

Preschoolers are excited to learn and explore and it can be tempting to try to speed up that learning by constantly correcting a child's mistakes. But intervening too much can squash your child's imagination and creativity. I see this quite often when kids play with the toys on my office floor.

Some parents can't stand to see a child put the bathtub on the roof of the dollhouse. They'll say, "No, the bathtub goes in the bathroom." Or if their child is coloring an elephant purple, they'll say, "No, elephants are gray, not purple. Here, use this crayon instead." But these things aren't mistakes. They're just examples of a preschooler's vivid imagination. And let's face it, kids are much more creative than most of us adults.

It's likely your child knows elephants are gray and bathtubs go in the bathroom anyway—at least in the adult world—so there's no need to turn playtime into mandatory lessons. There are no mistakes in imaginary play. It's okay to play with magical unicorns, people who can fly, and colorful animals who can talk. Facilitate learning and language by simply saying what your child is doing. Almost as if you're a radio announcer, say, "You're putting the horse on the boat. And look at that, the pig is watching TV in the barn."

For the most part, the mistakes you should be correcting during the preschool years should be focused on safety and social skills. Prevent your child from running into the road and correct her when she says something that could hurt someone else's feelings.

Let your preschooler do things that are tough for her to do. Even though she might spill the milk or put her shoes on the wrong feet, making those mistakes help her learn.

Teach School-Age Kids to Be Critical Thinkers

There used to be a widely held belief that we shouldn't let kids make mistakes because the wrong answer would be etched into their brains forever and they'd have trouble learning the right answer. So rather than ask the class, "What's 5 + 5?" the teacher would say, "5 + 5 = 10." But research shows the opposite is true. Kids remember more when they've been given an opportunity to retrieve an answer on their own. Even if they come up with the wrong answer, they'll be more likely to remember the correct answer at a later date.

Giving kids the answers impairs their ability to learn. Whether your child is working on his math homework or he's trying to fix his bicycle, letting him make a few mistakes is good for him. He needs to be challenged to do things on his own so he can develop crucial skills, like critical thinking and problem solving. So take a step back when your child doesn't know the answer. And remember that just because he asks you to help doesn't mean it's a good idea to assist.

Encourage him to try again or say, "Try to figure it out on your own first." Show him that you really want him to try, even if he doesn't get it right.

Pose questions back at him when he encounters problems. Here's an example:

Child: Mom, I was going to wear the red shirt that goes with these shorts but my shirt is in the laundry.

Parent: So what do you think you should do?

Child: I don't know.

Parent: Well, I bet you can think of some ideas.

Child: I could wear a different shirt, I guess. Or I could put on my jeans and wear my orange button-up shirt.

Parent: Oh, the orange shirt and jeans sound like a great choice.

Rushing in and giving advice prevents your child from learning how to solve problems. Let him identify a few solutions on his own. Then, when necessary, provide guidance, but remember it's okay to let him make a few mistakes along the way.

Teach Teens to Fight the Societal Pressure to Appear Perfect

Teens experience a tug-of-war relationship between the desire to fit in and the need to stand out. Many of them experience pressure to mask their mistakes and imperfections, fearing they'll be judged harshly. This idea that you should look beautiful, have a jam-packed social calendar, and be a star athlete often plays out on social media.

While you don't want your teen to air her dirty laundry on social media, make it clear that she can admit her mistakes. And sometimes being able to laugh at herself can help her see that a few blunders aren't likely to be all that life-altering.

Posting a picture of herself sweating, with a caption that says, "Oops, shouldn't have worn a sweatshirt on such a hot day," or sharing an image of her scraped knee with a note that says, "Perhaps high heels aren't always a good idea," could help her see that it's okay to acknowledge her mistakes. In fact, her peers are likely to be attracted to that type of transparency.

Hold regular conversations with your child about the importance of being authentic. Talk about how some people try to mask their weaknesses or cover up their mistakes, and point out how doing so can interfere with their ability to have genuine relationships. You can also point out famous failures. Talk about people like Thomas Edison. Although he's famous for his inventions that worked out, he invented many things that were dismal failures. He reportedly once said, "I have not failed ten thousand times—I've successfully found ten thousand ways that will not work."

Similarly, Walt Disney failed many times before Disney World became a success. Many of his cartoons, like Mickey Mouse, were rejected for years and few of his ideas were popular. Look for more examples of sports figures, entrepreneurs, musicians, and other historical figures who successfully recovered from their mistakes.

Kids Who Learn from Mistakes Become Wise Adults

Raised in Minnesota, my husband, Steve, played hockey as a child. One day, when he was in the third grade, he came home from practice and said, "Pop, I didn't even fall down once!" His father, Rob, responded by saying, "Well, I guess you weren't pushing yourself very hard, then." That helped Steve see from an early age that mistakes weren't bad. Instead they served as proof he was trying to reach his greatest potential.

Rob also taught Steve's sister, Cari, that mistakes weren't all that bad. When she graduated to a "big-girl" bed, her parents were thrilled. But Cari was terrified she might fall out. Rather than put rails on the bed or reassure her she wouldn't fall out, Rob held "falling-out-of-bed practice."

He lined the floor with pillows and had Cari practice rolling out of bed on purpose. That exercise taught her that if she mistakenly rolled out of bed, she'd be okay.

When you let your child make a mistake, you give him an opportunity to build mental strength. Making a mistake stirs up uncomfortable emotions and can lead to negative thinking and unproductive behavior. But it can also be your child's opportunity to get back up and try again. By giving your child enough guidance when he makes mistakes, you'll teach him how to turn those mistakes into valuable life lessons that he'll carry into adulthood.

Mentally strong people don't repeat the same mistakes over and over again. They acknowledge their missteps and learn from them. Then, they take their new knowledge and move forward, better than before.

Troubleshooting and Common Traps

While it's important to send the message that it's okay to make mistakes, it's also important not to let your child get off the hook for misbehavior by saying, "Oops, sorry. I didn't mean to." Clearly, there's a big difference between accidentally stepping on your toe and pushing his brother down the stairs. Differentiate between mistakes and deliberate violations. And don't let your child grow up thinking that apologies always fix mistakes. Sometimes mistakes can cause irreversible damage to relationships or people's lives.

Sometimes it's tempting to stay focused on mistakes that relate to competitive activities like academics or athletics. A failing grade or a lost game can clearly signal room for improvement. But many mistakes are social errors and teaching your child how to recognize and recover from those mistakes is crucial.

Talk to your child about interactions with other kids. When you go to the playground, host a birthday party, or attend a family function, debrief after those events.

Point out mistakes that hurt other people's feelings. And remember that it's not always what your child *does* that is a mistake. It can also be what he *doesn't* do. Not including a child in a game or not stepping in when another child is getting picked on are mistakes you should address as well.

Another common trap is the I-told-you-so phenomenon. If your child won't wear a jacket, don't say, "I told you it was cold," when he comes back inside to put on another layer. Instead ask him what he noticed or what he learned from the experience, or what he might do differently next time, but don't rub it in. Reminding him that you were right and he was wrong emphasizes the mistake. You want your child to learn from the experience, not feel shameful because of it.

Finally, make sure your child isn't growing dependent on you to fix her mistakes. I've seen kids scurry through their assignments because they're certain their parents will let them know if they've made any careless mistakes. They lose their incentive to look for their own mistakes before they turn in their work. So rather than assure your child you're going to fix things, ask him, "Are you sure you've checked your work?" and let him look for the mistakes.

WHAT'S HELPFUL

- Knowing the types of mistakes you should prevent
- Establishing consequences when your child won't learn from the natural consequences of a mistake
- Recognizing the difference between a mistake and a deliberate violation
- Debriefing with your child about his successes and failures
- Teaching your child to turn mistakes into learning opportunities
- Talking about your mistakes and giving your child examples of famous failures
- Viewing your role as a guide

WHAT'S NOT HELPFUL

- Letting your child fail without appropriate guidance
- Focusing on the outcome rather than the learning process
- Preventing mistakes to fast-track your child's path to success
- Sending the message that mistakes are bad
- Viewing your role as a protector

They Don't Confuse
Discipline with
Punishment

Jeff and Heidi brought their eleven-year-old son, Dylan, to therapy because they were exasperated with his behavior. Although he'd always been a handful, his defiance intensified as he grew older. And now he refused to listen and he seemed unaffected by consequences.

Jeff and Heidi were so eager to offer examples of Dylan's bad behavior that they talked over one another. They said Dylan refused to do chores, argued about bedtime, and constantly fought with his brother. Heidi said, "Here's an example from just earlier today. He spilled his grape juice on the carpet. He's not supposed to have drinks in the living room. So rather than ask for help cleaning it up, he just pushed the chair over the stain."

As soon as she was finished with her example, Jeff chimed in to say, "And yesterday I told him not to get up from the table until he was finished with his homework. I turned my back for one minute and he went into his brother's room and tried to take one of his handheld video games. I caught him before he had a chance to steal it."

Whenever he misbehaved, they took away something he liked and said he could have it back once he proved that he could "be good." But he never

*behaved long enough to earn anything back. So slowly, every privilege disap-
peared. "He has a bed and some blankets in his room, but that's about it at
this point. We had to take everything else away," Jeff explained. Dylan wasn't
allowed to use any electronics and he was grounded from seeing his friends
outside of school.*

*Heidi said, "We used to spank him but he's getting a little big for that, so
we don't know what else to do." Jeff chimed in and said, "My father used to
use the belt on me. I keep telling him he's lucky I don't do that to him. But I
might have to if he doesn't straighten out."*

*Dylan stared silently at the floor the entire time his parents talked. To
get him involved in the discussion, I asked him if he ever got into trouble at
school and he said, "Not really." Heidi said he occasionally got spoken to by
the teacher for talking during class and he had to stay in for recess a few times
because his work wasn't done, but he never required any serious disciplinary
action. I asked Heidi and Jeff why they thought he behaved so well in school
and Heidi said, "I guess he likes school, so he behaves for the teachers."*

*After a thorough assessment, I explained to Jeff and Heidi that Dylan
didn't have depression, anxiety, ADHD, or any other mental health problems. And at first, they were disappointed. They wanted to discover an underlying issue or "root cause" to his behavior. But I explained to them that
the good news was, a few tweaks to their parenting practices were likely all it
would take to turn his behavior around. And they were desperate enough to
try just about anything, so they agreed.*

*The fact that he behaved well at school showed he possessed the skills he
needed to manage his behavior in a structured environment. So the plan to
change Dylan's behavior didn't involve his participation in therapy. After all,
I wasn't going to talk him into following his parents' rules. But I could work
with his parents to help motivate him to behave.*

There were two main problems I wanted to address:

1. **Dylan had little incentive to follow the rules.** His parents took
   everything away from him and they weren't clear on what he
   needed to do to earn his things back. So he'd given up trying.

2. **Heidi and Jeff had a negative view of Dylan and that was affecting their parenting.** They labeled him as a "bad kid," so they expected him to misbehave all the time.

And there were three things I recommended they do to address those problems:

1. **Spend quality time with Dylan.** At first, they insisted they weren't going to play games or do fun things with him because he couldn't behave. But I suggested they spend positive time with him so he would be motivated to behave. Just fifteen minutes per day of their undivided attention playing catch or board games could improve his behavior.
2. **Catch Dylan being good.** I encouraged them to praise any good behavior they saw, no matter how small it might seem. Then, for extra reinforcement, they should say nice things about Dylan to one another or to Grandma or anyone else when Dylan was listening. If he could overhear his parents saying he was behaving well, he'd be extra motivated to keep up the good work.
3. **Give Dylan a fresh start every day.** To help Dylan stay motivated, he needed to know he could earn privileges each day. If he had a good day at school, he could watch TV. Or if he got his homework done, he could earn time to play on the computer.

Heidi and Jeff had expected they would need harsher punishments that would really "teach Dylan a lesson." But changing their interactions with him and using discipline, instead of punishment, helped turn his behavior around.

Jeff thought that the positive attention they had been giving Dylan was the most effective intervention of all. Many of Dylan's behavior problems stemmed from his attempts to gain their attention (even though it was negative). As soon as they started to give him daily doses of attention, he acted out less.

Slowly, Heidi and Jeff gained confidence in Dylan's ability to make better choices. And once they had confidence he could follow the rules, Dylan gained confidence in himself.

Do You Give out Harsh Punishments?

It's important to give your child effective consequences when she breaks the rules. But handing out harsh punishments can backfire. Do you respond positively to any of the following statements?

- ○ I try to shame my child into behaving.
- ○ I focus on trying to control my child rather than teaching him to control himself.
- ○ I have a zero-tolerance policy for misbehavior.
- ○ I punish bad behavior much more than I reward good behavior.
- ○ I frequently tell my child, "Because I said so!" when he asks the reasons behind my rules.
- ○ I don't trust my child to make good choices.
- ○ My child lies to get out of trouble.
- ○ I use physical punishment as my main form of discipline.
- ○ I think making my child suffer for misbehavior is the best way to teach him to do better.
- ○ When I'm angry I say or do things to my child that I later regret.

Why Parents Confuse Discipline and Punishment

Heidi and Jeff thought they had to give out harsh punishments to get Dylan to improve his behavior. The worse his behavior became, the harsher their punishments. And they got caught in a vicious cycle that seemed impossible to break.

Finding consequences that teach as opposed to consequences that punish can be tricky sometimes. When you struggle to recognize the difference, however, you're likely to make things worse.

PARENTS BELIEVE PUNISHMENTS WORK BEST

Almost every day I hear parents say things like "You can't discipline kids anymore" or "This is what's wrong with the world. You can't punish kids without getting into trouble." Perhaps you hear those things too. Or maybe you're one of those individuals who say those things. I agree that many of today's kids aren't getting nearly enough discipline. But I don't think the solution is harsher discipline. I think it's more of the right kind of discipline.

There's a big difference between punishment and discipline. Discipline is about training and teaching your child in a way that prepares him for the future. Punishment, however, is about inflicting a penalty that causes suffering.

Punishments focus on the mistake. They serve to make a child feel bad about his wrongdoing. Discipline, on the other hand, teaches him to do better next time.

Punishments may be physical, like slapping, spanking, or paddling. But punishment can also be verbal—like screaming, swearing, or name-calling.

Public humiliation or shame also falls into the punishment category. Announcing on Facebook that your child got all F's on his report card to embarrass him constitutes punishment.

PUNISHMENTS SOMETIMES STEM FROM DESPERATION

When an alligator snatched a two-year-old boy at a Walt Disney World beach in the spring of 2016, people around the world weighed in on whether the boys' parents were "bad parents." Parents who just lost their child in a horrible accident were villainized by people who insisted they'd never be "neglectful" like those parents. That news story came on the heels of the incident in which a child fell into a gorilla enclosure at the Cincinnati Zoo. Sadly, the gorilla was killed by zoo keepers who feared the child could be killed by the animal. The child escaped the incident without any serious injuries.

As video of the incident went viral, social media became flooded with comments about the parents' "poor parenting." Even though little information was known about the minutes leading up to the incident—like where the parents were in relation to the child or how the child fell—people began demanding the parents be charged with a crime. Even after investigators declared the parents weren't going to be charged with child endangerment or any other crime, they remained guilty in the eyes of public opinion.

News stories like these speak volumes about the type of world we live in. The Internet seems to give some people an open invitation to judge parents in a public forum. This type of judgment causes parents to feel like they're constantly being scrutinized. If your child throws a tantrum in the middle of the grocery store, what must other people think about your parenting? Or if he becomes disrespectful when you try to offer some words of advice at his baseball game, what will the other parents think? Instead of taking the time to teach a child to control herself, desperate parents sometimes seek to control her through whatever means they deem necessary.

PUNISHMENTS CAN BE TEMPTING TO USE

Instilling fear and inflicting pain can serve as short-term solutions. Unfortunately, punishments also tend to cause more long-term problems. But for parents who are only invested in getting their child to listen right now or be quiet this second, punishments can work.

Here are some common reasons why parents prefer punishment over discipline:

- **Punishments take less effort on the parent's part.** Spanking your child takes maybe twenty seconds of your time. But taking away electronics for twenty-four hours might mean you have to deal with a bored child for the rest of the day.

- **Punishments make some parents feel more in control.** If you can keep your child in line, whether it's with an intimidating look or a quick swat, you might feel empowered.
- **Punishments may make you feel better.** Screaming at your child because you're frustrated he won't quiet down or spanking him for embarrassing you in the middle of the grocery store might relieve some of your pent-up emotions.

Confusing Discipline and Punishment Could Be Bad for Your Child's Self-Worth

As Heidi and Jeff began handing out harsher punishments with Dylan, their relationship with him deteriorated and Dylan lost interest in trying to follow their rules. They were frustrated and overwhelmed by his noncompliance, but the punitive environment was making his behavior worse.

I see many cases like Dylan's parents—situations where parents feel desperate to force a child to behave. But I also see less dire situations that still involve harsh punishment. Even when those punishments are few and far between, they can still cause damage to children.

CORPORAL PUNISHMENT CAN BACKFIRE

In 1979, Sweden became the first country to ban physical punishment of children. At first, opponents argued that the country was going to end up in complete chaos as children wouldn't be able to learn appropriate behavior. But as the first generation of children grew up, there wasn't a rise in crime. In fact, theft convictions and drug-related crimes actually decreased. Alcohol use and youth suicide decreased as well.

Following Sweden, many other countries also banned physical punishments of children. Yet in the United States, spanking remains legal. In fact, nineteen states still allow school officials to paddle kids for misbehavior. In other states, hitting a child with a wooden object is considered child abuse. There isn't a clear line, however, that separates corporal punishment from physical abuse. Can a mother's boyfriend spank her kids? Can you hit your child with a belt? Is it okay to leave marks? Some states clearly outline what's acceptable, while others leave it open to interpretation.

Many cultural and religious differences influence whether parents spank. But I think almost all experts would agree, hitting your child because you can't control your temper isn't okay.

The American Academy of Pediatrics, the American Academy of Child and Adolescent Psychiatry, and the American Psychological Association are just a few of the major organizations that oppose physical punishments for kids. Multiple studies, including a fifty-year study by the University of Texas at Austin, found:

- **Spanking increases aggression.** Kids who are spanked are more likely to solve problems with aggression.
- **Spanking makes behavior problems worse.** Although spanking may seem to work in the short term, studies show it isn't effective in the long term. Behavior problems increase over time when kids are subjected to physical discipline.
- **Spanking has been linked to a lower IQ.** The more often children were spanked, the slower their development. But even children who are spanked infrequently are likely to have lower IQs.
- **Harsh punishment has been associated with an increased risk of mental illness.** Kids who are subjected to physical punishment are at a greater risk of mood disorders, anxiety disorders, personality disorders, and substance abuse issues. That increased risk starts in childhood and extends into adulthood.

Of all the studies that have been conducted on spanking, very few have found any benefits. A 2005 study published in the *Clinical Child and*

Family Psychology Review did find that occasionally spanking children between the ages of two and six when they refuse to go to time-out is more effective than other strategies. Placing a child in forced isolation for one minute was also found to be effective. But just because it was effective in the moment doesn't mean it made kids immune to the long-term effects of physical punishment.

YELLING CAN BE HARMFUL TOO

There are some parents who pride themselves on saying, "I've never hit my kids." But some of those parents yell and swear at their kids instead.

Research shows that harsh verbal discipline, such as cursing, yelling, and insulting your child, can be just as harmful as spanking. A 2013 study from the University of Pittsburgh followed 967 middle school students for two years. The kids who were subjected to harsh verbal discipline were more likely to have behavior problems and mental health issues.

Additionally, the researchers found yelling wasn't effective. Kids continued to misbehave. Even when they lived in homes that were generally loving and warm, the harsh words were damaging their motivation to follow the rules.

HARSH DISCIPLINE TURNS KIDS INTO GOOD LIARS

"She lies so much she doesn't even know when she's telling the truth anymore!" an irritated mother explained to me. She said her ten-year-old daughter, Olivia, lied all the time. "She'll say, 'No, I didn't eat the cupcake,' even when she's got frosting all over her face." The previous week, when her parents confronted her about her messy bedroom, she said burglars must have broken into the house and messed it up because she had cleaned it before she went to school. "Can you believe that?" her father exclaimed.

Olivia was so sneaky and deceitful that her parents never trusted anything she said. They were at a loss about what to do with her.

As I learned about their discipline practices, however, it became clear why Olivia wasn't telling the truth. Her parents had bad tempers. They yelled and screamed when they were angry. And in the past, they'd spanked Olivia when she was acting out.

They were inconsistent too. They'd take away her TV one day and make her do extra chores the next. Once, when Olivia said she was cleaning her room—but instead she was actually watching movies—her father got so mad he took her bedroom door off its hinges. And he never put it back on.

It was no wonder Olivia lied. Who on earth would want to tell their parents, "Hey, I messed up today," if there was a good chance Dad might take your door of the hinges? Olivia knew the difference between telling the truth and telling a lie, but honesty only led to serious punishments. So she'd learned that the best way to try and avoid the wrath of her parents was to tell a lie.

A 2011 study by McGill University found that kids who are subjected to harsh discipline lie more than other kids. And they become remarkably good at lying. By age three or four, they're able to tell sophisticated lies in an attempt to stay out of trouble. That means harsh punishment causes kids to take less responsibility for their misbehavior rather than more. They invest more energy into trying to avoid getting caught than trying to change their behavior.

PUBLIC HUMILIATION CAUSES KIDS TO FEEL BAD ABOUT WHO THEY ARE

There's a disturbing new trend among parents looking for strategies to get kids to behave—shaming them into submission. And many parents are turning to social media in hopes public humiliation will teach their children a lesson.

A California mother punished her preteen daughter by forcing her to stand on the street corner holding a sign that read I WAS DISRESPECTING MY PARENTS BY TWERKING AT MY SCHOOL DANCE. There was also the

Colorado mother who learned her thirteen-year-old daughter was posing as a nineteen-year-old on Facebook. She recorded herself confronting her daughter, and in the video, got her daughter to admit she still watches the Disney Channel. The mother then posted the video on social media.

Other parents have started shaming kids with bad haircuts. There's even a barber in Georgia who offers the "Benjamin Button Special," a haircut designed to make misbehaving kids look like old men.

It's interesting that so many parents who worry about the harmful effects of bullying end up bullying their own children. And just as it does when a child is bullied by peers, being bullied by a parent can have tragic consequences.

Obviously, these are extreme examples. But many parents do these things to a lesser extent by posting a picture of a child's messy bedroom on Instagram or by announcing a child's misbehavior on Facebook. A quick YouTube search for the phrase "child shaming" yields over 140,000 videos of parents making children hold up signs that say things like I'M A BULLY.

Publicly humiliating a child can cause serious psychological damage. And it could actually make behavior problems worse. Imagine two kids are faced with an opportunity to try drugs. One kid feels good about himself and the other kid thinks he's a bad person. Which one do you think is more likely to have enough respect for himself to say no?

Clearly, shaming your child damages your relationship too. Your child will view you as the mean ogre who inflicts pain and torture. Wouldn't you rather have a child who respects your opinion?

What to Do Instead

Heidi and Jeff had to interrupt the negative pattern they'd gotten into with Dylan. After spending more quality time with them, Dylan became more inclined to follow their rules. It only took a few small changes for them to start seeing really big behavior changes.

A slight shift in your approach to parenting can make a big difference to your child's behavior and to your relationship. The good news is, it's never too late to start using more effective discipline strategies.

ASSESS YOUR SKILLS AS A LEADER

Think about the worst supervisor or boss you've ever worked for. Perhaps you had a horrible boss when you landed your first job in high school. Or maybe the boss you work for now isn't so great. Spend a few minutes thinking about what made that person a bad leader. Take out a piece of paper and list all the descriptive words you can come up with, such as "rude," "inconsistent," or "demanding."

When you're done compiling your list, turn that piece of paper over. Now think about the best supervisor you've ever had. Perhaps you had a boss who was understanding and kind. Or maybe you worked for someone who was encouraging and motivating. Identify as many descriptive words as you can.

When you're done with both lists, think about how each of those supervisors affected the way you worked. Under which one did you perform at your peak? Then take a minute to think about which list describes how you parent your child. How many of the items from the "bad boss" list might be used to describe you? And how many items from the "good boss" list would your child say sound like you?

Whether it's in the office or in the home, good leaders inspire people to do their best work. If you are a good leader for your child, you'll bring out the best in him. But if your leadership style is lacking, he'll be less motivated to follow your directions.

ESTABLISH CLEAR RULES

Imagine what it would be like to drive around without any speed-limit signs. If you go too fast, you'll get pulled over by the police and ignorance about the speed limit won't excuse you from the penalties.

Having to guess the speed limit would be ridiculous, right? But that's what we do to kids quite often. We expect them to figure out the rules through observation. But the rules change depending on the situation. And that confuses kids.

Your four-year-old may struggle to understand why he can yell to his friend on the playground, but yelling to that same friend in the library causes you to leave early. And running up to Grandma to give her a hug is okay at home, but running to see her when she's in the hospital causes you to get mad.

When you're entering a new situation, make your expectations clear beforehand. Say, "At the library, we need to use walking feet and we need to talk in a whisper" or "In the airplane, we have to sit in our seats with our seat belts fastened and we have to use an inside voice."

Create clear household rules and hang them in a prominent location. Keep the rules simple—you don't want to create a two-hundred-page policy manual for your home.

Here are the five types of rules all kids need:

1. **Rules that promote morality.** Create rules such as "Tell the truth" and "Ask before taking anyone else's belongings."

2. **Rules that develop healthy habits.** Establish rules such as "Brush your teeth when you wake up and before you go to bed" and "Wash your hands before dinner." These types of rules give your child structure and build healthy habits into his daily routine.

3. **Rules that promote safety.** Rules should promote physical safety, such as "Wear a helmet when you ride your bike" as well as emotional safety, such as "Use kind words when you're talking to other people."

4. **Rules that encourage good social habits.** Create rules that help your child respect others by saying things such as "Knock on closed doors before entering" and "Wait until people are done talking before saying something."

5. **Rules that prepare kids for the real world.** Make rules that will equip your child to deal with the responsibilities of real life, such as "Twenty-five percent of your allowance needs to go into a savings

account" and "You can watch TV after you get your homework and chores done."

Make a list of household rules that apply to everyone in your home. Each child will likely have slightly different rules, in terms of curfew or bedtime and there's no need to list every little rule (unless you think it will really help your child). But make sure your child knows the consequences he can expect when he breaks the rules.

CREATE A SUPPORTIVE ENVIRONMENT

"I'll give him respect when he can show me some respect!" Rick exclaimed when I suggested he provide a little more nurturance and a lot less hostility toward his twelve-year-old son, Cameron. Rick and Cameron had been at odds for the last several months and their relationship had deteriorated to the point that they barely spoke to one another. Cameron was argumentative and defiant almost all the time and now they were at a standoff. Rick wasn't willing to budge until Cameron changed his behavior. But Cameron wasn't likely to change his behavior until Rick gave him a reason to do so.

My work with Rick didn't focus on giving Cameron harsher punishments. Instead it involved helping him show Cameron more love and empathy. At first, he was resistant to this because he didn't think the boy had earned it. But I showed him the research and challenged him to provide nurturance, which, in turn, gave Cameron motivation to change his behavior.

I see many parents who think demanding more respect and doling out harsher punishments will change a child's behavior. But that's not usually the case. In his book *Taking Charge of ADHD,* Russell Barkley shares the story of a teacher who used to say, "The kids who need the most love ask for it in the most unloving ways." Showing love and providing warmth can be the fastest and most effective ways to support your child's efforts in managing his behavior.

Studies link parental warmth to a variety of positive outcomes, such as helping kids develop a conscience. Additionally, when children have been exposed to extreme stress, warmth and affection reduce the psychological toll it can have on their lives.

Nurturing your relationship with your child should be the first step in any behavior management plan. Here's how you can show your child warmth:

- **Offer comfort.** Listen to your child when he's upset, give him a hug when he's having a rough time, and show empathy for him when he's feeling bad.
- **Encourage your child.** Cheer your child on when he's doing his best or when he's experiencing some self-doubt. Give him an optimistic voice when the voice inside his own head isn't positive.
- **Spend quality time together.** The only way to build and maintain a healthy relationship with your child is by spending quality time together. Go on adventures and engage in fun activities whenever you can.
- **Catch your child being good.** Don't just point out your child's mistakes and rule violations. Offer praise and positive reinforcement for good behavior.

When your child knows that your love isn't contingent upon his good behavior and he knows home is a safe place to tell the truth, your discipline will be much more effective. He'll be open to learning from the consequences you give him.

USE DISCIPLINE THAT TEACHES LIFE LESSONS

Andy lived with his wife and their three children. He worked hard so his wife could be a stay-at-home mom. And even though he was exhausted from his physically demanding job when he arrived home at night, he knew his wife needed a break when he walked through the door. So he devoted his evenings to playing with the kids, bathing them, and reading to them. He started counseling because his oldest son had some behavior problems and he wanted to learn how to help him. It was important to him that he do everything he could to be the best father possible.

I'd only been working with him for a few weeks when he expressed increased frustration about his son's behavior. None of his discipline practices seemed to work. He said, "Just this week I gave him a two-hour lecture about why he needs to be more respectful to his mother. When I got done, I asked him what he learned. He said, 'I learned that a vein pops out on your forehead when you get really mad.'"

When you give kids developmentally inappropriate consequences—like lecturing an eight-year-old for two hours—their behavior won't change. Similarly, when you hand out severe punishments, your child may only focus on his anger toward you, not on the mistake that he made.

Use discipline tools that will teach your child how to make a better choice next time. So rather than slap him for hitting his brother, look at his misbehavior as an opportunity to teach him something new. Time-out can teach him how to calm himself down when he's upset. Restitution, such as loaning his brother his favorite toy for twenty-four hours, can help him learn how to make amends.

Ask your child, "What could you do next time instead of hitting your brother?" or "What can you do to help yourself be patient when you're waiting for your turn?" Make sure your child has the skills he needs to manage his behavior better. If you've never taught him how to communicate in a healthy way or how to manage his anger safely, he'll continue to struggle, despite whatever consequences you give him.

How to Teach Kids to Make Good Choices

In the case of Dylan and his punitive parents, he needed an incentive to behave. A few changes to their parenting practices were all it took to turn his behavior around.

Make sure your discipline is an effective teaching tool. Invest time and energy into helping your child learn better ways to behave and you won't need to invest as much energy into dealing with punishments later on.

TEACH SELF-DISCIPLINE

Rather than insist on controlling your child, give him the tools he needs to control himself. Teach him how to manage his behavior. When he has the skills to make good choices for himself, he'll be able to make healthy decisions, even when you're not there to oversee him. Ask your child, "How do you think you're doing lately when it comes to following the rules?" Have open conversations about his behavior. Provide feedback about what he's doing well and tell him what things you want to work on.

Here's an example:

Parent: I've noticed you've been a lot nicer to your brother lately. How do you think you've been doing?

Child: I think I've been doing pretty good. I haven't gotten into any fights with him.

Parent: How have you managed to do that? What's the secret to your success?

Child: Well, when he bugs me I just tell him to give me some space or I walk away.

Parent: Oh, that's a good idea to just take a break from him when you need one. I've noticed you've been doing a good job using your words to tell him when you're starting to get annoyed.

Child: Yes, I try to tell him when I'm mad so I don't end up hitting him.

Parent: That's great. There is another thing I think we should work on, though. In the morning, you seem to be having trouble being ready for school on time. You get distracted by things when you're supposed to be getting ready and then we all have to rush out the door at the last minute. How do you think we can work on that?

Child: I don't know.

Parent: I think I'll start setting a timer for you. Then you'll know when you have to be done eating breakfast and when you should be dressed. Do you think that would help?

Child: Probably.

Parent: Well, let's try that tomorrow morning. Then, if you get everything done on time, you'll have a few minutes to play with something before it's time to leave.

Child: Okay.

Sometimes, just telling a child that you're developing a new goal for him can help turn his behavior around. Ask him what he thinks could help him do better and you might be surprised by the creative and helpful ideas he offers.

Teach self-discipline by using consistent positive consequences and negative consequences. Provide positive reinforcement for a job well done. Effective positive consequences can include a high five, praise, or some extra attention. Simply acknowledging your child's good behavior and saying thank you can go a long way. Kids love it when you notice that they're on the right track and giving some recognition encourages them to keep up the good work.

There also needs to be consistent negative consequences for misbehavior. While taking away TV might be an effective consequence for one child, another child might not be affected by it at all. Consider what matters most to your child and which consequence could work best.

MOTIVATE YOUR CHILD WITH A REWARD SYSTEM

Sometimes children lack the intrinsic motivation to learn new skills or do their chores. Giving them incentives to do better can be the best way to improve their behavior. However, there's a long-standing myth in the field of psychology that says rewarding kids for good behaviors decreases their intrinsic motivation. In the absence of a carrot to motivate them, they won't care about doing the right thing.

But studies have proven that just isn't true. As long as you're rewarding your child in a healthy way, she will become more motivated to work hard.

Here are a few tips for making rewards effective:

- **Establish a specific goal.** Rather than telling a child he can earn a treat for "being good," pick a specific behavior, like keeping his hands to himself.
- **Choose one to three behaviors at a time.** For preschoolers, identify one behavior to address. School-age children may be able to work on two or three behaviors at a time.
- **Make the rewards clear.** Tell your child in advance what he is going to earn and make sure he has a clear understanding of how he can earn it.
- **Provide rewards on a consistent basis.** Younger children may need a reward every hour (like a sticker), while an older child may be able to wait a week to earn a reward. Create a schedule of rewards that keeps your child motivated and invested.
- **Help your child be successful early on.** If your child thinks it's too hard to earn a reward, he'll give up early. Make sure he has some initial success and then he'll be motivated to keep going.
- **Focus on the behavior you'd like to see more often.** Rather than saying, "No screaming," frame it in a positive manner by saying, "Use an inside voice." Then reward your child for exhibiting the good behavior.

- **Introduce the reward system as something positive.** Don't tell your child, "You can't play video games anymore unless you behave." Frame it in the positive by saying, "I want to help you get along with your brother better. When you treat him with respect, you'll earn time to play video games."

Here are a few examples of effective reward systems:

- A four-year-old earns a sticker each morning if she stays in her own bed all night.
- A six-year-old gets to choose a board game to play with his parents if he gets his homework done before dinner.
- An eight-year-old earns one hour of electronics time after school when he gets ready for the bus in the morning without arguing.
- A ten-year-old earns a trip to the park after he makes his bed for five days.
- A twelve-year-old earns tokens for respectful behavior that he can exchange for rewards, like a later bedtime on the weekends or going to a movie.

This doesn't mean you shouldn't still give your child consequences when he breaks the rules, but he'll break the rules less often when he knows there's a reward at stake. And keep in mind that rewards don't have to cost any money. You can make privileges, like electronics time, a reward for good behavior.

Teach Preschoolers to Behave Better with Time-Out

Time-out can be an effective way to teach preschoolers to man-age their behavior. If your child becomes aggressive or overstimulated, send him to a quiet hallway or room away from the activity. During a few minutes of quiet time, he can figure out how to settle himself down. Place him in time-out for one minute for each year of age. So while a three-year-old needs a three-minute time-out, a five-year-old can handle a five-minute time-out. Just let him know the timer won't start until he's quiet.

The ultimate goal of time-out is for your child to learn to recognize when he's becoming overwhelmed or overstimulated and to be able to take a break on his own before he gets into trouble. Time-outs only work with kids who are given plenty of time-in. Otherwise they won't be affected by a few minutes away from everyone. So make sure you're giving your child plenty of one-on-one attention throughout the day.

If your child refuses to go to time-out, take away a privilege. Don't physically force your child to go to time-out. Say, "If you don't go to time-out, you won't be able to play with your doll for the rest of the afternoon."

Teach School-Age Kids to Behave Better with Logical Consequences

Logical consequences relate directly to the misbehavior. So if your child hits his brother over the head with his plastic sword, take his sword away for twenty-four hours. Or, if you catch him creating a social media account after you told him he couldn't, take away his computer privileges.

Tell kids when and how they can earn their privileges back. Saying, "You can have it when I can trust you again," is too vague. Make your expectations crystal clear. Say something like "You can have your electronics back once you've completed those two extra chores I assigned" or "You can get your video games back when you get caught up on your homework assignments."

Here are some more examples of logical consequences:

- An eight-year-old throws a ball in the house and breaks a lamp. He has to do chores to earn the money to buy a new one.
- A nine-year-old misbehaves during a trip to the park, so you leave the park early.
- A ten-year-old borrows her sister's favorite toy without asking. She then has to lend her sister her favorite toy for twenty-four hours.
- An eleven-year-old rides his bike outside the neighborhood. He loses his bike-riding privileges for twenty-four hours.

Teach Teens Problem-Solving Skills

When your teen exhibits behavior problems, problem-solve together how to remedy the situation. This is especially important if your teen violates the same rule more than once. Ask for your teen's input about what you can do to address the problem. Say something like "This is the second time you've been late for school. What can we do to make sure you're getting out of bed and out the door on time?" Brainstorm potential solutions together, like setting an alarm sooner or going to sleep earlier.

Of course, you may still need to take away privileges to help your teen learn more responsibility. But encouraging her to develop solutions can motivate her to avoid making the same mistake next time. It will also prepare her to become more independent, so she can problem-solve issues on her own when you're not there to give her consequences.

Disciplined Kids Become Forward-Thinking Adults

As a therapeutic foster parent and a therapist, I am often given some of the most troubled foster kids. That was the case with Chloe. She was a thirteen-year-old who had been in foster care for years. She'd lived in too many homes to count and she'd been kicked out of every single one. Most of the placements she'd been in were kinship placements, meaning various relatives had offered to become her foster parents. But none of them were able to keep her for more than a few months at a time because of her behavior problems.

Steve and I had met Chloe once before she came to live with us. She'd been staying with some distant relatives who were overwhelmed by her behavior, and she came to our home for a weekend respite visit when her foster parents needed a break.

Chloe behaved well the weekend she stayed with us. We had an older child staying in our home at that time and Chloe got along with her great. In fact, she was the perfect houseguest. But a different Chloe emerged when her foster mother arrived to pick her up on Sunday evening. As soon as she walked through the door, Chloe went from calm, kind, and cooperative to defiant, mouthy, and argumentative in an instant.

Less than a month later, I received a phone call from Chloe's state-appointed guardian. She said it was no longer an option for Chloe to stay in her current foster home. The foster parents said she was out of control and she needed a place to stay—starting tonight. After I talked it over with Steve, we agreed to let Chloe move in. The plan was for her to stay with us on a fairly short-term basis. There was an out-of-state relative who wanted to take her, but the legal process involved would take several months.

So our goal was to help her improve her behavior now, in hopes that her next move could be a successful long-term placement. She needed a forever home.

We created a token economy system that would allow her to earn tokens for good behavior. Then the tokens could be exchanged for privileges and rewards.

We created three daily goals based on behavior that she usually struggled with:

1. I'll use respectful language when I talk to people (she sometimes swore at people and called them names).
2. I'll use respectful touches only (she had a habit of hitting when she was mad).
3. I'll ask to borrow things rather than take anything without permission (she stole things sometimes).

At the end of each day, we'd review her behavior. For each goal she met, she could earn one token. That meant she could earn up to three tokens per day and twenty-one tokens per week.

Then we identified privileges and rewards she was interested in earning. We assigned each one a point value. Staying up an extra thirty minutes on a nonschool night, for example, was just one point. But going to her favorite restaurant was thirty points.

I wanted to make sure she could earn a daily reward if she wanted to, but I also wanted her to have the option to save up for bigger-ticket items. She offered input into what she thought the rewards should be worth—and she assigned pretty fair point values. But then she asked, "How many points do I have to get to see my brother?" Not only did the question break my heart but it showed me that time with family had probably been used as a punishment in the past.

I assured her that visiting with her brother (who lived in another foster home) wouldn't require any tokens—tokens would just be for extra privileges. We used some chips from a game that looked like coins and she collected them in a jar next to her bed. Every day she counted them and talked about what she wanted to earn.

Her behavior that summer was one of the most amazing transformations I'd ever seen. She earned every token possible—except for one. It seemed impossible to think she usually got kicked out of foster homes after only a few weeks.

The token system showed Chloe—and all the adults in her life—that with the right incentives, she could behave. She just needed a little extra motivation to stay on track. And many of the rewards she wanted to earn were things she probably got in her previous homes already—like time to use her electronics.

A few months later, Chloe moved in with that relative who had expressed interest in her. And eventually, that relative adopted both Chloe and her brother.

When you focus on teaching your child how to do better, rather than inflicting pain for mistakes she made in the past, she'll have the tools she needs to reach her greatest potential. She'll gain confidence in her ability to make healthy choices and she'll strive to become better each day.

Mentally strong people don't dwell on the past. While they do reflect on it—so they can learn from it—they don't punish themselves for past mistakes. Instead, they keep their focus on doing better next time.

Troubleshooting and Common Traps

Insulting your child's character by labeling him a jerk, thief, or idiot can be quite damaging. When I address how name-calling can be harmful, some parents sarcastically ask, "Why, because I might damage his self-esteem?" But it's actually worse than that. Calling your child names will affect his core beliefs about himself.

Let's say you start calling your child stupid. Well, after a while, he'll start to believe that he *is* stupid. And a child who believes he's stupid won't perform well in school. Then, when he gets bad grades, his belief that he's stupid gets reinforced. It's a vicious downward spiral.

Avoid saying, "I'm so disappointed in you." Instead send a message that says, "I'm disappointed you made a bad choice." Show your child that you still love her in spite of her behavior.

Paying attention to your emotions and how they're likely to affect your decisions can help you make the best discipline choices for your child. When you're feeling good, you might have the energy to address certain behavior problems effectively. But on a day when you're tired, stressed out, and overwhelmed, you might be tempted to just let little behavior problems go until you eventually scream at your child to stop.

When you're annoyed, frustrated, and angry, it's an opportunity to role-model how to deal with those emotions in a healthy way. If you scream, spank, or make outrageous threats because you can't control your temper, you'll be teaching your child to do the same.

Take a self-time-out when you need one. Or if you're feeling too flustered by your child's behavior to even think of a consequence, say, "I'm going to tell you what your consequence is going to be in a few minutes." Then take some time to cool down so you can give an effective consequence.

Sometimes parents fall into the trap of making all of their discipline practices revolve around material possessions. Buying toys for good behavior and taking away toys for bad behavior places a lot of emphasis on material goods. Studies show placing too much emphasis on material goods may teach children to value their stuff. Materialistic adults are more likely to be compulsive spenders, have gambling problems, financial problems, and lower marital satisfaction. So while it is good practice to take away your child's bicycle or his electronics as a consequence, you should be careful that your child doesn't think those are the most important things in life. Look for consequences that involve experiences or extra work once in a while, like an earlier curfew or extra chores.

WHAT'S HELPFUL

- Being a good leader for your child
- Creating a loving environment
- Keeping your emotions in check
- Establishing clear rules
- Using positive consequences to encourage good behavior
- Providing negative consequences that teach self-discipline
- Using reward systems
- Ensuring that discipline is about teaching

WHAT'S NOT HELPFUL

- Inflicting suffering on your child
- Relieving your frustration and anger by yelling or punishing your child
- Using corporal punishment
- Trying to control your child rather than teaching him to control himself
- Taking away privileges indefinitely
- Using harsh punishments that demotivate your child

They Don't Take
Shortcuts to Avoid
Discomfort

Nicole called my office and said, "I'm not even sure which kid to bring in first. All three of them don't listen." I suggested she come in by herself so we could create a plan together. She agreed and she scheduled an appointment for the following week. She worked a part-time job and served as the primary caregiver for her three children, ages nine, seven, and four. Her husband, Brian, worked long hours and some days, the children were in bed before he got home.

Nicole spent her afternoons racing from sports practices to Boy Scouts. By the time they sat down to eat dinner together, everyone was exhausted. The boys argued with each other, her four-year-old threw tantrums, and no one listened to anything Nicole said. Then Nicole spent the rest of the evening struggling to get the kids to do their homework, take baths, and pick up after themselves.

I asked her how she responded to their misbehavior and she said, "I'm usually too tired to argue with the kids. If they refuse to pick up after them-selves, I just do it myself. If they're crying because they want something, I give it to them. When Brian is home, it isn't so bad, though. The kids listen to him better, probably because they don't spend as much time with him as they do me."

But after I heard more about Nicole's life, it became clear that the problems were:

1. **Her kids misbehaved regularly.** Nicole's kids struggled to follow the rules, and despite her attempts to give them structure, they were noncompliant when she told them what to do.
2. **Nicole didn't follow through with discipline strategies.** By evening, Nicole was tired. And she didn't feel like enforcing her rules or giving out consequences when the kids misbehaved.

My recommendations included:

1. **Establish clear rules and consequences as a couple.** They needed to work together to create household rules.
2. **Develop consequences for misbehavior.** They needed a discipline plan and they had to follow through with negative consequences when the kids weren't listening.
3. **Nicole needed strategies to recharge her batteries.** Nicole needed to identify strategies that would help her feel more energized, even at the end of the day, so she could follow through with consequences when the kids misbehaved.

Nicole agreed to my recommendations. She and Brian created household rules and established consequences for the kids, and she felt prepared to enforce them.

She identified strategies that would help charge her batteries. Brian agreed that he would try to come home earlier two nights per week so he could relieve Nicole of her parenting duties. Nicole also decided to carve out some time for herself. Rather than go straight to day care to pick up her daughter, she'd grab coffee with a friend or run some errands on her own at least one afternoon per week. Building a little alone time into her schedule could help her feel less drained.

Once she began to view discipline as a long-term investment, she was less tempted to take shortcuts. She knew if she could teach her kids to do their chores now, she'd spend a lot less time doing their chores for them in the future.

Slowly, the kids' behavior changed. And Nicole no longer felt like she needed to take whatever shortcut she could to survive the day.

Do You Take Shortcuts That Backfire in the Long Term?

Taking the path of least resistance can be necessary—and even helpful—sometimes. But taking shortcuts that avoid discomfort can create more problems if you're not careful. Do any of these points sound familiar?

○ I give in to my child when he's whining or screaming.

○ Sometimes I don't enforce the rules because it just feels like too much work.

○ When things get tough, I give up.

○ I let my child play with electronics longer than I should because I don't want to deal with her behavior.

○ I'm too busy or too tired to address my child's behavior problems.

○ I avoid talking to my child about uncomfortable and awkward subjects.

○ If I'm embarrassed by my child's behavior, I'll do just about anything to make him stop acting out.

○ When it comes to sticking to goals, I'm not a very good role model for my child.

○ I relieve my stress in unhealthy ways sometimes, such as by drinking too much or eating too much.

Why Parents Take Shortcuts

Like many parents, Nicole ran out of energy and patience by the end of the day. So she focused on getting through the night with as little resistance from the children as possible.

Time and energy are finite resources. Whenever you feel like you don't have enough, you may be tempted to take shortcuts, despite the long-term ramifications.

SHORTCUTS MAKE LIFE EASIER RIGHT NOW

Today's world is filled with tempting shortcuts that promise quick and easy results. There are diet pills that will help you lose weight fast. There are pills that claim to help you gain muscle overnight. And there are plenty of get-rich-quick schemes that promise overnight success. Everyone takes shortcuts to avoid discomfort at one time or another. Maybe you've stepped off the treadmill long before you ever reached your goal because you felt tired. Or maybe you took out a loan so you didn't have to save up the money to go on vacation.

It's not just "average" people who get sucked into taking unhealthy shortcuts. There are many athletes who have tried to take shortcuts to success. Rather than train longer, or harder, some turn to illegal drugs to give them a quick competitive advantage.

Remember the track star Marion Jones? She was a hero during the 2000 summer Olympics when she won three gold and two bronze medals. But then, in 2006, she tested positive for steroids. She was stripped of her medals and banned from competing in the 2008 Olympics. And then there was Lance Armstrong. Known for his incredible cycling abilities, he was hailed a hero when he returned to the sport after beating cancer. He spent years denying allegations that he was using performance-enhancing drugs. After winning seven consecutive Tour de France races, he finally admitted he'd been doping the entire time.

Wealthy celebrities sometimes seek financial shortcuts and fall prey to get-rich-quick schemes. Director Steven Spielberg and actor Kevin Bacon invested their money with Bernie Madoff, who promised huge returns. Despite his "too-good-to-be-true promises," Bacon and Spielberg handed over their money, which they subsequently lost in Madoff's Ponzi scheme.

The news is filled with stories of people trying to alleviate their problems in unhealthy ways as well. Whether it's the lure of more money, more success, or becoming more attractive, there's a shortcut for everything. And many parents take shortcuts when it comes to raising their children. Giving candy to a screaming child might be one way to make his bad behavior stop when you're dining in a fancy restaurant. Or letting your child play on his electronics for hours on end may make your life a little easier today. While some parenting life hacks make great sense, others can be quite damaging to kids.

MOST PARENTS ARE STRETCHED THIN

It can feel like everyone else has a clean house, neatly pressed clothes, and plenty of time left over to coach sports and head the PTO. And when it feels like there just aren't enough hours in the day to keep up, you might be happy to take any shortcut you can get. You might be tempted to let your child watch TV for five hours, as long as she's quiet, so you can get some work done. Or maybe it's easier to just look the other way when your child is reaching for another cookie. After all, he'll play quietly when he's chewing.

In an attempt to gain some control in their frazzled life, some parents—especially mothers—are abusing prescription stimulants. Whether they're looking for a quick weight-loss fix or they're hoping to gain more energy, it's become such a widespread problem that stimulants have been dubbed "mommy's little helper." When taken for a legitimate condition like ADHD, stimulants can be helpful. But when abused, stimulants can lead to a host of medical conditions (not to mention legal issues).

While you might never go to that extreme, there's a good chance you take some type of unhealthy shortcut. Consider what things you might do to get rid of your pain right now, even if they cause bigger problems down the road.

SHORTCUTS LEAD TO LONG-TERM PROBLEMS

Working smarter rather than harder is great practice. And an occasional shortcut isn't harmful. Feeding your child a donut as you rush out the door in the morning isn't a big deal as long as you only do it once in a while. But if you do it every day, your child may suffer consequences. Although it's easier to give in after the fifth time your child asks, "Can I please have another cookie?" letting him have his way is unhealthy. He'll learn to pester you louder and longer the next time and you'll have to do twice as much work to teach him that those strategies aren't effective.

There are two types of unhealthy shortcuts: problem-related shortcuts and emotion-related shortcuts. Both provide temporary relief in the moment, but ultimately lead to bigger problems.

Here's an example of each.

Molly has been trying to get her thirteen-year-old son to clean his room for the past week. Clothes are strewn all around, there's trash everywhere, and dishes and cups are scattered across the floor. She's tired of arguing with him to get it cleaned up.

> **Problem-related shortcut:** She could clean her son's room for him. That would solve the problem for today.

> **Emotion-related shortcut:** Rather than argue with him and or be forced to look at the mess, she could take the family out for dinner as a way to escape the issue. She'll feel better temporarily.

Both shortcuts will help Molly get through the day. However, both could have long-term ramifications.

If Molly takes the problem-related shortcut and cleans her son's room for him, he'll learn it's okay to be irresponsible. If she uses the emotion-related shortcut, her son will learn his mother will reward him for having a messy room by taking him out for dinner. Either way, he won't learn any important life lessons.

Parents Who Take Shortcuts Have Kids Who Take Shortcuts

Kathy brought her six-year-old son, Sam, to therapy, saying, "He won't sleep in his own bed at night." For the past several years he had refused to sleep in his own room, but Kathy and her husband were tired of him invading their bed. "He cries and screams if I try to make him sleep in his own bed. Even if I get him to start out in his bed, it only lasts five minutes before he's right back in our room," she explained.

Kathy came to the next appointment without Sam so we could problem-solve how to get him to sleep in his own room. She agreed to sleep on a mattress on the floor in Sam's room for a few nights as a way to get him used to sleeping in his own bed. She returned the following week and said, "That didn't work. He cried when I told him he had to sleep in his own bed. Isn't there some medication you can give him that will just knock him out at night?"

Like many parents I have worked with over the years, Kathy was so desperate to change Sam's behavior she was willing to try anything—except patience. Sam didn't have trouble sleeping; he just didn't want to sleep in his own bed. And that was only because his parents had allowed him to sleep in their bed for years.

I explained to her that it was going to take more than one or two nights of working with Sam to get him to sleep in his own bed successfully. There weren't any healthy shortcuts to make it happen faster.

Instead the solution was going to be persistence and patience. She had to teach Sam that he could sleep in his own bed and she was likely going to have to take things one step at a time.

Fortunately, she agreed to keep trying. And she and her husband used a variety of tools to help Sam get used to sleeping on his own—including a new bedtime routine and a reward system. But most importantly, they had to be consistent in their message when they told Sam he could no longer sleep in their bed.

That meant walking him back into his own room when he tried to get in their bed, even if it was midnight and they were tired. Allowing him to sleep in their bed just for one night would undo the progress they'd made. So they had to hold firm. And their persistence paid off once Sam adjusted to sleeping in his own room.

Their willingness to stick to the plan showed Sam that change takes hard work and perseverance. And that was an important life lesson for Sam to learn.

Your child learns how to handle discomfort by watching you. If you take the easy way out every time you're faced with difficult circumstances, he will start to take shortcuts of his own.

- A ten-year-old copies his friend's homework because it will take hours to figure it out on his own.
- A twelve-year-old refuses to practice playing the piano because he's struggling to learn the notes.
- A fourteen-year-old snacks constantly in between meals because he wants to avoid feeling hungry.
- A sixteen-year-old starts skipping meals because she wants to lose weight for the prom.
- An eighteen-year-old starts stealing money from the cash register at work because she wants to buy a new car.

Whether your child wets his toothbrush so you think he brushed his teeth or he rushes through his homework so he can play outside, short-cuts solve problems in the moment. The long-term consequences may not become apparent for weeks, months, or even years down the road. And even then, most kids won't be able to link those consequences to their behavior.

What to Do Instead

In dealing with her children's behavior, Nicole had to recognize how her shortcuts were adding to their problems—not solving them. Then she had to establish parenting strategies that supported her long-term goals. Insisting that her kids did their chores, holding them accountable, and refusing to give in would help them learn important life lessons.

Look for alternatives to the shortcuts you take. Commit to developing strategies that are the healthiest for your child in the long term, not just what's easiest right now.

IDENTIFY THE SHORTCUTS YOU TAKE

Cynthia brought her nine-year-old son, Daniel, to therapy because he was angry and aggressive toward his six-year-old brother, Jackson. The fighting had gotten out of control, and most recently, Daniel had started hitting Jackson. She said, "I think he needs anger management classes." But after I heard a little more about what was going on, it didn't sound like Daniel was hitting his brother out of anger. Instead he was using aggression as a way to get his needs met.

Over the years, whenever Daniel and Jackson fought, Cynthia would intervene and say, "Daniel, just give him what he wants so he'll stop crying" or "Daniel, let him have that toy so he won't scream." Now Daniel was tired of giving in to his little brother. So he'd started taking a stand because his mother refused to intervene.

Daniel didn't need anger management classes. Instead Cynthia needed help setting limits and establishing consequences for Jackson. That meant not letting Jackson get his way—even when he screamed.

Over time, Daniel grew to trust that his mother was going to handle the situation, without telling him to give in to his brother's demands every time. And as his trust increased, his aggression decreased. That didn't mean he didn't still get frustrated by his pesky little brother sometimes, but he no longer hit him to resolve the issue.

Cynthia had become so accustomed to making Daniel give in to his brother that she didn't even recognize the shortcut she was taking. Pacifying Jackson, even when it was unfair to Daniel, had become a habit. And ultimately, she was teaching Jackson that pestering his brother and crying loudly were effective ways to get whatever he wanted.

Think about the shortcuts you take. Which ones might be saving you some time and energy in the short term while causing you more pain in the long term?

Here are some questions to consider:

- Do you use punishment instead of discipline because it takes less effort?
- Do you ignore behavior problems because it takes too much energy to address them?
- Do you do things for your kids rather than teach them how to do those things for themselves?
- Do you solve your kids' problems rather than teach them how to solve their own issues?

CREATE A PLAN TO AVOID FUTURE SHORTCUTS

Seven-year-old Hazel had the whiniest voice I'd ever heard. And it drove her parents crazy. Anytime she said things like "But Mom, that's not fair" or "I want to go now!" her parents would spring into action. They'd do whatever they could to make her stop whining. And now they were paying for it. Hazel had figured out that whining was a great way to get her needs met. Their hope in bringing her to therapy was that I would have a magic cure. But the solution wasn't quite that painless. Hazel's parents needed to change their behavior if they wanted to change Hazel's behavior.

I encouraged them to tell Hazel that from now on, she was going to have to use a "big-girl voice" when she made a request. And if she pestered, begged, and whined, they weren't going to respond to her. Instead they would turn away and act as though they couldn't see her or hear her whines. Then, as soon as she stopped whining, they could give her attention again by praising her for being quiet. But under no circumstances were they to give in when she whined.

They agreed to that plan when they left the office. But when they returned the following week, they said, "Hazel just didn't get it. She doesn't know how to communicate without whining." I asked a few more questions and I learned that when they tried to ignore her, she whined louder and longer. And they had started caving in because they thought Hazel couldn't possibly communicate any better.

So I reminded them that things were likely to get worse before they got better. That whining louder and longer was Hazel's desperate attempt to make whining more effective—and so far it was working. I encouraged them to do whatever it took to ignore Hazel's whining. And if they could do it successfully for a week, they'd likely see some behavior changes. Even though those changes might not seem for the better at first, they should stick with the plan, because over time things would improve.

Sure enough, Hazel's whining decreased once her parents had a clear plan—and they were able to stick with it. It was hard on them at first. They essentially had to "untrain" Hazel. She'd learned that whining would help her get what she wanted. And they had to stop taking shortcuts that reinforced that belief.

If you've gotten in the habit of taking shortcuts, develop a plan to help you stop. Otherwise you'll likely stay stuck in the same old behavior patterns.

Ask yourself the following questions:

- What do I need to stop taking this shortcut?
- What can I do differently?
- How can I stick to my plan even when it's really hard to do?
- When am I most likely to take a shortcut and how can I plan ahead for those situations?

FIND HEALTHY WAYS TO CHARGE YOUR BATTERIES

We recognize that the batteries in our electronics need to be charged regularly. But, for some reason, we expect ourselves to keep going all the time. But just like our smartphones, at some point we have to stop and charge our batteries to function at our best.

When you feel energized, you'll be less likely to turn to shortcuts to get through the day. So it's important to look for healthy ways to charge your batteries.

Make self-care a priority. You'll be role-modeling for your child that it's important to take care of yourself while also making sure that you're taking the steps to become the best parent you can be.

Discover what activities help you feel recharged. Here are a few examples:

- Exercise
- Find a hobby
- Spend time with friends
- Read a book
- Go on a date night
- Write in a journal

Some parents say they don't have time to take care of themselves or that they feel too selfish to do things without the kids. But engaging in self-care is the key to avoiding unhealthy shortcuts.

Imagine a car that is almost out of gas. The driver looks at a map and discovers the nearest gas station is fifty miles away if he continues on the highway. If he takes a shortcut, he could get there in twenty miles, but that route involves taking a desolate, winding road that few people ever drive on. The driver might be tempted to take the shortcut because he's not sure he has enough gas.

Parenting can be similar. You need enough gas in your tank so that you can take the best route to your destination. If you are running low on fuel, you might have to depend on shortcuts. The best way to fill your parenting gas tank is by taking care of yourself. Then you'll have the energy to withstand the long, hard road that will help you raise a responsible child.

How to Teach Kids to Resist Tempting Shortcuts

In the case of Nicole and her misbehaving kids, she was teaching them bad habits. Crying, whining, and arguing got their needs met. She had to commit to teaching them more appropriate skills so they could grow up to become responsible adults.

In chapter eight we discussed the importance of not shielding kids from pain. But it's not enough to just let your child experience pain. You also have to make sure he doesn't take any unhealthy shortcuts to deal with his pain.

HELP YOUR CHILD ESTABLISH CHALLENGING GOALS

Make sure your child is always working on some type of goal. The key is to create challenging yet realistic goals. Here are some examples:

- **Fitness goals:** "I want to be able to run a mile without stopping." (Try to keep the focus away from weight, as you don't want your child to think getting healthy is only about a number on a scale.)
- **Educational goals:** "I want to read fifty books during summer vacation."
- **Financial goals:** "I want to save up enough money to buy a new skateboard."
- **Behavioral goals:** "I want to get all my chores done before dinner for a whole week."
- **Social goals:** "I want to make a friend that I can spend time with outside of school."

Once he has a goal for himself, help him work toward accomplishing it. Kids often start out feeling excited about a goal, but they tend to lose momentum quickly. Here's how you can help your child accomplish his goal:

- **Encourage your child to write down his goal.** Written goals are much more likely to be achieved. Hang your child's goal in a prominent place in his bedroom so he can be reminded of what he is trying to accomplish.
- **Break the goal down into smaller objectives.** Thinking about a big goal can be overwhelming. Help your child identify small steps he can take today to help him work toward his goal.
- **Find a way to track your child's progress.** Create a chart, place check marks on a calendar, or give him a journal to keep track of his progress. It will teach him to hold himself accountable and it can keep him motivated.

Working toward his goals will be uncomfortable at times. And he'll be tempted to take shortcuts when the going gets tough.

Provide him with guidance and support to help him experience success. Each time he overcomes an obstacle or achieves something new, he'll gain confidence in his ability to persevere.

HELP YOUR CHILD CREATE A CONSTRUCTIVE MANTRA

Whether it's one day or one month into the process, your child will likely struggle to keep working toward his goal. It's at that point he may be tempted to quit or take a shortcut.

Helping your child continue to work toward his goal, even when he doesn't feel like it, teaches him he's stronger than he thinks. The more he practices working through tough times, the more he'll learn he can behave contrary to how he feels.

Kids are better equipped to ward off negative thoughts when they have a helpful mantra in place. Here are some examples:

- **"Keep moving my feet."** If your child is trying to run a mile or he's complaining that his legs are too tired while you're walking around the grocery store, tell him to concentrate on taking one more step at a time.

- **"I can wait."** When your child is waiting in a long line or when he's tempted to interrupt a conversation, reminding himself to be patient can help him tolerate the wait.

- **"I'm a tough kid."** If your child is about to get a shot or he's going to undergo something difficult, reminding himself that he's tough can help him be brave.

- **"Just one cupcake."** If you told your child he can only eat one cupcake, he can remind himself of that over and over to resist the temptation when he wants to eat a second one.

Proactively help your child develop a short saying he can repeat to himself when things get tough. A helpful mantra could prevent your child from thinking things like "I can't stand this!" or "This is too hard. I quit." Those types of thoughts will lead him to take a shortcut.

Then reinforce his efforts by using that phrase when he's struggling. If he hears you say, "Keep moving!" it'll remind him to tell himself that he can keep going.

Teach Preschoolers to Use the "Batman Effect"

Preschoolers love to take any shortcut they can. After all, they're impatient and impulsive by nature. So waiting in line, taking turns, and following the rules can be hard. So don't be surprised if your preschooler interrupts every few minutes because he doesn't want to wait for his turn to talk. It's also common for preschoolers to grab a cookie after you've said no because she doesn't want to wait until after dinner to have a treat.

But the good news is, delayed gratification is a skill that can be taught. With practice, your child's self-control muscle will improve. Start teaching him from an early age that he can put off feeling good now so he can feel great later. As he gains confidence in his ability to delay gratification, he'll be less likely to take unhealthy shortcuts.

One of the best ways to do that is to use the "Batman effect." In a 2016 study published in *Child Development,* researchers found that children persisted at tasks longer when they pretended to be a hardworking character like Batman, Dora the Explorer, or Bob the Builder. In a series of experiments, children were given boring, repetitive tasks that required their full attention. They were given the option to take a break to play video games or keep working. The children who took on the role of a character worked longer on the boring tasks.

So when your child is faced with a boring or difficult task, say, "I bet a superhero could get this room clean! Show me how Superman would clean this room." Occasionally check in and ask, "How's it going in there, Superman?"

When your child pretends to be some of his favorite positive fictional characters, he'll emulate their work ethic. Since hardworking characters resist unhealthy shortcuts, he'll be more likely to persevere.

Teach School-Age Kids to Engage in Behavioral Experiments

Self-doubt can lead school-age kids to question their ability to stay the course. A child may think, "I'll never be able to wait until

Friday to earn my reward" or "It doesn't matter how many times I study my spelling words. It's just too hard." Kids who experience self-doubt dwell on their discomfort until they finally cave in. They stop looking for healthy solutions and seek immediate ways to help themselves feel better. If your child gives up (or you give in) each time he insists he can't possibly endure another minute of discomfort, he'll underestimate his capabilities.

Teach him to challenge his negative thinking by performing a behavioral experiment. When you overhear him say things like "I can't do this," tell him to take a brief break or a few deep breaths and try again. Encourage him to prove his negative thinking wrong.

A simple exercise to demonstrate this is to ask him how far he thinks he can run. If he's like most kids, he might overestimate his capabilities at first. But then, when he starts feeling tired, he might give up right away.

Run around a track with him if you can. Ask him to tell you when he starts to think his legs are too tired to go any farther or when he feels like quitting because he can't catch his breath. Then encourage him to keep going, just a little bit longer, to prove to himself that he's stronger than he thinks.

Talk about this exercise afterward and discuss how our brains sometimes try to get us to quit earlier than we need to. Even if he doesn't reach the goal he set for himself, discuss how he can keep going and keep trying hard without taking a shortcut.

Teach Teens the Truth About Shortcuts

The teen years are filled with opportunities to take unhealthy shortcuts. And peer pressure can be a major factor in a teen's decision to indulge in some unsavory activity. Your sixteen-year-old might skip meals because she wants to lose weight for the prom or your eighteen-year-old might be tempted to take a friend's prescription pills because they'll help him stay up all night studying.

Warn your teen about the dangers of taking shortcuts in life. But saying, "Don't smoke because it's unhealthy" or "Stay away from alcohol because it's bad to drink" can backfire. If your teen's friend says, "I got drunk this weekend and it was so much fun," your child will think you must not know what you're talking about because his friend's experience was positive.

Acknowledge that shortcuts provide some temporary relief. Then warn your teen about the dangers. Say, "Drinking alcohol can be fun sometimes. But it's illegal for you to drink. And it's not good for your developing brain and it could lead you to make some risky decisions." Or say, "Playing video games all night will help you feel better right now because you won't have to worry about your schoolwork. But if you don't get your work done tonight, you'll only be more anxious tomorrow."

Giving a balanced view can help your teen see you as more credible because she'll see that you were right about the upside to taking a shortcut. Then she'll be more likely to recall the warnings you issued as well. That can be instrumental in helping her make the healthiest choices for herself.

Kids Who Learn to Resist Unhealthy Shortcuts Become Persevering Adults

Today's kids are digital natives. They've never known what it's like to order something from a catalog and wait weeks for it to arrive. And they've never had to wait for a movie to arrive in the video store before being able to watch it. They can gain instant access to everything from their friends to their trivia questions in a matter of seconds. So when it comes to making decisions in their lives, they're tempted to take shortcuts. They want everything to happen in an instant.

That's why it's essential for kids to have role models who teach them the importance of staying the course, even when it's difficult. When they know they can handle taking the high road rather than the easy way out, they gain confidence in their ability to reach their goals, no matter how long it takes.

Stanford's famous marshmallow experiment shed some light on the importance of delayed gratification. Researchers gave kids a choice between eating one marshmallow now or a larger reward (like two marshmallows or a mint) twenty minutes later. The children waited in a room by themselves, testing their self-control.

Researchers found that the children who exhibited enough self-control to wait for the larger reward at age four generally fared better in life. They had higher SAT scores and were less likely to be overweight or use drugs thirty years later.

Teaching your child persistence now could help him resist the temptation to take shortcuts later in life. A child who understands the importance of self-control may be able to stick to his goals longer, and is more likely to persevere when the going gets tough.

Mentally strong people don't expect immediate results. Whether they're paying off debt or improving their physical health, they know change doesn't happen overnight. They stay the course and resist unhealthy shortcuts along the way.

Troubleshooting and Common Traps

Although it might be tempting sometimes, don't collude with your child to take a shortcut. Even though you could finish his math homework in about ten minutes, don't do it for him. And just because you're an engineer doesn't mean you should do his science-fair project for him. If you become a partner in crime in taking a shortcut, you'll send your child the wrong message. He'll assume that some shortcuts are okay to dodge hard work sometimes.

Another common trap is that parents aren't always consistent in giving kids rewards to entice them to delay gratification. If you say, "I'll match the amount of money you earn for your bicycle by the end of the month," it's essential that you follow through. Otherwise your child won't have any incentive to work toward other rewards that you promise him in the future.

It can also be hard sometimes to distinguish between a "mood booster" like we talked about in chapter nine or an unhealthy shortcut. The difference depends on how it will affect your child long term. For example, if your child has a hard day at school and he comes home in a bad mood, going for a short bike ride is a helpful mood booster.

When he feels happier, he may be better able to concentrate on his homework. But riding his bike all night to avoid studying for the test he dreads taking tomorrow is an unhealthy shortcut.

So ask yourself, "Is what he's doing right now going to help or harm him in the long term?" A mood booster will contribute to his long-term goal while a shortcut will sabotage his long-term effort.

WHAT'S HELPFUL

- Helping your child create challenging goals
- Building credibility with your child about the dangers of shortcuts
- Helping your child conduct behavioral experiments
- Recharging your batteries so you can be at your best
- Assisting your child in creating a mantra
- Teaching delayed gratification
- Acknowledging the temptation to give in to shortcuts

WHAT'S NOT HELPFUL

- Giving in to your child's bad behavior
- Colluding with your child to take shortcuts
- Letting your child give up on goals without any guidance
- Ignoring your child's unhealthy shortcuts
- Allowing yourself to get run-down
- Staying focused on the short-term gains without looking at your long-term goals

They Don't Lose Sight of Their Values

Fifteen-year-old Kyle was kicked out of a special program that allowed him to take college classes while still in high school because he'd been caught cheating. Kyle's parents brought him in for counseling for two reasons: they wanted to figure out "where they went wrong" and they were worried about his future. Kyle's mother said, "We taught him better than this. We've always told him to be honest." But now his parents were questioning everything. They worried that the only reason he'd been getting good grades was that he'd been cheating all along.

I met with Kyle for a few sessions to hear more about what happened and to find out how he planned to move forward. He said he knew cheating was wrong and he shouldn't have done it. He was disappointed in himself and he was upset that he'd squandered his opportunity to get free college credit. Kyle admitted he'd cheated a few times before, but he said, "No more than any other kid my age." He said most of his friends cheated from time to time and he'd never known anyone to get caught. So he never imagined his professor would catch him.

As we talked about what led to his decision to cheat, he said, "Without enough time to do a good job on my paper, I might have failed that project. And my parents would be disappointed if I failed."

Kyle's parents had sent the message that high achievement was essential. Although they'd say things like "Do your best," their behavior implied that his best wasn't always good enough. They hired tutors to give him a competitive advantage and enrolled him in an expensive SAT prep course. And they invested a lot of time into talking about Ivy League schools.

They constantly praised him for being smart. They bragged to friends and family that he was an exceptional student who always got straight A's. Their emphasis on achievement taught Kyle that his grades were more important than anything else. He knew his parents expected him to get as many college credits as possible while he was still in high school. So he thought cheating was his best option.

The main problems appeared to be:

1. **Kyle cheated.** Kyle couldn't go back and change this fact. But he could decide how to deal with it. He needed to create a plan for himself moving forward.
2. **Kyle was confused about his family values.** Kyle wasn't sure exactly what price he was willing to pay for his achievement.

My recommendations included:

1. **Kyle and his parents should clarify their values.** Kyle's parents needed to decide what they really expected from Kyle. And Kyle needed to do some work to identify his values as well.
2. **The family should ensure their behavior was in line with their values.** Once they identified their values, the family needed to make sure their priorities exemplified their beliefs.

Kyle's parents joined his next therapy session and we examined their family values. Although they wanted him to succeed academically, they said it was more important for him to be honest. We addressed some of the ways their behavior may have sent mixed messages.

To move forward, the whole family had to look closely at their values. Did his parents value honesty over achievement? I didn't want them to just give answers that they thought were socially appropriate. It was up to them to decide what was most important in their own lives.

I encouraged Kyle to spend some time thinking about his own values. Perhaps the things he valued most were not in line with his parents' values.

The family returned the following week and all of them said that they did indeed value honesty over achievement. But they saw how they'd gotten their priorities mixed up over the years. They talked about good grades and high achievement all the time. Yet the subject of honesty rarely came up. They saw how their emphasis on good grades sent the message that they'd be disappointed in him if he failed.

And Kyle's parents admitted they probably would have been upset if his grades weren't good. But now they realized one bad grade would have been better than cheating.

Together, they were committed to trying to realign their priorities. Even though Kyle was only a few years away from being an adult, they wanted to spend those years trying to live according to their values so they could teach him what was important in life. I spent the next few weeks helping them create a plan.

They eventually came to the point where they were able to feel a little bit thankful that this incident happened. It was going to cost them more money because Kyle wouldn't get college credit for free—but they now realized that being honest and good people were more valuable than money.

Are You Parenting According to Your Values?

Everything you do, from how you spend your money to how you spend your time, speaks volumes about what's important to you in life. Sometimes parents' priorities get mixed up and they inadvertently send the wrong messages about values to their kids. Do you answer affirmatively to any of these points?

○ I'm not sure what my personal values are.

○ I don't know how to teach my child about values.

○ It's nearly impossible to prioritize the things that matter in my life.

○ If I asked my child about our family values, he'd have no idea what I was talking about.

○ I get caught up competing with other parents and I lose sight of my own values.

○ I send my child mixed messages about what's really important.

○ I rarely reflect on whether my child is learning my values.

○ I sometimes get so focused on what's going on right now that I forget to step back and look at the bigger parenting picture.

○ When I am making parenting decisions, I don't think much about the life lessons I want my child to learn.

Why Parents Lose Sight of Their Values

Although it was unintentional, Kyle's parents had taught him to think his reputation was more important than his character. They wanted to set their son up for a happy, successful life. They thought paying for tutoring and SAT prep courses would help him stay competitive with his peers. They never imagined it would place him under so much pressure to succeed that he'd be tempted to cheat.

If you aren't clear on your values, you may be sending your child mixed messages about what's important in life. And even if you know your values, sometimes it's hard to live in accordance with them.

IT'S EASY TO GET CAUGHT UP IN THE COMPETITION

My friend Sarah called a few weeks ago and said, "My kid is a brat." Sarah had thrown her eight-year-old daughter, Morgan, a birthday party and witnessing her daughter's behavior at the event was an eye-opening experience. When one of Morgan's friends showed up with a card, Morgan ran over and said, "You didn't bring a gift? You only got me a card? That's really rude." The other child, apparently embarrassed, explained there was a gift card inside the envelope.

Sarah said she rushed over and apologized to the little girl and her mother but she knew an apology wasn't enough. "It didn't occur to Morgan that *she* was the rude one!" she exclaimed. She said she was tempted to yell at her daughter for being ungrateful and acting like a spoiled brat but then a lightbulb went on and she realized, "I'm the one that taught her to be like this." She knew she had to make some serious changes to the way she was raising her daughter.

Sarah spent months planning Morgan's birthday party. She'd scoured Pinterest for party ideas and spent weeks shopping for party favors and creating homemade decorations that transformed their backyard into a tropical resort.

She said, "Apparently, I should spend more time making sure I'm raising a nice kid rather than worrying about whether I'm impressing her friends with the party favors." She recognized that it wasn't just about today's party. It was a problem with her parenting that was evident in other areas of her life.

Obviously, Sarah isn't alone in this problem. It's easy to get caught up in the competition aspect of parenting. Social media makes it especially tempting.

There used to be a mentality that held that it takes a whole village to raise a child. Friends, neighbors, extended family, and adults in the community pitched in and helped out. And most adults felt some sort of responsibility to ensure kids were being raised well. But in the age of social media, there seems to be a competition in the race to raise the "best kid." Parents are showing off their children's holiday gifts, sports trophies, and academic accomplishments.

And rather than saying, "Thanks to everyone who helped me raise my child," too often parents are saying, "Look at how great my child is— thanks to me." And other parents then feel the pressure to ensure their child is equally successful.

Social media has led to an interesting paradox: parenting issues have become more public. Yet rather than support one another, people are more likely to shame one another. Post a picture of your kids enjoying a meal at a fast-food restaurant and someone is likely to warn you about the dangers of processed foods. If your child sustains an injury at the playground, someone will likely blame you for being irresponsible. Let your kids play outside by themselves, and you might hear how dangerous it is to allow kids to be unsupervised.

Unfortunately, shaming and unhealthy competition causes some parents to second-guess their values. And while it's good to consider your parenting practices and consider alternatives, if you change the way you parent, it should be because you decide it's what's best for your family. Not because you worry about what other parents are going to think.

It's hard to show that your child has good values over the Internet. How do you post a picture of him being honest? Or being generous? It's much easier to brag about his achievements by showing him holding up his latest trophy or newest award.

PARENTS LOOK AT THEIR KIDS THROUGH ROSE-COLORED GLASSES

The vast majority of parents assume their kids are doing better than they really are. That may lead them to pat themselves on the back for a job well done as they assume they've instilled healthy values in their offspring.

But studies show parents are looking at their kids through a distorted lens. Here are just a few examples:

- **Parents overestimate their child's academic achievements.** Based on parental reports, the average GPA for high school students is between 3.15 and 3.24. But national transcript data shows the average GPA is actually between 2.95 and 3.0.
- **Parents are unaware their kids are sexually active.** According to parental reports, only about 17 percent of teens are sexually active. But the Centers for Disease Control and Prevention reports

that 42 percent of all high school boys and 43 percent of high
school girls have reported having sex.

- **Parents are oblivious that their children are drinking.** Based
  on reports from parents, only one out of ten high school students
  consumes alcohol. Yet studies show 72 percent of high school
  students have consumed alcohol and 42 percent admit to drinking
  in the last thirty days.
- **Parents underestimate their teen's size.** According to parental
  reports, 13 percent of children are "somewhat overweight" and only
  3 percent are "greatly overweight." Yet according to the National
  Centers for Health Statistics, more than one-third of American
  children are overweight and 17 percent of them are obese.

Clearly, most parents think their child is better than average, even
though this is statistically impossible. They believe their child is smarter,
healthier, and makes better choices than other kids. It's this rose-colored
view of children that may lead parents to conclude their kids have adopted
their values.

It's easy to assume that if your child is well behaved and he's doing well in
school, he must have some set of clear morals. So many busy families take
for granted that their child has adopted their values. But just because your
child is doing well on the outside doesn't mean he's internalized your values.

Losing Sight of Your Values Muddles
Your Child's Moral Compass

In Kyle's case, his parents sent mixed messages over the years. Although
they said one thing, their behavior said something else. Kyle thought he
had to succeed at all costs, even if it meant cheating, and his decision to
cheat was a costly one.

It's likely that all parents lose sight of their values sometimes. When
you do, it's essential to take steps to address the problem. Otherwise your
family may experience some serious consequences.

KIDS ARE CONFUSED ABOUT THEIR PARENTS' VALUES

A father once brought his son into my therapy office because the boy lied every day. However, in addressing some of his behavior problems, I learned that this father frequently bought the twelve-and-under movie tickets for his thirteen-year-old son. When I pointed out to him that lying to get a cheaper movie ticket was sending a message to his son that dishonesty was okay, he said, "Yeah, but it saves us three dollars every time we go to the movies." While that may be true, he was paying a bigger price in terms of the life lessons he was teaching his son.

Kids learn far more from what you do than what you say. And your child isn't going to see a stark difference between lying to get into the movies for a lower price (or the buffet or the amusement park) and cheating on a math test. Dishonesty is dishonesty.

But it's easy for parents to get so caught up in the moment and in their personal objectives that they lose sight of the life lessons they're teaching their children.

If you go to any children's sporting events you're likely to see evidence that some adults have lost sight of what's important in life. Parents are screaming at umpires in Little League games for "making a bad call" and coaches are yelling at little kids for making mistakes on the soccer field. And it isn't just one or two "bad" parents who are being poor sports. There are many parents in the stands complaining that their child doesn't get enough playing time or saying rude things about the coaches' decisions.

Although those same parents may say, "Just do your best" or "It doesn't matter who wins or loses," it's their behavior that speaks volumes about what they truly believe.

A 2014 survey by Harvard's Making Caring Common Project discovered that parents' and teachers' top priority was for kids to be caring. Respondents ranked kindness as more important than achievement. But that's not the message kids were actually getting. About 80 percent of teens said their parents and teachers valued achievement or happiness over kindness. Teens were three times more likely to agree with the statement "My parents are prouder if I get good grades in my classes than if I'm a caring community member in class and school."

In the moment it's easy to forget what's important. But it's in those little moments that kids learn what's actually important to you in life.

How do you treat someone who has made a mistake? How do you respond when a cashier gives you back too much change? What do you do when someone treats you poorly? Your behavior speaks louder than your words.

A LACK OF VALUES IS AT THE ROOT OF MANY PROBLEMS

Ninety-six percent of parents say a "strong moral character" is very important, if not essential, to their children's future. Yet many of them aren't devoting enough time toward helping kids develop the moral fiber they need to become good people.

When most parents think about the lack of values in some children's upbringing, they picture kids who join gangs, do hard-core drugs, and end up in jail. News reports are filled with tragic tales of kids who get mixed up in a life of crime and violence because they endured horrific home lives. But those aren't the only kids who seem to lack a moral compass. College-bound teens, star athletes, and kids with "good parents" are also a little lost these days. Here are just a few statistics about today's youth:

- 43 percent of sixteen- and seventeen-year-old teens admit to cheating on tests in school.
- One in four students is bullied during any given school year.
- Nearly half of all middle and high school students report being sexually harassed at least once by their peers.

Those are the things that happen to kids while they're still in high school, living under their parents' watchful eyes. What do you think happens when they go off to college or enter the workforce?

When kids only follow the rules because they don't want to get into trouble, they're not likely to behave when they think they won't get caught. So it's important to consider whether your child has internalized your values. Is he following the rules because you told him to? Or is he invested in doing the right thing even when no one is looking?

What to Do Instead

It wasn't enough for Kyle's parents to simply say they valued honesty. They had to do some soul-searching to find out if it was actually true. They had spent years living as though achievement were more important than anything else. If they wanted to live according to their values, they had to make some changes.

That's not to say they couldn't still make academic success a priority. But they had to be careful that they didn't continue teaching Kyle that his grades were the epitome of success. They acknowledged that they'd lost sight of their values and they needed to realign their priorities. If you want to raise a child with strong morals, it's essential that you actively teach him your values.

THINK ABOUT YOUR VALUES

It's easy to say, "I want a kind and generous kid." But it's harder to ensure that your behavior aligns with those values. Consider how you might respond to the following scenarios:

- Your teen says he gave his jacket to a kid at school whose family can't afford one. Would you commend him for his generosity or scold him for giving away a jacket you paid for?
- Would you rather your child's teacher say he's the kindest kid in the class or that he's the smartest math student she's ever seen?
- If your teen had to choose between doing yard work for a company who would pay him or doing yard work for an elderly

neighbor who can't afford to pay, how would you prefer he spends his Saturday?

- If your child asks you to buy a specific brand of shoes because all the other kids are wearing them, would you buy them so he fits in or would you encourage him to buy something else so he stands out?

- If your child was in the middle of doing his homework when a friend called crying, would you want him to take time out to talk or would you prefer he finish his homework first?

Coming to terms with your actual values is a bit uncomfortable. "I value achievement over kindness" may seem like it's not the socially appropriate thing to say. But for some parents, it's a reality.

ASK YOURSELF WHAT LIFE LESSONS YOU'RE TEACHING YOUR CHILD

One day, the parents of a ten-year-old girl I'd been working with for a while came into my office asking if they should allow their daughter to quit the soccer team. It was a few weeks into the season and she said she didn't want to play anymore. The mother was happy to let her quit. But the father thought they should make her stick it out. They were looking for a third opinion to be the "tie breaker."

I explained there wasn't one right answer when it comes to parenting issues such as this one. Instead it was up to them to examine their values and decide what life lessons they wanted to teach their child. If they wanted her to learn that it's important to honor commitments and finish what she started, they could tell her she had to finish out the season. That could teach her that her teammates were counting on her to be on the team. The potential downside would be that she might be hesitant to try new things in the future for fear she'll have to stick it out even if she doesn't like it.

If, however, they wanted her to learn that it's important to try new things and move on when something isn't a good fit, they could let her quit. Allowing her to quit might help her see that life is full of opportunities and you have to decide which ones are best for you. Additionally, she might learn that youth sports are about having fun, and if it's not fun, there's no need to keep playing.

The potential downside could be that she doesn't learn to persevere when things get tough. Perhaps she doesn't want to put in the practice to get better, which could in turn help her enjoy playing more. Or maybe she thought she was going to be successful right away and she's only quitting because this didn't happen.

Most parenting decisions don't have a right or wrong answer. Your response should depend on the life lesson you think your child needs to learn. What's right for one family and one child may not be the best choice for everyone.

Think about what values are the most important to you, such as kindness, friendship, community service, achievement, and spiritual beliefs. Clearly, this isn't a comprehensive list of every value you may hold near and dear. But it can get you started. Add whatever things you value the most and try to think about which things you think are the most important.

You can't begin to teach your child your values until you know for sure what your values are. Then, once you're clear on what is most important to you, tough parenting choices become a lot easier.

CREATE A FAMILY MISSION STATEMENT

Organizations usually have mission statements that outline the reasons they exist. That mission statement helps them make decisions that fulfill their purpose. For similar reasons, it makes sense for families to develop a mission statement. Writing it down and referring back to it often can help you make important life decisions as well.

A family mission statement is what makes your family different. Without a clear purpose, you're a group of people who happen to live under the same roof. When you create a mission statement, you come together to work on a common goal and you have a shared purpose.

The adults in the household should talk about the family's purpose privately, brainstorming ideas about what you believe the family's mission is. Then hold a family meeting to get input from the children. Ask the following questions:

- What makes us a family?
- What kinds of things are we able to accomplish as a family?
- How can we use what we have to make the world a better place?
- How can we help other people?
- What types of things are most important to us?

Write down everyone's input. Then spend some time creating a short mission statement that encompasses what's most important to your family. Keep it simple and memorable. If you make it too long or complicated, you'll defeat the purpose.

Here are some sample family mission statements:

- Our purpose is to love God and serve other people. We work to help each other become better by creating an atmosphere of love and learning. We strive to spread hope and joy.
- Our family believes in hard work. We seek to be honest, kind, and caring. We're grateful for what we have and we love each other at all times.
- In our house, we make memories. We maintain positive attitudes, treat each other with respect, and stick together at all times.
- We dream big. Work hard. Love much. Laugh often. And serve others joyfully.

Once you've completed your mission statement, post it in a prominent location. I've worked with some families who create posters with beautiful typography and hang them on the wall. I've even seen some families get them stenciled on a wall in their home.

Just remember, you might want to change your mission statement someday. As your kids grow older or your family's needs shift, you may find that your current statement needs to be edited. Feel free to change it as needed. When you're making decisions as a family, refer back to your mission statement. Does your next family vacation support your mission statement? Are your spending habits serving your purpose? Are you spending your time in a way that is fulfilling your mission?

DECIDE HOW TO PASS ON YOUR VALUES

I once worked with a father who used to drive his children to school every day. But one day his son complained that it was embarrassing to get dropped off in their "old car." After that, the father let his son walk to school. It wasn't to punish him for being rude. He wanted his son to realize that transportation was a privilege. And so was going to school. He wanted him to appreciate having a ride.

Think about what values you want to be handed down in your family. What do you hope your child will teach your grandchildren someday?

It's also important to consider how you learned your values. And how you can teach your child—who is going to have very different experiences in life—the values you hold near and dear. Perhaps you learned about the importance of hard work because you were raised by parents who worked long hours. And you want to teach your child about hard work, but at the same time you don't want to be at your office all the time because you want to spend time with your family. Or maybe you lost a parent at a young age. And that helped you see the importance of family. How can you teach your child to cherish family time without enduring the same hardship?

ACKNOWLEDGE YOU MADE MISTAKES

When you lose sight of your values at one time or another, acknowledge that you've lost your way. Point out the problem to your child and apologize when necessary.

Here are some examples of ways in which a parent may address the issue:

- "I'm so sorry I yelled at your coach tonight. I lost my temper and I was wrong. I always tell you that it doesn't matter if you win or lose and tonight I lost sight of what is important. I'll never do that again."
- "I want to apologize for something I've been doing lately. I get after you for not eating healthy. But I haven't been a very good role model. I've been eating fast food for lunch. Starting tomorrow, that's going to change. It's important for me to take care of my body better and I want all of us to be healthy."
- "We've gotten so wrapped up in our jobs lately that we haven't spent much time together as a family. That's not right. Family is most important. I'm going to start coming home earlier in the evenings and I'm going to do less work from home."

If you don't address the discrepancies between what you say and what you do, your child will be confused. But you can't just say you're going to change. You have to actually do it if you want your child to learn an important life lesson.

How to Teach Kids to Live According to Their Values

In the case of Kyle and his decision to cheat, he was unclear about whether he valued success or honesty more. His parents had never spent any time purposely teaching him about their values.

Instilling your values in your child shouldn't be a passive activity. Be intentional about the life lessons you want your child to learn.

SHARE HOW YOU ARRIVE AT IMPORTANT DECISIONS

Your behavior alone may not always send a clear message to your child about your values. Sometimes you need to explain what went into your decisions.

Consider the following scenarios:

- One dad values his family. To give his children the best life possible, he works seventy hours a week so his wife can be home with the kids. He loves his children and he wants to make sure they have an opportunity to go to college. He wants to teach them that hard work is the key to success.
- Another dad values his family. So he works twenty hours per week. His family doesn't have much money. But they have a lot of time together. He wants his children to know that material possessions aren't important. It's quality time together that is the most important thing in life.

People may be quick to judge which father actually loves his family the most. While one person might choose the father who works a lot to ensure that his kids have a good future, someone else might say he's neglecting them. Someone else might say the father who works part-time loves his family the most and he's raising them "right." But another person might say he's lazy and he doesn't care enough about his family to work hard.

Explain the thinking process behind your decisions. What went into your decision to take a new job? Did you want to earn more money? Did it offer more flexible hours that would give you time with your family? Is it a position you feel more passionate about?

TALK ABOUT OTHER PEOPLE'S VALUES

If your child says his friend's house is bigger or the neighbor drives a nicer car, talk about it. Explain your values about money and talk about how you decide when to make purchases.

Many of the children he goes to school with will likely have different rules in their homes. When your child says, "That's not fair! My friends get to do that stuff," turn it into an opportunity to talk about your values.

Here are a few examples:

Child: Mom, how come Hayden's family doesn't go to church?

Mom: Hayden's family may have different beliefs than we do. In our family, it's important to practice our faith, and we believe the way to do that is to go to church.

Child: Alex's parents aren't married.

Dad: There are lots of reasons why adults don't get married. It was important to your mother and me to get married, though. We wanted to get married before we had kids.

Child: Why didn't Alex's parents want to do that?

Dad: I'm not sure. Perhaps getting legally married wasn't important to them.

Child: Does that mean they won't ever get married?

Dad: Not necessarily. If it becomes important to them someday, they might.

Child: How come Izzy lives in such a nice house and we don't?

Parent: Good question. Her parents might make more money than we do. Or they might be willing to borrow more money from the bank than we are. Or it might be important to them to live in a nice house.

Child: Why isn't that important to you? It'd be fun to live in a mansion!

Parent: We'd have to work more if we wanted a nicer house. And we'd rather spend time together as a family and doing things we like to do than more time at our jobs.

When your child understands your values, he'll naturally gravitate toward friends with similar values. But, of course, there may be times he chooses a friend or two with very different values. And while those friends may influence him, they'll have much less influence over him than you will as long as you're proactively teaching your values in a healthy way.

Teach Preschoolers About Your Values

Start introducing your values to your preschooler by talking about the reasons behind why you do certain things. Say, "I'm buying Grandma some flowers, and together, we're going to bring them to her because it's important to be generous," or say, "We're going to go walk the neighbor's dog for her today because she broke her leg and it's important to help people."

Get your child involved in doing those things with you whenever possible. Whether you're teaching her hard work or community service, she'll start internalizing those values when you make it a priority to get her involved.

Praise her behavior when it is in line with those values as well. Don't reserve praise for good behavior like "Picking up your toys." Instead praise her for exemplifying behavior that is consistent with your values, such as being kind, hardworking, honest, or generous.

Establishing family traditions can be one of the best ways to show your preschooler that you're a cohesive group. Whether you're a single parent of an only child or you have a blended family with children of all ages, identify a few family activities you can do together. A tradition could be as simple as eating pizza every Friday night or holding a family game night once a month. It doesn't have to be extravagant or costly. Instead it should be about doing something as a family.

Teach Your School-Age Child to Make Choices According to His Values

When asked if cheating or bullying is wrong, most school-age kids will say yes. But that's because they know it's what adults want to hear. But in reality, many kids are cheating, bullying, and violating many other moral standards. That's why it's important to give your child opportunities to practice living according to your values. The way he spends his money, the language he chooses when he talks to his friends, and the choices he makes about how he spends his time will show you the type of values he's developing.

Here's how you might talk to your child:

Parent: I'm upset to hear that you were involved in vandalizing the other team's field after the game.

Child: I know. It was a stupid mistake.

Parent: What made you think it was an okay idea?

Child: I don't know.

Parent: Well, what was going through your mind when you were doing it?

Child: My friends were doing it and they told me to do it too. So I thought it wasn't a big deal.

Parent: What do you think about people who destroy property?

Child: I usually think they're not very nice people.

Parent: Right. Now tell me, were you afraid you wouldn't look cool if you didn't do something all your friends were doing?

Child: Yes, I guess so.

Parent: What's more important, looking cool or being a nice person?

Child: Being a nice person.

Parent: Yep. But sounds like you got those mixed up today, huh? I know it's hard sometimes, but it's important to remember what matters most. Being nice comes before looking cool all the time, okay?

Each time your child's behavior isn't in line with your values, consider it a sign that he needs more help in that area. Provide a consequence when necessary and create a plan for how you can make changes to reinforce your values better.

Teach Your Teen How to Deal with Ethical Dilemmas

It's important that your teen not simply parrot back your values because you told him those things are important. Instead help your teen become a critical thinker who can figure out how to address the temptations of adolescence. Drugs, alcohol, sex, bullying, and joining inappropriate conversations on social media are just a few issues teens may face. It's important for her to understand the consequences of her choices and to know where you stand in terms of your values.

Simply telling your teen, "I expect you to say no to drugs and alcohol," can go a long way. Parents who think, "All kids try marijuana at one point or another," tend to have kids who smoke marijuana. But a parent who outright says, "I expect you to say no," has made her values clear.

It's common for teens to rebel a bit at some point or another. Sometimes they rebel against authority, but at other times they simply rebel against their own childhoods as they try to prove they're no longer the same little kids they used to be.

You can prevent your teen from rebelling against major issues by giving her a little more freedom over minor issues. Let her choose how she wears her hair or let her pick her own style of clothing (as long as it's appropriate). If you let her express her independence in safe little ways, she'll be less likely to rebel in a major way down the road.

Acknowledge that sometimes, there isn't a clear right or wrong answer and that's why it's important to know your values. For example, if a friend confides in your teen about something potentially dangerous, should she remain loyal to her friend? Or should she break that trust and talk to an adult? Or what should you do if a teacher makes a grading error in your teen's favor? Or what if you're with a friend when he steals something from a store?

Use the latest news headlines to strike up conversations about various social and political issues. Be open to hearing your teen's opinion—even when you don't agree—and examine other people's points of view.

Kids Who Understand Their Values Become Adults Who Embrace Change

Malala Yousafzai was raised in Pakistan. Her father owned several schools and was an educational activist. From an early age, Malala valued education.

In 2009, the Taliban issued an edict that said girls could no longer attend school. They began destroying schools in the local area.

Malala became a fierce advocate for girls' education. Consequently, the Taliban issued a death threat against her. But, she didn't back down.

In 2012, when Malala was 15, a gunman shot her when she was traveling home from school. Despite a bullet wound to the head, Malala survived. And she continues to speak out about the importance of education. Her courage and advocacy has gained international attention and she became the youngest person to receive the Nobel Peace Prize.

Now a young adult, Malala continues her mission. She opened a school for Syrian refugee girls in Lebanon and continues to fight for free, quality education to children all over the world.

And while your child hopefully won't ever face the same dangers Malala faced, it's important to know she can stand up and do the right thing. A child who understands her values will want to create positive change in the world, even when it's not the popular thing to do.

Mentally strong people don't shy away from change. Instead, they become change makers who are inspired to create a better life for themselves and a better world for other people.

Troubleshooting and Common Traps

Occasionally, there may be a difference between what you say and what you do. At least, it may appear that way to your child.

For example, if you go to a neighbor's home for dinner and the food tastes terrible, you might still send a thank-you note saying you had a lovely time. Or, if an acquaintance asks, "Do you like my new car?" you might say yes even if you're not a fan.

If you've taught your child to value honesty, you'll want to point out that there's no need to be so brutally honest that you hurt other people's feelings. Instead, show your child that you also value kindness and respect.

Another common trap is that sometimes parents assume a child has adopted their values because he behaves well or because he has good grades. But just because a child doesn't get into trouble doesn't mean he's behaving according to your values.

If you've taught him to value kindness, for example, his good grades don't indicate that he's going out of his way to befriend the new kid in school or that he's standing up for the kids who are getting picked on.

He might still be cheating on tests or he could be lying about where he's going.

Don't simply assume your child is doing well because you haven't heard otherwise. Make it a priority to stay vigilant and to continue looking for teachable moments.

Finally, technology causes some parents to lose sight of their values. Family time turns into everyone texting other people. Or a family vacation becomes more about looking perfect in the pictures you're going to post on social media rather than genuinely enjoying one another's company.

No matter how technology continues to evolve, make sure you're staying true to your values. Periodically step back and review your activities to make sure they're in line with your beliefs.

WHAT'S HELPFUL

- Knowing your values
- Assessing whether your behavior is in line with your values
- Looking for teachable moments to instill your values
- Talking about ethical dilemmas
- Giving your child an opportunity to practice living according to your values
- Pointing out examples of times when your child behaved in accordance with your values
- Creating a family mission statement

WHAT'S NOT HELPFUL

- Sending mixed messages about what's important to you
- Getting your priorities mixed up
- Being unclear about what you really value
- Expecting your child to passively learn your values
- Assuming your child's good behavior means he's adopted your values
- Getting caught up in parenting competitions

CONCLUSION

When Rick Hoyt was born in 1962, oxygen deprivation led to serious health problems. Rick was diagnosed as a spastic quadriplegic with cerebral palsy. Doctors told his parents, Dick and Judy, to institutionalize him. They said there was no hope for recovery and he would always be a "vegetable." Dick and Judy refused to comply with the doctors' recommendation. They brought Rick home and decided to raise him like a "regular" child. As he grew older, they took him sledding and swimming. They taught him the alphabet and some basic words. And eventually, they realized his eyes followed them around the room. Even though he couldn't walk or speak, they thought he was quite astute.

Dick and Judy were desperate to find a way to help their child communicate. When he was ten, engineers at Tufts University built Rick a specialized computer. A cursor highlighted each letter of the alphabet and Rick was able to select the letter by tapping his head on his wheelchair. His first words were "Go, Bruins!"

Dick and Judy fought to integrate him into public school. When Rick was thirteen, they were finally able to get administrators to see past his physical limitations and they allowed him to enroll in school.

In 1977, Rick told his father he wanted to participate in a five-mile benefit run for a Lacrosse player who had become paralyzed in an accident. Dick, middle-aged and out of shape, agreed to push Rick in his wheelchair and the two finished second to last. But that night Rick said, "Dad, when I'm running, it feels like I'm not handicapped." And those words inspired Dick to keep on competing.

Dick had a special wheelchair built so he could push Rick more easily, and they began running together. Now, forty years later, they've run over

1,100 races together. They've completed marathons, triathlons, and they even ran across the entire United States in forty-five days.

Now in his mid-seventies Dick says he still isn't ready to retire. Team Hoyt continues to participate in races all over the country.

Dick and Judy Hoyt could have given up on their son. Or, they could have done everything for him—to his own detriment. But they didn't.

They challenged Rick to become his best. And the child who was once referred to as a "vegetable" grew up to become a man with a degree in special education from Boston University.

Helping your child become mentally strong isn't about making him the best at everything. It's about giving him the skills and tools he needs to become the best version of himself.

Mentally Strong Parents Raise Mentally Strong Kids

Your passion to work on building your own mental strength will be the single most important factor in encouraging your child to grow stronger. When your child knows you make self-development a priority, he'll follow suit. Your child is always watching to see what kind of choices you make. The way you treat other people, the way you spend your money, and the way you spend your time speak volumes. And of course, he'll see how you deal with mistakes and setbacks too. To be a good role model you don't have to pretend you have superhero mental strength. Instead let your child know you're an imperfect human being. And even though you struggle with negative thoughts, uncomfortable emotions, and unproductive behavior, you're striving to become a little better today than you were yesterday.

Be Your Child's Mental Strength Coach

Just like it's important to teach your child to take care of her body, it's equally important to teach her to take care of her mind. The best way to do that is by coaching her. Give her exercises to practice. Provide feedback and guidance. Cheer her on when she's doing her best. And provide correction when she goes out of bounds.

Your ultimate goal should be to work yourself out of a job. So as the years go by, your role should shift. Rather than telling her what to do, start asking her what she thinks she should do. Instead of giving her the answers, help her find the answers for herself. Eventually, she'll learn how to coach herself. She'll be able to change her negative thinking patterns and she'll recognize her unproductive behavior. And she'll be able to control her emotions, so her emotions don't control her.

The biggest challenge you may face is finding the right balance. You have to allow your child to experience enough struggles that he'll develop mental strength. And you have to let him endure bad times so he'll fully appreciate good times.

Helping your child build mental strength is a journey, not a destination. As your child grows, his challenges will grow bigger right along with him. That's why it's important to view your mental-strength-building strategies as a work in progress.

There may be days where you declare victory and times when you feel like a failure. But the ups and downs of childhood and the journey to grow stronger are going to be tumultuous. When you see your child struggling, or when you think you haven't made any progress at all, remind yourself that mental strength training is a lifelong process.

Being mentally strong doesn't mean you will have all the answers. So don't be afraid to acknowledge when you're not sure how to help your child deal with a specific problem or issue. Asking for help isn't a sign of weakness. In fact, asking for support shows you are motivated to become even better.

Keep in mind that building mental strength won't make your child immune to depression, anxiety, or mental health problems. If her mood or behavior is interfering with her education, family, friendships, or fun, talk to her doctor. A referral to a professional counselor could be in order.

Avoiding the thirteen things mentally strong parents don't do will ensure you aren't engaging in the habits that will rob your child of mental strength. When you refuse to do those things, you'll be helping your child build the mental muscle that he'll need to become the strongest and best version of himself.

REFERENCES

INTRODUCTION

"American Psychological Association Survey Shows Teen Stress Rivals That of Adults." American Psychological Association (February 11, 2014). Accessed March 2, 2017. http://www.apa.org/news/press/releases/2014/02/teen-stress.aspx.

Howie, L. D., P. N. Pastor, and S. L. Lukacs. "Use of Medication Prescribed for Emotional or Behavioral Difficulties Among Children Aged 6–17 Years in the United States, 2011–2012." *NCHS Data Brief*, no. 148. Hyattsville, MD: National Center for Health Statistics. 2014.

CHAPTER 1

Abbott, Jim, and Tim Brown. *Imperfect: An Improbable Life*. New York: Ballantine Books, 2012.

Aquino, K. "Structural and Individual Determinants of Workplace Victimization: The Effects of Hierarchical Status and Conflict Management Style." *Journal of Management* 26, no. 2 (2000): 171–93.

Campbell, Bradley, and Jason Manning. "Microaggression and Moral Cultures." *Comparative Sociology* 13, no. 6 (2014): 692–726.

Chorpita, Bruce F., and John R. Weisz. *Match-ADTC: Modular Approach to Therapy for Children with Anxiety, Depression, Trauma, or Conduct Problems*. Satellite Beach, FL: PracticeWise, 2009.

Dyer, John R. G., Christos C. Ioannou, Lesley J. Morrell, Darren P. Croft, Iain D. Couzin, Dean A. Waters, and Jens Krause. "Consensus Decision Making in Human Crowds." *Animal Behaviour* 75, no. 2 (2008): 461–70.

Hiroto, Donald S., and Martin E. Seligman. "Generality of Learned Helplessness in Man." *Journal of Personality and Social Psychology* 31, no. 2 (February 1975): 311–27.

Horwitz, Steven. "Cooperation Over Coercion: The Importance of Unsupervised Childhood Play for Democracy and Liberalism." *SSRN Electronic Journal*, June 22, 2015.

"Our Mission." Kids Kicking Cancer. Accessed January 13, 2017. http://kidskicking cancer.org/our-mission/.

Schwartz, David, Kenneth A. Dodge, and John D. Coie. "The Emergence of Chronic Peer Victimization in Boys' Play Groups." *Child Development* 64, no. 6 (December 1993): 1755–72.

Seligman, M. E. P. "Learned Helplessness." *Annual Review of Medicine* 23, no. 1 (February 1972): 407–12.

Viano, Emilio. *Crime and Its Victims: International Research and Public Policy Issues: Proceedings of the Fourth International Institute on Victimology* (NATO Advanced Research Workshop). New York: Hemisphere Pub. Corp., 1989.

CHAPTER 2

Betancourt, Laura M., Wei Yang, Nancy L. Brodsky, Paul R. Gallagher, Elsa K. Malmud, Joan M. Giannetta, Martha J. Farah, and Hallam Hurt. "Adolescents With and Without Gestational Cocaine Exposure: Longitudinal Analysis of Inhibitory Control, Memory and Receptive Language." *Neurotoxicology and Teratology* 33, no. 1 (January & February 2011): 36–46.

Cavassuto, Maria. "Jennifer Lopez and Felicity Huffman: Men Don't Feel 'Mommy Guilt' With Their Kids." *Variety* (May 27, 2016). Accessed January 13, 2017. http://variety .com/2016/tv/news/jennifer-lopez-felicity-huffman-mommy-guilt-1201784050/.

Froh, Jeffrey J., William J. Sefick, and Robert A. Emmons. "Counting Blessings in Early Adolescents: An Experimental Study of Gratitude and Subjective Well-Being." *Journal of School Psychology* 46, no. 2 (2008): 213–33.

Lack, Evonne. "Top 7 Mommy Guilt Trips—and How to Handle Them." BabyCenter (February 14, 2017). Accessed March 2, 2017. https://www.babycenter.com/0_top-7 -mommy-guilt-trips-and-how-to-handle-them_3654967.bc.

Milkie, Melissa A., Kei M. Nomaguchi, and Kathleen E. Denny. "Does the Amount of Time Mothers Spend with Children or Adolescents Matter?" *Journal of Marriage and Family* 77, no. 2 (2015): 355–72.

Oudekerk, Barbara A., Joseph P. Allen, Elenda T. Hessel, and Lauren E. Molloy. "The Cascading Development of Autonomy and Relatedness from Adolescence to Adulthood." *Child Development* 86, no. 2 (October 23, 2014): 472–85.

"Parenting/TODAY Moms Survey: Are Your Children Spoiled?" *Parenting*. Accessed January 13, 2017. http://www.parenting.com/article/are-your-children-spoiled?

Passanisi, Alessia, Irene Sapienza, Silvia Budello, and Flavio Giaimo. "The Relationship Between Guilt, Shame and Self-Efficacy Beliefs in Middle School Students." *Procedia - Social and Behavioral Sciences* 197 (July 25, 2015): 1013–17.

Ratnapalan, S., and Batty, H. "To Be Good Enough." *Canadian Family Physician* 55, no. 3 (2009): 239–240.

Sani, Giulia M. Dotti, and Judith Treas. "Educational Gradients in Parents' Child-Care Time Across Countries, 1965–2012." *Journal of Marriage and Family* 78, no. 4 (April 19, 2016): 1083–96.

CHAPTER 3

Ang, Rebecca P., and Noradlin Yusof. "The Relationship Between Aggression, Narcissism, and Self-Esteem in Asian Children and Adolescents." *Current Psychology* 24, no. 2 (June 2005): 113–22.

Brummelman, Eddie, Sander Thomaes, Stefanie A. Nelemans, Bram Orobio De Castro, Geertjan Overbeek, and Brad J. Bushman. "Origins of Narcissism in Children." *Proceedings of the National Academy of Sciences* (2015).

Brummelman, Eddie, Sander Thomaes, Stefanie A. Nelemans, Bram Orobio De Castro, and Brad J. Bushman. "My Child Is God's Gift to Humanity: Development and Validation of the Parental Overvaluation Scale (POS)." *Journal of Personality and Social Psychology* 108, no. 4 (April 2015): 665–79.

Decety, J. "The Functional Architecture of Human Empathy." *Behavioral and Cognitive Neuroscience Reviews* 3, no. 2 (2004): 71–100.

Ojanen, Tiina, Danielle Findley, and Sarah Fuller. "Physical and Relational Aggression in Early Adolescence: Associations with Narcissism, Temperament, and Social Goals." *Aggressive Behavior* (March & April 2012).

Ornaghi, Veronica, Jens Brockmeier, and Ilaria Grazzani. "Enhancing Social Cognition by Training Children in Emotion Understanding: A Primary School Study." *Journal of Experimental Child Psychology* 119 (March 2014): 26–39.

Pfeifer, Jennifer H., Marco Iacoboni, John C. Mazziotta, and Mirella Dapretto. "Mirroring Others' Emotions Relates to Empathy and Interpersonal Competence in Children." *NeuroImage* 39, no. 4 (February 2008): 2076–85.

Shiota, Michelle N., Dacher Keltner, and Amanda Mossman. "The Nature of Awe: Elicitors, Appraisals, and Effects on Self-Concept." *Cognition & Emotion* 21, no. 5 (July 19, 2007): 944–63.

Stucker, Matthew. "Girl Costs Father $80,000 with 'SUCK IT' Facebook Post." CNN (March 4, 2014). Accessed March 2, 2017. http://www.cnn.com/2014/03/02/us/facebook-post-costs-father/.

Twenge, Jean M., and W. Keith Campbell. *The Narcissism Epidemic: Living in the Age of Entitlement*. New York: Free Press, 2009.

CHAPTER 4

Burstein, Marcy, and Golda S. Ginsburg. "The Effect of Parental Modeling of Anxious Behaviors and Cognitions in School-Aged Children: An Experimental Pilot Study." *Behaviour Research and Therapy* 48, no. 6 (June 2010): 506–15.

"In U.S., 14% of Those Aged 24 to 34 Are Living With Parents." Gallup, Inc. (February 13, 2014). Accessed January 13, 2017. http://www.gallup.com/poll/167426/aged-living-parents.aspx.

"National Child Kidnapping Facts." *Polly Klaas Foundation*. Accessed March 7, 2017, http://www.pollyklaas.org/about/national-child-kidnapping.html

Lester, Kathryn J., Andy P. Field, and Sam Cartwright-Hatton. "Maternal Anxiety and Cognitive Biases Towards Threat in Their Own and Their Child's Environment." *Journal of Family Psychology* 26, no. 5 (October 2012): 756–66.

Parker, Kim. "Who Are the Boomerang Kids?" Pew Research Center's Social & Demographic Trends Project (March 15, 2012). Accessed January 13, 2017. http://www.pewsocialtrends.org/2012/03/15/who-are-the-boomerang-kids/.

Phillip, Abby. "Family Taught Boy About 'Stranger Danger' by Kidnapping Him at Gunpoint, Police Say." *Washington Post* (February 6, 2015). Accessed January 13, 2017. https://www.washingtonpost.com/news/morning-mix/wp/2015/02/06/mo-family-charged-with-teaching-boy-about-stranger-danger-by-kidnapping-him-at-gunpoint/.

Reese, Diana. "Update: McDonald's Denies Firing South Carolina Mom Sent to Jail for Taking Daughter to Park While at Work." *Washington Post* (July 23, 2014). Accessed

March 1, 2017. https://www.washingtonpost.com/blogs/she-the-people/wp/2014/07/23 /south-carolina-mom-goes-to-jail-loses-job-for-taking-daughter-to-park-while-at -work/?utm_term=.afb89b8a4c0f.

Sandberg-Thoma, Sara E., Anastasia R. Snyder, and Bohyun Joy Jang. "Exiting and Re- turning to the Parental Home for Boomerang Kids." *Journal of Marriage and Fam- ily* 77, no. 3 (February 28, 2015): 806–18.

"School Violence: Data & Statistics." Centers for Disease Control and Prevention (No- vember 30, 2016). Accessed January 13, 2017. http://www.cdc.gov/violenceprevention /youthviolence/schoolviolence/data_stats.html.

Seligman, Laura D., and Thomas H. Ollendick. "Cognitive-Behavioral Therapy for Anx- iety Disorders in Youth." *Child and Adolescent Psychiatric Clinics of North America* 20, no. 2 (2011): 217–38.

Skenazy, Lenore. "I Let My 9-Year-Old Ride the Subway Alone. I Got Labeled the 'World's Worst Mom.'" *Washington Post* (January 6, 2015). Accessed January 13, 2017. https:// www.washingtonpost.com/posteverything/wp/2015/01/16/i-let-my-9-year-old-ride-the -subway-alone-i-got-labeled-the-worlds-worst-mom/.

"The Burden of Stress in America." (2014). Accessed January 12, 2017. http://www.rwjf .org/content/dam/farm/reports/surveys_and_polls/2014/rwjf414295.

"Young Do Not Feel Grown Up Until 29, Survey Shows." *The Telegraph* (September 3, 2015). Accessed January 13, 2017. http://www.telegraph.co.uk/news/newstopics/how aboutthat/11840925/Young-do-not-feel-grown-up-until-29-survey-shows.html.

CHAPTER 5

Barton, Alison L., and Jameson K. Hirsch. "Permissive Parenting and Mental Health in College Students: Mediating Effects of Academic Entitlement." *Journal of American College Health* 64, no. 1 (2016): 1–8.

Jago, R., T. Baranowski, J. C. Baranowski, D. Thompson, and K. A. Greaves. "BMI from 3–6 Y of Age Is Predicted by TV Viewing and Physical Activity, Not Diet." *Interna- tional Journal of Obesity* 29, no. 6 (June 26, 2005): 557–64.

Lamborn, Susie D., Nina S. Mounts, Laurence Steinberg, and Sanford M. Dornbusch. "Patterns of Competence and Adjustment among Adolescents from Authoritative, Authoritarian, Indulgent, and Neglectful Families." *Child Development* 62, no. 5 (1991): 1049.

Langer, S. L., A. L. Crain, M. M. Senso, R. L. Levy, and N. E. Sherwood. "Predicting Child Physical Activity and Screen Time: Parental Support for Physical Activity and General Parenting Styles." *Journal of Pediatric Psychology* 39, no. 6 (2014): 633–42.

Underwood, Marion K., Kurt J. Beron, and Lisa H. Rosen. "Continuity and Change in Social and Physical Aggression from Middle Childhood Through Early Adolescence." *Aggressive Behavior* 35, no. 5 (September & October 2009): 357–75.

Williams, Lela Rankin, Kathryn A. Degnan, Koraly E. Perez-Edgar, Heather A. Hen- derson, Kenneth H. Rubin, Daniel S. Pine, Laurence Steinberg, and Nathan A. Fox. "Impact of Behavioral Inhibition and Parenting Style on Internalizing and Externaliz- ing Problems from Early Childhood Through Adolescence." *Journal of Abnormal Child Psychology* 37, no. 8 (2009): 1063–75.

CHAPTER 6

Breheny Wallace, Jennifer. "Why Children Need Chores." *Wall Street Journal* (March 13, 2015). Accessed March 3, 2017. https://www.wsj.com/articles/why-children-need -chores-1426262655?mod=WSJ_hpp_MIDDLENexttoWhatsNewsThird.

Brummelman, Eddie, Sander Thomaes, Meike Slagt, Geertjan Overbeek, Bram Orobio De Castro, and Brad J. Bushman. "My Child Redeems My Broken Dreams: On Parents Transferring Their Unfulfilled Ambitions onto Their Child." *PLoS ONE* 8, no. 6 (June 19, 2013).

Chua, Amy. "Why Chinese Mothers Are Superior." *Wall Street Journal* (January 8, 2011). Accessed March 2, 2017. https://www.wsj.com/articles/SB1000142405274870411150 4576059713528698754.

Chua, Amy. *Battle Hymn of the Tiger Mother*. New York: Penguin, 2012.

"Epi-Aid 2015-003: Undetermined Risk Factors for Suicide Among Youth, Ages 10–24." (2014). Accessed March 3, 2017. http://www.fairfaxcounty.gov/hd/hdpdf/va-epi-aid -final-report.pdf.

Flett, Gordon L., Kirk R. Blankstein, Paul L. Hewitt, and Spomenka Koledin. "Components of Perfectionism and Procrastination in College Students." *Social Behavior and Personality: An International Journal* 20, no. 2 (1992): 85–94.

Harding, Jim. "Father Jailed for Sharpening Helmet." *Chicago Tribune* (April 20, 1997). Accessed March 2, 2017. http://articles.chicagotribune.com/1997-04-20/sports/9704 200367_1_cito-helmet-sharpening.

Hopkinson, Christina. "My Arrogance Nearly Killed My Baby: Christina Hopkinson Thought She Was the Perfect Mother, Until Her Son Nearly Starved When Breastfeeding Went Horribly Wrong." Accessed March 5, 2017. http://www.dailymail.co .uk/femail/article-2990435/New-mother-Christina-Hopkinson-says-competitive -parenting-nearly-killed-baby.html#ixzz4aCtlim5P.

Jenni, Oskar G., Aziz Chaouch, Jon Caflisch, and Valentin Rousson. "Infant Motor Milestones: Poor Predictive Value for Outcome of Healthy Children." *Acta Paediatrica* 102, no. 4 (2013). doi:10.1111/apa.12129.

Mcbride, H. E. A., and L. S. Siegel. "Learning Disabilities and Adolescent Suicide." *Journal of Learning Disabilities* 30, no. 6 (November & December 1997): 652-59.

Norman, Neil. "Dark Side of Oz: The Exploitation of Judy Garland." *Express* (April 5, 2010). Accessed March 2, 2017.

Ramey, Garey, and Valerie Ramey. "The Rug Rat Race." (April 2010). Accessed March 2, 2017. doi:10.3386/w15284.

Ruiz, Michelle. "6-Year-Old Cece Price Is a Famous Internet Comedian, but Her Mom Won't Rest Until She's on TV." *Cosmopolitan* (June 8, 2015). Accessed March 2, 2017. http:// www.cosmopolitan.com/entertainment/a40048/cece-price-internets-most-fascinating/.

Sherry, Simon B., Joachim Stoeber, and Cynthia Ramasubbu. "Perfectionism Explains Variance in Self-Defeating Behaviors Beyond Self-Criticism: Evidence from a Cross-National Sample." *Personality and Individual Differences* 95 (June 2016): 196–99.

Törnblom, Annelie Werbart, Andrzej Werbart, and Per-Anders Rydelius. "Shame Behind the Masks: The Parents' Perspective on Their Sons' Suicide." *Archives of Suicide Research* 17, no. 3 (2013): 242–61.

Wang, Yanan. "Morning Mix CDC Investigates Why So Many Students in Wealthy Palo Alto, Calif., Commit Suicide." *Washington Post* (February 16, 2016). Accessed March 3, 2017. https://www.washingtonpost.com/news/morning-mix/wp/2016/02/16/cdc-investigates-why-so-many-high-school-students-in-wealthy-palo-alto-have-committed-suicide/?utm_term=.7b5e89083a65.

CHAPTER 7

Bryan, Christopher J., Allison Master, and Gregory M. Walton. "'Helping' Versus 'Being a Helper': Invoking the Self to Increase Helping in Young Children." *Child Development* (October & November 2014).

Bryan, Christopher J., Gregory M. Walton, Todd Rogers, and Carol S. Dweck. "Motivating Voter Turnout by Invoking the Self." *Proceedings of the National Academy of Sciences of the United States of America* 108, no. 31 (2011).

Gardner, Phil. "Parent Involvement in the College Recruiting Process: To What Extent?" *Collegiate Employment Research Institute* (2007). Accessed January 13, 2017. http://ceri.msu.edu/publications/pdf/ceri2-07.pdf.

Peluchette, Joy Van Eck, Nancy Kovanic, and Dane Partridge. "Helicopter Parents Hovering in the Workplace: What Should HR Managers Do?" *Business Horizons* 56, no. 5 (September & October 2013): 601–9. doi:10.1016/j.bushor.2013.05.004.

Rogers, Fred. "Tragic Events." The Fred Rogers Company. Accessed March 3, 2017. http://www.fredrogers.org/parents/special-challenges/tragic-events.php.

Wallace, Jennifer Breheny. "Why Children Need Chores." *Wall Street Journal* (March 13, 2015). Accessed January 13, 2017. http://www.wsj.com/articles/why-children-need-chores-1426262655.

CHAPTER 8

Ciarrochi, Joseph, Amy Y. C. Chan, and Jane Bajgar. "Measuring Emotional Intelligence in Adolescents." *Personality and Individual Differences* 31, no. 7 (2001): 1105–19.

Dufton, L. M., M. J. Dunn, and B. E. Compas. "Anxiety and Somatic Complaints in Children with Recurrent Abdominal Pain and Anxiety Disorders." *Journal of Pediatric Psychology* 34, no. 2 (June 24, 2008): 176–86.

Eslami, Ahmadali, Akbar Hasanzadeh, and Farid Jamshidi. "The Relationship Between Emotional Intelligence Health and Marital Satisfaction: A Comparative Study." *Journal of Education and Health Promotion* 3, no. 1 (February 2014): 24.

Gilleland, J., C. Suveg, M. L. Jacob, and K. Thomassin. "Understanding the Medically Unexplained: Emotional and Familial Influences on Children's Somatic Functioning." *Child: Care, Health and Development* 35, no. 3 (May 2009): 383–90.

Howard, Jennifer. "Faculty on the Front Lines." *Chronicle of Higher Education* (Fall 2015).

Kerr, Matthew A., and Barry H. Schneider. "Anger Expression in Children and Adolescents: A Review of the Empirical Literature." *Clinical Psychology Review* 28, no. 4 (April 2008): 559–77.

Sarah Maraniss Vander Schaaff. "How Should Parents Discuss Major World Catastrophes with Their Children?" *Washington Post* (March 26, 2014). Accessed January 13, 2017. https://www.washingtonpost.com/opinions/when-the-protective-shell-around-your

-kids-cracks/2014/03/26/a0dd0c9c-b43a-11e3-8020-b2d790b3c9e1_story.html ?tid=a_inl.

Shamsuddin, Noorazzila, and Ramlee Abdul Rahman. "The Relationship Between Emotional Intelligence and Job Performance of Call Centre Agents." *Procedia - Social and Behavioral Sciences* 129 (May 15, 2014): 75–81.

"Students Who Feel Emotionally Unprepared for College More Likely to Report Poor Academic Performance and Negative College Experience." The Jed Foundation (October 7, 2015). Accessed January 13, 2017. https://www.jedfoundation.org/first-year-college -experience-release/.

Umberger, Wendy A., and Judy Risko. "'It Didn't Kill Me. It Just Made Me Stronger and Wiser': Silver Linings for Children and Adolescents of Parents with Chronic Pain." *Archives of Psychiatric Nursing* 30, no. 2 (April 2016): 138–43. doi:10.1016 /j.apnu.2015.08.001.

Wegner, Daniel M., David J. Schneider, Samuel R. Carter, and Teri L. White. "Paradoxical Effects of Thought Suppression." *Journal of Personality and Social Psychology* 53, no. 1 (1987): 5–13.

Worland, Justin. "Why a Free Speech Fight is Causing Protests at Yale." *Time* (November 10, 2015). Accessed January 13, 2017. http://time.com/4106265/yale-students-protest/.

CHAPTER 9

Bushman, Brad J. "Does Venting Anger Feed or Extinguish the Flame? Catharsis, Rumination, Distraction, Anger, and Aggressive Responding." *Personality and Social Psychology Bulletin* 28, no. 6 (June 1, 2002): 724–31.

Supportive Relationships and Active Skill-Building Strengthen the Foundations of Resilience: Working Paper No. 13. Center on the Developing Child at Harvard University (2015). www.developingchild.harvard.edu.

Dufton, L. M., M. J. Dunn, and B. E. Compas. "Anxiety and Somatic Complaints in Children with Recurrent Abdominal Pain and Anxiety Disorders." *Journal of Pediatric Psychology* 34, no. 2 (June 24, 2008): 176–86.

Friedersdorf, Conor. "The Perils of Writing a Provocative Email at Yale." *The Atlantic* (May 26, 2016). Accessed March 3, 2017. https://www.theatlantic.com/politics /archive/2016/05/the-peril-of-writing-a-provocative-email-at-yale/484418/.

Jones, Damon E., Mark Greenberg, and Max Crowley. "Early Social-Emotional Functioning and Public Health: The Relationship Between Kindergarten Social Competence and Future Wellness." *American Journal of Public Health* 105, no. 11 (2015): 2283–90.

CHAPTER 10

Barker, Jane E., Andrei D. Semenov, Laura Michaelson, Lindsay S. Provan, Hannah R. Snyder, and Yuko Munakata. "Less-Structured Time in Children's Daily Lives Predicts Self-Directed Executive Functioning." *Frontiers in Psychology* 5 (June 17, 2014).

Haimovitz, Kyla, and Carol S. Dweck. "What Predicts Children's Fixed and Growth Intelligence Mind-Sets? Not Their Parents' Views of Intelligence but Their Parents' Views of Failure." *Psychological Science* 27, no. 6 (April 25, 2016): 859–69.

Kornell, Nate, Matthew Jensen Hays, and Robert A. Bjork. "Unsuccessful Retrieval Attempts Enhance Subsequent Learning." *Journal of Experimental Psychology: Learning, Memory, and Cognition* 35, no. 4 (July 2009): 989–98.

Lemoyne, Terri, and Tom Buchanan. "Does 'Hovering' Matter? Helicopter Parenting and Its Effect on Well-Being." *Sociological Spectrum* 31, no. 4 (June 9, 2011): 399–418.

Reed, Kayla, James M. Duncan, Mallory Lucier-Greer, Courtney Fixelle, and Anthony J. Ferraro. "Helicopter Parenting and Emerging Adult Self-Efficacy: Implications for Mental and Physical Health." *Journal of Child and Family Studies* 25, no. 10 (June 6, 2016): 3136–49.

Schiffrin, Holly H., Miriam Liss, Haley Miles-Mclean, Katherine A. Geary, Mindy J. Erchull, and Taryn Tashner. "Helping or Hovering? The Effects of Helicopter Parenting on College Students' Well-Being." *Journal of Child and Family Studies* 23, no. 3 (2014): 548–57.

Voorhis, F. L. V. "Costs and Benefits of Family Involvement in Homework." *Journal of Advanced Academics* 22, no. 2 (February 2011): 220–49.

CHAPTER 11

Barkley, Russell. *Taking Charge of ADHD*. New York: The Guilford Press, 2013.

"Corporal Punishment." AACAP (July 30, 2012). Accessed March 2, 2017. https://www.aacap.org/aacap/Policy_Statements/2012/Policy_Statement_on_Corporal_Punishment.aspx.

Deci, E. L., R. M. Ryan, and R. Koestner. "The Pervasive Negative Effects of Rewards on Intrinsic Motivation: Response to Cameron (2001)." *Review of Educational Research* 71, no. 1 (Spring 2001): 43–51.

"Denver Mom Shames Daughter for Facebook Posts, Racy Photos in Video Going Viral." KNXV (May 20, 2015). Accessed March 2, 2017. http://www.abc15.com/news/local-news/water-cooler/denver-mom-shames-daughter-for-facebook-posts-racy-photos-in-video-going-viral.

Fredén, Jonas. "Smacking Children Banned." Sweden.se (December 14, 2015). Accessed March 2, 2017. https://sweden.se/society/smacking-banned-since-1979/.

Gershoff, Elizabeth T. "Spanking and Child Development: We Know Enough Now to Stop Hitting Our Children." *Child Development Perspectives* 7, no. 3 (September 10, 2013): 133–7.

Gershoff, Elizabeth T., and Andrew Grogan-Kaylor. "Spanking and Child Outcomes: Old Controversies and New Meta-Analyses." *Journal of Family Psychology* 30, no. 4 (June 2016): 453–69.

Gómez-Ortiz, Olga, Eva María Romera, and Rosario Ortega-Ruiz. "Parenting Styles and Bullying. The Mediating Role of Parental Psychological Aggression and Physical Punishment." *Child Abuse & Neglect* 51 (January 2016): 132–43.

Larzelere, Robert E., and Brett R. Kuhn. "Comparing Child Outcomes of Physical Punishment and Alternative Disciplinary Tactics: A Meta-Analysis." *Clinical Child and Family Psychology Review* 8, no. 1 (2005): 1–37.

Mackenbach, Joreintje D., Ank P. Ringoot, Jan Van Der Ende, Frank C. Verhulst, Vincent

W. V. Jaddoe, Albert Hofman, Pauline W. Jansen, and Henning W. Tiemeier. "Exploring the Relation of Harsh Parental Discipline with Child Emotional and Behavioral Problems by Using Multiple Informants. The Generation R Study." *PLoS ONE* 9, no. 8 (August 13, 2014).

Payne, Ed. "Try 'Old Man' Haircut for Misbehaving Kids." CNN (February 5, 2015). Accessed March 2, 2017. http://www.cnn.com/2015/02/05/us/feat-barber-shames-mis behaving-kids/.

"Physical Punishment and Mental Disorders: Results from a Nationally Representative US Sample." *Pediatrics* 130, no. 2 (June 2012).

Rapaport, Daniel. "California Mother Publicly Scolds Daughter for Twerking." ABC News (September 10, 2013). Accessed March 2, 2017. http://abcnews.go.com/blogs /headlines/2013/09/california-mother-publicly-scolds-daughter-for-twerking/.

Richins, Marsha L., and Lan Nguyen Chaplin. "Material Parenting: How the Use of Goods in Parenting Fosters Materialism in the Next Generation." *Journal of Consumer Research* 41, no. 6 (February 9, 2015): 1333–57.

Simons, Dominique A., and Sandy K. Wurtele. "Relationships Between Parents' Use of Corporal Punishment and Their Children's Endorsement of Spanking and Hitting Other Children." *Child Abuse & Neglect* 34, no. 9 (September 2010): 639–46.

Smith, Brendan L. "The Case Against Spanking." (April 2012). Accessed March 2, 2017. http://www.apa.org/monitor/2012/04/spanking.aspx.

Straus, Murray A., and Mallie J. Paschall. "Corporal Punishment by Mothers and Development of Children's Cognitive Ability: A Longitudinal Study of Two Nationally Representative Age Cohorts." *Journal of Aggression, Maltreatment & Trauma* 18, no. 5 (July 23, 2009): 459–83.

Suchman, Nancy E., Bruce Rounsaville, Cindy Decoste, and Suniya Luthar. "Parental Control, Parental Warmth, and Psychosocial Adjustment in a Sample of Substance-Abusing Mothers and Their School-Aged and Adolescent Children." *Journal of Substance Abuse Treatment* 32, no. 1 (January 2007): 1–10.

Talwar, Victoria, and Kang Lee. "A Punitive Environment Fosters Children's Dishonesty: A Natural Experiment." *Child Development* 82, no. 6 (October 24, 2011): 1751–58.

Wang, Ming-Te, and Sarah Kenny. "Longitudinal Links Between Fathers' and Mothers' Harsh Verbal Discipline and Adolescents' Conduct Problems and Depressive Symptoms." *Child Development* 85, no. 3 (September 3, 2013): 908–23.

"Where We Stand: Spanking." HealthyChildren.org (November 21, 2015). Accessed March 2, 2017. https://www.healthychildren.org/English/family-life/family-dynamics /communication-discipline/Pages/Where-We-Stand-Spanking.aspx.

CHAPTER 12

Mischel, W., Y. Shoda, and M. Rodriguez. "Delay of Gratification in Children." *Science* 244, no. 4907 (May 26, 1989): 933–8.

Mischel, Walter, Yuichi Shoda, and Philip K. Peake. "The Nature of Adolescent Competencies Predicted by Preschool Delay of Gratification." *Journal of Personality and Social Psychology* 54, no. 4 (April 1988): 687–96.

Murray, Joanne, Anna Theakston, and Adrian Wells. "Can the Attention Training Technique Turn One Marshmallow into Two? Improving Children's Ability to Delay Gratification." *Behaviour Research and Therapy* 77 (February 2016): 34–39.

Shoda, Yuichi, Walter Mischel, and Philip K. Peake. "Predicting Adolescent Cognitive and Self-Regulatory Competencies from Preschool Delay of Gratification: Identifying Diagnostic Conditions." *Developmental Psychology* 26, no. 6 (November 1990): 978–86.

"Study Focuses on Strategies for Achieving Goals, Resolutions." Dominican University of California. Accessed January 13, 2017. http://www.dominican.edu/dominicannews /study-highlights-strategies-for-achieving-goals.

White, Rachel E., Emily O. Prager, Catherine Schaefer, Ethan Kross, Angela L. Duckworth, and Stephanie M. Carlson. "The 'Batman Effect': Improving Perseverance in Young Children." *Child Development* (2016).

CHAPTER 13

"Culture of American Families: Executive Report – IASC." (2012). Accessed January 13, 2017. http://www.iasc-culture.org/survey_archives/IASC_CAF_ExecReport.pdf.

"Are Teens Cheating Their Way to Higher GPAs?" Gallup, Inc. (April 15, 2003). Accessed January 13, 2017. http://www.gallup.com/poll/8200/teens-cheating-their-way-higher -gpas.aspx.

"Sexual Risk Behaviors: HIV, STD, & Teen Pregnancy Prevention." Centers for Disease Control and Prevention (July 18, 2016). Accessed March 2, 2017. https://www.cdc .gov/healthyyouth/sexualbehaviors/.

"Student Reports of Bullying and Cyber-Bullying: Results from the 2013 School Crime Supplement to the National Crime Victimization Survey." *PsycEXTRA Dataset.*

"The Children We Mean to Raise." Making Caring Common. Accessed January 13, 2017. http://mcc.gse.harvard.edu/the-children-we-mean-to-raise.

Yousafzai, Malala, and Christina Lamb. *I Am Malala: The Girl Who Stood Up for Education and Was Shot by the Taliban.* New York: Back Bay Books, 2015.

CONCLUSION

"About Team Hoyt." Team Hoyt. Accessed January 13, 2017. http://www.teamhoyt.com /About-Team-Hoyt.html.

ACKNOWLEDGMENTS

I never imagined my original article, "13 Things Mentally Strong People Don't Do," would turn into one book, let alone two. I'm grateful to my agent, Stacey Glick, who read that article and suggested I write a book.

And many thanks to my talented and dedicated team at Harper-Collins. Amy Bendell, Alieza Schvimer, and Lisa Sharkey are just a few of the amazing professionals who helped make this book a reality.

Thank you to all the readers of my first book who asked how to teach kids about mental strength. Many of your comments and questions shaped the ideas I wrote about in this book.

I'm also grateful to the clients and foster children I've met over the years who have taught me valuable lessons about mental strength.

And thank you to my friends, family members, teachers, and mentors, who have served as mentally strong role models throughout my life.

BOOKS BY AMY MORIN

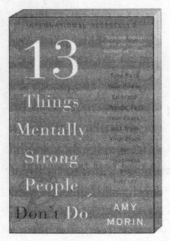

13 THINGS MENTALLY STRONG PEOPLE DON'T DO

Take Back Your Power, Embrace Change, Face Your Fears, and Train Your Brain for Happiness and Success

Expanding on her viral post that has become an international phenomenon, a psychotherapist offers simple yet effective solutions for increasing mental strength and finding happiness and success in life.

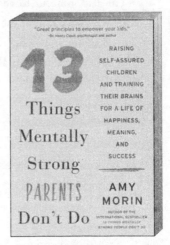

13 THINGS MENTALLY STRONG PARENTS DON'T DO

Raising Self-Assured Children and Training Their Brains for a Life of Happiness, Meaning, and Success

Drawing on her experiences and insight, *13 Things Mentally Strong Parents Don't Do* combines case studies, practical tips, specific strategies, and concrete and proven exercises to help children of all ages—from preschoolers to teenagers—build mental muscle and develop into healthy, strong adults.